Praise for *Female Nomad & Friends*

"Rita Golden Gelman's book pulsates with life's flavors—both in the stories and the recipes that accompany them. Remarkably, all royalties will be donated through two Rotary clubs to provide scholarships for young adults in a Delhi slum. As a Rotarian myself, I salute Rita and savor her book. So will you."

—Karin Treiber, Ph.D., Rotarian, Minneapolis, MN

"Thanks to Rita and her friends, the world just got a little smaller. This inspirational book simultaneously illustrates how large and small our global community has become. By sharing recipes, customs, and lives, we are ushered through an exotic world of experiences."

—John O. Hishmeh, executive director, Council on Standards for International Educational Travel

"These wonderfully poignant stories speak to the inner nomad in all of us, reminding us of the joy and warmth we feel when sharing laughter, tears, and meals across cultures."

—Sara LaRosa, returned Peace Corps Volunteer, Tonga 2006–2008

Praise for *Tales of a Female Nomad*

"I loved so much of your book, especially the part about how many of your adventures happened because you simply trusted people. You have renewed my faith in people and I'm going to trust more!"

—Marisa Atamian-Sarafian, Oakland, CA

"Your book consistently captivated me and filled me with the warmth of humanity. I was honored to vicariously participate in your experiences and appreciated your humble and personable approach. But most of all, I learned something about not only the fascinating places, but the nature of reality itself."

—Tantra Bensko, Rainsville, AL

"I'm in my mid-thirties and struggle with having made some unconventional choices. It is really validating to read such an intimate and honest account from another woman who didn't follow a traditional path or do what others expected."

—Elizabeth Olds, Washington, DC

"Your writing, your spirit, your priorities, your outlook . . . just wonderful!"

—Nancy Zaffaro, West Linn, OR

"I LOVE LOVE LOVE IT!!!!!!!! Your life has been incredible."

—Allie Hammond, Knoxville, TN

"I am 18. After reading your book, I felt like the life I want to have, this interesting, magical, spontaneous, unpredictable life, can actually come true."

—Chelsea Bickford, Lodi, CA

"It is so refreshing after reading so many cautionary tales of how to keep safe while traveling to read about someone giving everybody a chance and taking each day as it comes. You are so inspirational to all women who feel that something is missing in their lives and feel there must be another way to live."

—Gloria Knipe, New Zealand

"Everyone believes i'm crazy for traveling the way i do, and after reading your book, they have a much better understanding, although most still think i'm crazy!"

—Elena Slagle, Sacramento, CA

"I have just blown through your book in record time and find it the most refreshing and personally inspirational read I have had in ages."

—Nora Dunn, nomad

ALSO BY RITA GOLDEN GELMAN

Tales of a Female Nomad:
Living at Large in the World

TALES OF

BREAKING FREE

AND

BREAKING BREAD

AROUND THE WORLD

THREE RIVERS PRESS

NEW YORK

Female Nomad & Friends

RITA GOLDEN GELMAN

With Maria Altobelli

Illustrated by Jean Allen

Published in the United States by Three Rivers Press,
an imprint of the Crown Publishing Group,
a division of Random House, Inc., New York.

www.crownpublishing.com

Three Rivers Press and the Tugboat design are registered trademarks of
Random House, Inc.

Grateful acknowledgment is made to Red Wheel/Weiser LLC for
permission to reprint "The Filipino Elvis" from *Psychic Surgery and Faith
Healing: An Exploration of Multi-Dimensional Realities, Indigenous
Healing, and Medical Miracles in the Philippine Lowlands* by Jessica Bryan.
Copyright © 2007 by Jessica Bryan. Reprinted by permission of Red
Wheel/Weiser LLC, Newburyport, MA and San Francisco, CA.
www.redwheelweiser.com.

Library of Congress Cataloging-in-Publication Data
Gelman, Rita Golden.
Female nomad & friends : tales of breaking free and breaking bread around
the world / by Rita Golden Gelman, with Maria Altobelli; illustrated by
Jean Allen.—1st ed.
    p. cm.
1. Gelman, Rita Golden—Travel.   2. Women travelers.   3. Voyages
and travels.   I. Altobelli, Maria.   II. Title.   III. Title: Female nomad
and friends.
  G465.G443 2010
  910.4092—dc22   2009044278

ISBN 978-0-307-58801-2

Printed in the United States of America

Design by Ellen Cipriano

10 9 8 7 6 5 4 3 2 1

First Edition

Stories

Mixed Messages

Language

Passion

Food

Recipes

We are forty-one authors in this anthology, with forty-one ways of expressing ourselves. The editors have tried to retain the voices, styles, slang, even the punctuation idiosyncrasies of the various authors. *Female Nomad & Friends* is a celebration of diversity and a tribute to our shared humanity. We hope you enjoy traveling with us.

Female
Nomad &
Friends

How Female Nomad & Friends Came to Be and What It's All About

Rita Golden Gelman

It was not planned; it kind of snuck up on me when I wasn't looking. E-mail was the vehicle.

Let me back up a little. Well, maybe a lot, because this book actually started in 1987, when I divorced, gave everything away (no storage), and took off with a backpack to start a new life. My kids had left home, my husband was an ex, and it was finally "my time." I no longer wanted to live in one tiny dot on the giant map of the world. I wanted to explore, to adventure, to connect with the diversity of life on earth. I was ready to live my dream.

I turned off the volume of voices that said, *You are running away!* I knew I wasn't. I was running toward the excitement and learning that comes with *connecting*. I wanted to speak other languages, experience different belief systems, share ceremonies and foods, music and art, clothes and the daily lives of people who were different from me—people with different eyes, body shapes, skin color, behavior patterns, religions, ideas. I knew that travel would also reinforce those shared traits that make us all members of one human family: the laughter, the tears, the need for community, the love of children, and that special tingle of pleasure we all feel when we touch each other's hearts.

Connecting is still the central theme of my life. Instead of living within the constraints that tie us to a place, I chose to break free of the world I was living in. In 1987 I opened my life to otherness; it became addictive. I still have no fixed address and hardly any possessions.

I financed my addiction by writing children's books. I didn't earn much, but that was okay because living in the developing world doesn't cost much if you live with the locals. And the rewards are extraordinary: new things to learn, new friendships to develop, and new ways of life to explore.

In May 2001 my first adult book, *Tales of a Female Nomad: Living at Large in the World,* was published. It's about the first fifteen years of my new life. On the second-to-last page, against all editorial advice, I included my website and e-mail address. Back then it was rare to see an e-mail address in a book. My editor was afraid I'd be swamped. I was, and I loved it.

Twenty-four hours after the book appeared in the stores, the e-mails began to arrive. (Apparently a lot of people read the last pages first.) The e-mails have slowed down after all these years, but I still "meet" new readers every day, and I write back to all of them. There are thousands of letters in my computer.

Readers have shared and continue to share their dreams and fears, their adventures and longings, their joys and pain. They share their lives as I shared mine in the book. It is a special kind of e-connecting, and I have been deeply enriched by the readers I've met both virtually and face to face.

Everyone who reads the *Nomad* book knows that I have no

permanent home; many e-mails include an invitation to visit, to occupy the guest room, to sleep on the couch. I often accept. As a friend of mine likes to say, I've "slept around a lot." I've also shared tons of lunches and dinners and coffees with e-mailers. And I've accepted hundreds of invitations to speak to organizations, to book clubs, and to classes at all levels. Because of the book and that e-mail address, I've given talks in Antigua, Guatemala; New Delhi, India; Arusha, Tanzania; Paramaribo, Suriname; Vancouver, Canada; and hundreds of U.S. cities. The generosity and warmth of the people I've met is overwhelming.

There are recurrent themes in my e-mails that led to the creation of *Female Nomad & Friends.* Lots of readers have written to tell me that I'm living their dreams, but they've never had the courage to act. And now they're thinking, *If she can do it, why can't I?* A second theme is from people who are doing it. Their parents and friends think they're crazy. They write, "Thanks for showing me I'm not the only crazy one."

I'm happy to own both the ordinariness and the craziness, especially if they encourage people to get out there and experience the exhilaration that comes from *connecting.*

The *connecting* doesn't have to happen in a foreign culture. Often people read the book and decide to interact in a more meaningful way with the world around them. One of my favorite e-mails was from a woman in the San Francisco area. I no longer recall her name, but I remember her words, "I finished your book and walked across the street to introduce myself to the Vietnamese family who had been living there for three years."

Yessssss.

Others have ventured farther. They felt encouraged to

travel, to study abroad, to volunteer in Africa, to join the Peace Corps, teach English, build houses with Habitat for Humanity, sign up with Doctors Without Borders, and yes, even leave bad marriages in order to live their dreams.

Many of the letters I receive conclude with "I can't wait for a sequel."

Sorry. The sequel is not going to happen. The same personality aberration that is such a good fit for my nomadic existence guides the rest of my life as well. Along the way I've climbed mountains, gone scuba diving, eaten dragonflies, cuddled orangutans, worshipped in a mosque, meditated on a beach, and chanted myself into a hypnotic state in an ashram. I had acupuncture in Thailand, danced with women in the villages of Bali, sung with tribes in the jungle of Irian Jaya. Most recently I have gone paragliding in Peru. (Flying over Lima was amazing.) I am insatiably curious and hungry for new experiences. There's no time to do things over, like write a sequel. I'm ready to move on.

In my e-mails I'm often asked, "How about a cookbook?" I had a lot of fun writing about the many times I've cooked with women on fires all over the world and talking about the foods I've eaten, but there are no cookbooks in native "kitchens." The women pour, toss, stir, and smell. Then they taste. And pour, toss, and stir some more. Me too. I cook by feel, by look, by sound, by taste. I love to eat, and I like to read cookbooks, but I'm a pretty hit-or-miss cook. And I've never been very good at following directions or sticking to measurements.

Then one day I was visiting my friends Lars and Nirin in Nantes, France. Lars is a chef. While we were eating his

eggplant-onion-zucchini tartes on a base of exquisite puff pastry, I told him about my cookbook-petitioning e-mailers.

"I couldn't fill a book with recipes," I said. "I have, maybe,
ten good ones from my travels. A cookbook needs hundreds."

"Oh, no, it doesn't," said Lars in his musical Swedish accent. "Combine the recipes with stories. Look at this."

Then he took a big coffee-table book from a bookcase; it
was written in Swedish. On every page was the story of an event
in Swedish history; each story was accompanied by a recipe.

"Write a story and add a recipe," he advised. "The stories
will fill up the pages, you won't need so many recipes, and
everyone will be happy." He reminded me of a story of mine
he had read and suggested several recipes that could accompany it. (See "The Perfect Seatmate," page 183. Lars's suggestion was that I should follow that story with recipes for finger
foods. You have to read the story to get why this is funny.)

I considered his suggestion for maybe five minutes. I knew
I didn't have enough stories to fill a book either, so I dropped
that idea and went on with my life.

Then about a month later I realized that I wanted to *read*
the book he described, not *write* it! Why not get other people
to write it? Hmmm. I liked the idea. I had a website that was
getting a lot of hits. I could ask for submissions from all those
readers who had told me they wanted to write about their travels. I threw out the challenge: Send me stories about *connecting*
and *risk-taking* around the world, with recipes.

The call went out in 2003. The stories dribbled in slowly,
and I kept popping them into an e-file. By the end of 2006 I
decided it was time to choose. That's when I realized that the
project entailed a lot, *a whole lot,* of organization.

I would have to choose the stories, edit them, communicate with the authors, re-edit, get permissions, solicit bios, edit the bios, and more.

And then there were the recipes. Originally I'd asked for a recipe with every story, as Lars had suggested. Once I'd edited the fifty or so story-finalists, I'd have at least fifty recipes to test and retest and retest!

It is not a secret that I am organizationally challenged. Just thinking about the job ahead made me wobbly. I rarely think things through, and this time I knew I was in over my head.

I should have written a sequel, I was thinking, when Maria Altobelli offered to help. I had met her through an e-mail she'd sent me after she read the nomad book. She's an American expat who lives in Pátzcuaro, Mexico, with her husband, Paul. I'd visited them several times. Maria is a writer, a fabulous cook, and superorganized. It was an offer I couldn't refuse. I flew to Mexico.

From December 2006 through March 2007 we read and edited. Nearly every day, all day.

Putting the book together was a lot more demanding than either of us expected. But we loved reading the stories. Together we realized that most of the stories were from people who had left their comfort zones and stepped into the unfamiliar. These writers had been willing to take risks, break rules, face the unknown.

Risks are not the same for everyone. For some, walking out the front door or talking to a stranger is a risk. For others, risk is about moving to a new place, saying yes to an invitation, reaching out to help a stranger, or traveling to a country where they don't know the language.

For the most part, the risks in these stories are neither

dangerous nor foolhardy but rather the kind of risks that spark the part of you that screams from within, *Hey, look at me! I can't believe I'm doing this!*

A number of the stories are written by professional writers, but many are not. Maria and I chose stories where the writer's soul shines through the words. We wanted the reader to feel that the writer was a friend, sharing a part of her- or himself. We were looking for stories with "heart." And that's what we got. You will leave wanting to know the writers and possibly wanting to *be* them.

Along the way we broke all our rules.

We started out thinking we wanted two or three pages at the most. But some of our favorite stories were lots longer. Why not? We were in charge. Where better to flaunt rules than in a book that encourages the reader to break them? Occasionally we found a story we liked that wasn't even close to the themes of connecting and risk-taking, but if it made us laugh or cry or feel good, we slipped it in.

We set a cut-off date. Then three months later a good story arrived. We took it, of course.

Sometimes Maria and I disagreed, but we decided that our readers would have different opinions as well. Not everyone had to like every page.

Once we edited the stories, we had to deal with the recipes. At first we thought every story needed a recipe. But in the end we decided to include a limited number of superspecial recipes. Maria, who is a much better cook than I, has written about our process of testing. See "Breaking Bread: About the Recipes" on page 12.

Maria and I finally had a book we loved. Now we needed a publisher. My agent sent it to the Crown Publishing Group, a division of Random House; they had published *Tales of a Female Nomad*. We had a sale! That was February 2009.

Way back when I was soliciting stories, I had told the potential authors that the profits from the book would go into a special fund that would send high school graduates from the slums in New Delhi to vocational schools. None of us would be making any money from this project.

In 2005 I had raised money to send six kids, all of them graduates of twelfth grade, to Jetking Institute for computer hardware, software, and networking study. I wanted to use the royalties from the new anthology to expand the program.

The authors loved the idea.

It isn't easy to grow up in a slum in New Delhi. I'm familiar with the one that is directly across from the American Embassy School in a beautiful neighborhood in the embassy district called Chanakyapuri. Vivekenand Camp Part 2, referred to as a *jhuggie,* which means "hut, slum," was born thirty-five years ago when the school was being built. The workers came from their villages and built cardboard and plastic and rusted-metal shacks on the empty land across from the construction site. They never left.

By the time I arrived, many of the shacks had been converted into stone or wood or stucco, and they were filled with families, 228 of them (more than a thousand kids) illegally parked on land that did not belong to them. They lived in constant danger of being bulldozed out of their homes by the government.

I spent nearly a year in New Delhi and many hours in Vivekenand Camp Part 2. When I arrived in 2003, only one young man in the history of the *jhuggie* had graduated from high school. Lal Singh had become a role model. When I left a year later, three more were about to graduate. And three more in ninth grade were determined to finish. They were smart and motivated, and they dreamed of going to college or vocational school, or both. They knew that Lal Singh had gone to computer school and that he had a real job.

All six of those young men completed high school and computer training, and today they all have jobs.

Carol Lemley, the teacher in the American Embassy School who introduced me to the *jhuggie,* recently told me that there are now twenty young people from Vivekenand who have finished high school and gone on to further schooling; four of them are girls.

When I was there, more than fifteen hundred people were sharing three water pumps, eight toilets, pirated electricity, and open, smelly drainage ditches. Most families lived in one-room shacks with—well, I'll let one of the boys tell you in his own words. He wrote this while he was still in high school.

> *It's pretty pathetic when your whole life depends on one stupid exam, and you're the only one who cares.*
>
> *I mean, try memorizing dates of India's war against the British or thinking about quadratic equations when there's a cricket game on television, your mother is on the floor cooking dinner, your brother is fighting with your sisters, your sisters are pulling on you to make him stop, and your father is drinking again and you know that in a couple of hours he's going to start yelling at your mother and maybe begin swinging. Oh, and all of this is going on in a hut that is eight feet wide and ten feet long. That's our whole house. Welcome to my life.*

Most young people are taken out of school as soon as they are old enough to contribute to the family income by working in construction for one or two dollars a day. That is their future. This young man miraculously passed the feared twelfth-grade exam, graduated, and attended Jetking. He is now taking courses in college. And he has a job! (He requested that I not use his name.)

The ten kids that I came to know in this *jhuggie* are some of the nicest, most respectful, most caring and motivated kids I have ever known. Part of their motivation is due to the proximity of the American Embassy School and the love and encouragement they have had from some caring teachers (especially Carol).

The author royalties from this book are funding scholarships for slum kids who manage to graduate from high school. Each author received two copies of the book; no one was paid any money.

Let me share with you some details. I always like knowing the inner workings of things; I figure you might too. The "advance on royalties" paid by Crown was $55,000. After the agent's 15 percent fee was deducted, a total of $46,750 was sent to the Rotary Club in Delhi (via a Rotary Club in Maryland) that will be administering the scholarships. Delhi Rotarian Manjit S. Sawhney is vetting and mentoring the young men and women who qualify.

To give you an idea of the cost of schooling in India, here are the latest figures: Jetking costs around $1,200 for a thirteen-month course, up from $780 a few years ago. A three-month English course at the British School of Language costs $120; and it costs $195 per year for college at Delhi

Open University. The money from this book will change a lot of lives.

There will be even more money if this book earns out its advance. All additional royalties will find their way to the Delhi Rotary and new students. So please pass along the word, encourage your friends to buy a copy, and they too will be contributing dramatic life improvements to some very deserving young men and women.

Some stories here will make you laugh out loud, and others will bring tears to your eyes. They offer rapture and rape, the bizarre and the beautiful, insensitivity and tenderness. The stories are alive and pulsing. I hope they will inspire you to break free, break rules, take risks, and take off.

Happy journey, wherever it may take you.

Rita Golden Gelman
At Large in the World

Breaking Bread: About the Recipes

Maria Altobelli

My aunt Carolina cooked fantastic meals, scooping ingredients up with her hand, pinching with her fingers, and eyeballing liquid as she poured. One day as my dad, friends, and I sat at the kitchen table, she set down a steaming bowl of pasta with tomato sauce. Talk stopped as we breathed in the tantalizing aroma.

I bit into a meatball and had to ask, "So how much garlic do you use?"

She made a face. "You like garlic, you use more. You don't like so much, you use less." She shrugged and gave me a withering look. "God forbid you leave it out entirely."

So I grew up with a total disregard for measuring and a healthy respect for garlic.

My own cooking style today borders on controlled chaos, but that's not the way to write a cookbook. The recipe testers for this book tried out measurements, tasted, adjusted, served the dishes to friends and family, and laboriously wrote everything down. Rita and I tried and discarded recipes, refined and retested others. We made a final list and tested again and again with friends, relatives, and readers in Mexico, Australia, and across the United States.

Professional chef Victoria Allman, whose story "Riding Out the Storm" appears on page 279, also tested the recipes on the yacht *Cocoa Bean*. The crew of ten and numerous guests and family of the yacht owners served as judges. We selected the dishes that got raves.

One of our favorite methods for testing was a tasting party. Everyone invited received a recipe and brought the finished product to the party. We tasted each dish one by one and made comments about it. Later, Rita and I adjusted the recipes to fit the comments and tried them again.

Everyone loved those tasting parties. They were always a group effort. We all had so much fun, we want to encourage you to throw one. Get ready for an afternoon or evening of good eating and camaraderie.

In deference to those of you who have a fondness for measuring cups and spoons, we have included the measurements. The recipes work as written. For those of you who look at meal preparation as a blank canvas to fill with inspiration, the list of ingredients suggests colors for your palette. Keep in mind that many of the recipes in this collection are traditionally served fiery hot. Let your taste buds, and not the recipes, dictate the amount of heat you add to the dish. If you are wary, start with less, taste, and add.

Cooking is about creativity, so we encourage you to play, be imaginative, and do a lot of tasting. Don't worry all the time about being exact. Scoop, pinch, eyeball. And if you like garlic, use more.

The recipes here border on the exotic, but we've tried

to include something for every palette. Using the recipes as a guide, break free from the measurements, break rules, and most important, break bread, sharing the new tastes you create with others.

Maria Altobelli
Pátzcuaro, Mexico

Connecting

My Favorite Organization Ever

Rita Golden Gelman

Being a part of Servas is like having family all over the world. It's actually better than family. People join Servas because they want you to visit them when you are in their country. Not always the case with family.

Since I have no home, I'm always a traveler and never a host. Servas visits are for two nights, and everyone (hosts and travelers) is screened in a face-to-face interview. Servas charges a small annual membership fee, and travelers pay a deposit for host lists in the countries they want to visit. During the visits, however, no money changes hands.

My first Servas visit was with Gabi and Batsheva in Tel Aviv in 1988. Before the trip, I saw their names in the Israel host book; I wrote asking if I could stay with them when I visited.

They welcomed me as they would an old friend. They fed me, toured me, guided me, and shared their stories as I shared mine. I helped with the cooking and clean-up and bought a meal or a snack here and there.

After only one day we felt so close that we decided their

single son, then living in the Dominican Republic, and my single daughter, then living in New York, should marry! Never happened, but we did have fun planning the meeting and discussing the wedding. It was wonderful getting to know them. Their love for each other made being with them a pleasure.

Gabi and Batsheva met in an orphanage. Their parents were killed by the Nazis. During and after the war, the surviving kids were taken from Europe to an orphanage in Palestine. The two found themselves among the oldest children there and ended up working on the same projects and caring for the younger kids together. They fell in love. Batsheva had a sister, Tova, who was also in the orphanage. I never met Tova, but Gabi and the two sisters shared a special closeness as the only survivors of both families. The sisters meant everything to each other.

As we shared our stories, Gabi, Batsheva, and I developed a special bond. Servas is like that. A level of intimacy is quickly established, and you always leave feeling as though you have made a new friend—or extended your family.

Several years later I returned to Israel for my cousin's wedding. I called Gabi and Batsheva. Gabi answered the phone. He was excited to hear from me, but he explained that Tova had recently died and Batsheva was devastated. He didn't think she felt ready for guests. The two women had been incredibly close, he reminded me. I suggested that maybe this time I could take care of Batsheva. They talked it over and decided it was a good idea.

I didn't exactly take care of her, but I did some cooking and a little cleaning; and Batsheva was able to share her happy Tova stories, as well as her pain.

On the second day of my visit, Batsheva received a letter from a Servas friend in Brazil. Claudia had heard about Tova's death and written a sympathy note. She had included her e-mail address. I offered to write to Claudia on my computer. In the e-mail I introduced myself to Claudia, and then Batsheva dictated her response while I typed. I left the next day, sad, but pleased that I had been able to help.

Four years later in Argentina, I once again connected with people through Servas. I was staying in my friend Gera's home in San Miguel, outside of Buenos Aires, so I didn't need a place to stay, but I wanted to meet people in Buenos Aires. I took out my host list and called a few people. The response was fantastic. Servas members invited me to share meals, parties, and excursions.

After I had met a number of hosts, they told me that a group of them planned on taking a boat across the river the next Sunday to meet Uruguayan hosts. Would I like to come? Of course.

Our two groups got together in the charming Uruguayan town of Colonia and wandered for a few hours before lunch. Everyone wanted to talk a little to everyone else, so two of us would walk and talk for a while, and then we'd switch. The first two Uruguayans I met insisted that I come back as their Servas guest (which I did). I was able to converse with them in Spanish, although they both spoke better English than I did Spanish.

The third person I met asked me not to speak Spanish. "My Spanish is not very good," she said. "My English is better."

"But aren't you from Uruguay?" I asked.

"No, I'm not. I'm from over the border in Brazil."

It was at that point that we introduced ourselves. "My name is Rita. I'm from the United States."

"Oh, my God," she said. "I can't believe it. I'm Claudia."

Yes, she was *that* Claudia! We hugged like old friends. And cried. And a month later I was a Servas guest in Claudia's house in Brazil.

If you're a traveler and a connector, check it out. It's an amazing organization: www.servas.org or www.usservas.org.

*AFTER TWENTY-FOUR YEARS of nomadding, Rita Golden Gelman is still happily without a permanent home. Her current passion is **LET'S GET GLOBAL,** a national movement she founded in 2009 to encourage and assist U.S. youth to have international experiences after high school, before they begin the next phase of their lives: www.letsgetglobal.org. U.S. Servas Inc. is the fiscal sponsor of LET'S GET GLOBAL. Visit Rita's personal website at www.ritagoldengelman.com.*

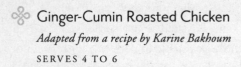 Ginger-Cumin Roasted Chicken

Adapted from a recipe by Karine Bakhoum

SERVES 4 TO 6

---

    2 small chickens or one large chicken

    3 tablespoons extra virgin olive oil

Sea salt or kosher salt and freshly ground black pepper, to taste

    1 tablespoon grated ginger

    ½ teaspoon cayenne pepper

    2 tablespoons cumin

½ lime, juiced

2 tangerines, cut in half and seeded (2 to 3 oranges, depending on juice content, can be substituted for tangerines)

24 large cloves garlic, inner skins left on

½ cup cognac (optional) or ¼ cup water

1 cup pitted Kalamata olives

3 rosemary sprigs (for garnish)

Preheat oven to 475°F.

Place the chicken in a large roasting pan, and rub with olive oil, letting the oil coat the bottom of the pan. Season with salt and pepper.

Combine the ginger, cayenne pepper, cumin, lime juice, and juice of ½ tangerine in a small bowl to make a paste.

Pat the paste evenly over the chicken.

Scatter the garlic cloves around the chicken, mix with the oil on the bottom of the pan, and place the pan in the oven.

After 15 minutes, squeeze ½ tangerine over the chicken and return to oven at the same temperature for another 15 minutes.

After the second 15 minutes, squeeze another ½ tangerine on top, and reduce the oven temperature to 350°F.

Bake 20 minutes, then add the cognac and olives to the pan. If not using cognac, add ¼ cup water and squeeze the remaining ½ tangerine over the chicken. Brush with the juice from the bottom of the pan, and bake another 10 minutes.

Place on a serving platter. Scatter the olives and whole garlic around the chicken. Pour the pan juices on top. Garnish with the rosemary sprigs.

....

Sometimes the pan juices evaporate too quickly, and I add a few extra tablespoons of tangerine or orange juice along the way. I also brush the chicken with the flavored pan juices each time I baste with the tangerine juice. The chicken skin gets pretty dark—but it's delicious. I usually skip the cognac; it's still great. This is an easy and delicious way to entertain. Once I added Dijon mustard to the ginger mix. It was a little different but still wonderful. I like this with spinach or asparagus and buttery mashed potatoes. —rgg

....

....

For the garlic lover, more garlic cloves can be added. The garlic roasts to a soft consistency and can be popped out of its blackened skin easily. It's wonderful. Don't omit the olives. They are an important addition to the dish. A large chicken will take longer to cook than two small ones. Make sure the internal temperature of the chicken is 165°F. For just two people, two thigh/ drumsticks or a chicken half can be roasted instead of the whole chicken. The chicken is often served with couscous. —ma

....

Peeing, Drugs, and a School

Maria Altobelli

The war in Vietnam or the Peace Corps in Bolivia? My future husband Paul had to choose. For a man opposed to war, the decision was easy. For two years he worked and sweated in Bolivia's eastern jungles and loved every minute. He started by clearing a patch of abandoned land in the tiny, mud-street village of Ascención de Guarayos. He and a rowdy group of boys made a rudimentary soccer field. Road repair, bridge construction, an electric co-op, and an endless supply of projects filled his days. His most impressive achievement was building an elementary school with the help of the villagers. His stint finished in midproject, so he asked for a six-month extension. Then another. He figured if he got one more, he would never leave. So he got on a plane and flew back to Minnesota. We got married, and for years I heard plenty about Bolivia.

Some of his stories made me want to go there. There was the guy who missed the New Year's Eve festivities with his buddies. The next morning he rode a horse bareback and bare-ass naked into the compound where his friends were staying. He fired a pistol repeatedly into the air as he circled the courtyard. With a final volley and a few whoops, he reined back on the horse and galloped off into the New Year.

That was cool. I wanted to visit.

Instead we moved to Mexico, but the idea of going to Bolivia wedged itself into my subconscious.

In 2004 Paul and I decided to go to Ascención de Guarayos. The trip once involved several days on horseback working through the jungle, or hanging around the regional capital of Santa Cruz waiting for a bush pilot to make a supply run. Fun options at twenty-five but not so appealing now that we were in our fifties.

The new, paved road to Ascención was the clincher. The modern bus made it even better. The five-hour bus trip should have been a snap. After all the time we'd lived in Mexico, bus travel had become part and parcel of our lives. However, a weak bladder and the absence of a usable bathroom on the bus quelled my enthusiasm. Before the bus even left the station, I saw several passengers check out the cubicle, grimace, and close the door without stepping inside. I immediately had to pee.

I crossed my legs and watched two guys get on the fully booked night bus. They started an animated discussion with the driver. The traditional handshake, where a folded bill is passed unobtrusively from palm to palm, must have occurred since the two dudes came to the back of the bus where we were. They arranged various packages in the space behind us designed for oversize luggage, squished down on the floor between the packages and our seats, and went to sleep.

All I could think of was Law 1008. It made jail mandatory for the mere suspicion of possession of any drug or illegal substance. The two guys could have been innocently going home after a week's work in Santa Cruz, or they could have been transporting drugs, firearms, or dynamite destined for the next antigovernment demonstration.

What would we say to the cops if we were stopped at one of numerous checkpoints in the country? I imagined a conversation on the side of the deserted tarmac in the blackness of the remote Bolivian countryside. "What dope? I know the packages were stashed behind our seats, but they must have belonged to the two guys who were sitting on the floor behind us. Yeah, I know they're not here now, but they were."

Now I really had to pee. I sucked tight any muscle I could remotely connect with my bladder.

Getting off that bus in Ascención de Guarayos at 4:00 A.M. was a huge relief.

The next morning we tried to teach a group of young boys in the plaza the finer points of *bolero,* a traditional stick-toss game we brought from Mexico. One boy became an instant expert, and before long he was showing off to quite a crowd.

Paul made small talk with the other boys. "So where do you guys go to school?"

"The Pablo Kundzins School," they answered, intent on their new game.

"But I'm Pablo Kundzins," Paul said with surprise.

It turned out a government edict a few years back ordered all schools in Bolivia be given an actual name rather than the number they had been assigned. When it came to the school in Ascención, a heated battle developed. One group wanted the school named for a popular music instructor from the Guaraní, the local indigenous group. Another equally strong contingent held out in favor of a local teacher who worked his way up the ranks and became a prominent politician.

To end the dispute, someone suggested naming the school for the Peace Corps volunteer who had helped get the funds for the project and then worked shoulder to shoulder with the townsfolk on the construction. Everyone figured Paul was long dead anyway, so it was a safe bet.

Kundzins had been impossible for anyone to pronounce during Paul's three years in town, so the spelling on the school didn't exactly jibe with his name. We later saw the banner with *Escuela Pablo Cuncins* emblazoned in dark blue. What the heck? The newly resurrected dead shouldn't be choosy.

Days later, we waited in the bus for the return trip to Santa Cruz. A short, stooped man with a lined, leathery face climbed up the steps of the bus with difficulty. He limped down the aisle and stopped in front of Paul.

"Do you remember me?" he asked.

We had been awake for almost our entire stay in Ascención, revisiting Paul's old haunts and reestablishing contacts. Our eyes could hardly focus.

Paul looked at the hunched, middle-aged man in rumpled clothes in front of us. "I'm sorry," Paul mumbled. "I don't. Help me out."

"Maybe you would remember my wife, the one who had so much trouble with her pregnancy."

Speechless, Paul reached for the man's hand. "Manuel Ortumpi! Yes, yes, I remember."

Good Lord, I thought. *Even I remember.* I had heard the story of his wife enough times. She was pregnant with her first child. The baby simply refused to be born. The mother needed to get to Santa Cruz fast, but the only way out of town was the plane owned by the Evangelical minister who wanted the equivalent of $250 before he would even think about moving.

In a time and place where the majority of the town's population lived on a family income equivalent to $75 a *year,* $250 was an impossible sum. Pleas and promises of future payment were to no avail. Paul and the desperate young husband began canvassing door to door, getting a few *bolivianos* (coins) at each stop. The priest emptied the poor boxes in the church and dug into his own pockets. Paul added what was left of his monthly Peace Corps pay. They were still over a hundred dollars short.

Paul went to find Yeguaroba, a young man who was one of the most respected members of the community. Paul explained the situation to him. "Maybe you could come along and act official," Paul suggested.

"Wait a minute. Let me get my gun. After all, we have quite a bit of money to deliver," Yeguaroba said.

When Paul, the frantic husband, and Yeguaroba got to the minister's house, Paul dumped the pile of rumpled *bolivianos* on the desk. "I believe we have enough," he said.

The minister started to count through the pile. Yeguaroba looked official and fingered the trigger of his ancient carbine. "We have enough," he said, moving the gun upward. "Better start the plane. We're in a hurry here."

The baby died while still inside the young mother, but the Santa Cruz doctors saved the woman's life. When Paul left Ascención de Guarayos, she was still in delicate health.

"I just wanted you to know," Manuel Ortumpi said. "My wife recovered. We have three grown sons."

The two held onto each other's hands a long moment. "Thank you," Manuel said simply. With a last handshake, he walked off the bus and was lost in the crowd outside.

The motor started up, and we slowly pulled out of town.

MARIA ALTOBELLI and her husband, Paul Kundzins, were bit-ten in their twenties by the travel bug and have never looked for a cure. The two continue their vagabond ways, and now live in cen-tral Mexico with assorted canines. Her story, "A Desert Mirage" (see page 298) is an excerpt from a book about the Mexico she has seen over the last thirty-five years. Her website is www.mexicoin smallbytes.com. Contact Maria at mexicobytes@yahoo.com.

A Pair of Shoes

Janie Starr

Petrona Chavaj, the cook at Ecológico Uxlabil, has invited me to her house for a farewell lunch. For the last two weeks I have been staying at the lodge on the banks of Lake Atitlán in Guatemala. Petrona and I have become friends. Her ten-year-old son Estuardo, the family comic, has agreed to serve as my guide because I'm not sure I can find my way on my own.

As we walk from the lakeside lodge, we climb the trash-strewn path past windowless nylon shacks. Estuardo waves and smiles at the people we pass. This is his kingdom, and I am his guest.

In between greetings of *Hola* and *¿Cómo estás?* we talk like new pals. He tells me that he, his dad, and his oldest sister, Cris, are the only swimmers in the family, that he can run faster than his dad, and that he likes to watch the Discovery Channel on Saturdays.

"Why only Saturdays?" I ask.

"Because *la televisión* is off limits on school nights. *Mis padres* make me study." He could have been one of my own sons, bending to the wishes of Mom and Dad. Except that he is a small, dark indigenous child, wearing hand-me-down jeans, a too-small T-shirt with a red swoosh emblazoned across the front, and a dusty pair of tight-toed scuffed black leather shoes, the kind grown men wear.

As we trek along, Estuardo warns me to stay out of the scrub bushes because pit vipers and other snakes lurk there.

After a twenty-minute walk, we arrive at the house. I thank Estuardo, and he gives me his widest toothy grin before running off to watch his program on the ancient television set. Petrona beckons me into a small, dark, one-room building that serves as both kitchen and eating area. Chickens and dogs move in and out of the room. Petrona wipes her hands on her apron and sets a mound of food before me: crispy fried fish, rice, and kidney beans prepared with an herb I cannot identify.

"*¡Coma!*" Eat, eat, she says as she dishes out plates for the three children who are home.

"I'd like to wait for you, Petrona, so that we can eat together."

I watch as the kids run in, grab their plates, and scurry off to another small building.

Petrona fixes her plate and sits down beside me. I feel honored to be in her home.

"This is so good; it's different from the bony fish I had at the hotel. Is it hard to come by?"

"*Sí*, but I have a friend who sells me fish to cook for the guests, and he brought me this one especially for you."

I worry what this lunch has cost her, but her hospitality does not speak of sacrifice. It is a meal between two women who have become friends.

"Next time you come, you will stay with us. It is *muy humilde,* but we would like to have you."

I thank her and work one of the few bones out of my teeth.

Petrona has an open, readable face. When she speaks to me, her eyes deepen and widen and her weathered skin smooths out into a sweet smile. Unlike her husband Gaspar, whose entire face lights up, whose eyes sparkle, and who laughs out loud like Estuardo, Petrona's smile is tinted with sadness.

"Estuardo is a troublemaker like his dad." She says this with pride, and I picture the time I felt Estuardo reach from behind my chair to cover my eyes with his small brown hands as I sat eating dinner.

As we finish our lunch, I ask Petrona about Estuardo's school. The family is Catholic, so I am surprised to learn that Estuardo attends the Evangelical school near their house.

"It's the best choice we have as long as he is in *básico.*" I take that to mean elementary school. "The state schools don't even have books for the kids. Next year we can switch him to the Catholic school where his sister goes."

Then she tells me about the boxes of shoes that church members from the States sent to San Juan after the mudslides caused by Hurricane Stan destroyed so many homes. The boxes were filled with piles of sneakers, enough for all the children.

"The day they passed out the shoes, they gave a pair to every single child except Estuardo."

"They did *what*?" I ask, wondering if I understood her Spanish.

"They said he didn't need them since we have an American

friend, who, they believed, paid for his tuition." Her eyes fill with tears and her voice becomes stronger. "No one paid for Estuardo except me. I work from four in the morning until late in the day to pay for him to attend this school."

She wipes her eyes, and all I can say is, "How *injusto.*" I think, *What kind of person denies a child a pair of shoes?* "How did Estuardo react?"

"He cried and cried and begged for me to buy him new tennis shoes. I can't afford to send him to the dentist when he has a toothache. Where would I find the money to buy him a pair of shoes?"

I am having trouble reconciling the beaming urchin who makes me laugh with the weeping boy Petrona depicts.

She explains how angry she got at the teacher and the missionaries. She told them that she alone had paid his tuition. They must not have believed her because they never gave Estuardo his pair of shoes.

"I would never lie," Petrona said. I believe her.

"Petrona, I'm going to leave a few things here when I go. I had planned to leave my shoes as well." We both look down at my size-five red canvas sandals, with the thick tire soles. "Do you think Estuardo might be able to fit into these?"

Her eyes fill up again, "*Gracias,* Juanita. *Sí.* I know he would."

"Boys wear them too," I add because I don't think Estuardo would want to wear girls' shoes.

I know my offer is as much about making *me* feel useful as it is about making any significant difference in a young boy's life.

I look at my watch; I need to get back to my room to pack.

"I will wash the sandals and leave them with Gaspar before I go. He's still working at the lodge, right?"

Petrona tries to talk me out of cleaning them, but I insist. They are dusty, and the treads are wedged with dirt and who-knows-what else.

We hug each other goodbye, and now we are both teary. Then Petrona runs into a back room and brings out a golden scarf threaded with purple that she had woven.

"*Un regalito,* Juanita. A small gift for when it gets cold where you live."

"Oh, *gracias,* Petrona. It is beautiful."

She wraps the scarf around my neck, and we hug and kiss again. Then Estuardo escorts me down the hill.

When we arrive back at the lodge, Estuardo jumps into the porch hammock with his dad, who is taking his afternoon siesta. I wave to Gaspar and climb the three flights of stairs to my room.

I wash the sandals, and when I go back downstairs and hand them over, Estuardo leaps into my arms, and I twirl him around. Then he jumps down, jerks off his worn-out old-man's cracked-leather shoes and pulls on the too-big sandals. Even Gaspar has tears in his eyes.

Estuardo gives me one final grin, and then he takes off running. He disappears in a flash of red as he kicks up his heels and turns the corner toward the lake.

CURRENTLY A PRESENTER *for Al Gore's Climate Project and coordinator of Sustainable Vashon's Solar Initiative, Janie Starr has a long history of community activism. Her memoir,* Bone Marrow Boogie: The Dance of a Lifetime, *documents her successful travels through lymphoma. Her passion for experiential learning leads her to explore Spanish-speaking countries. She struggles between the urge to pack up and go and her commitment to shrink her carbon footprint. Living on a Pacific Northwest island is an adventure in itself. Her publications include* "A Trip to Cuba," Timeline; "Laura," Cup of Comfort for Women; *and* "Adele: Mother-in-Love," ducts.org. *Contact Janie at starrboogie@earthlink.net.*

Tower of Babel

Kelly Hayes-Raitt

I got married today.

Although I am traveling with an American women's delegation to meet Iraqi women who tell us about their experiences living under a brutal dictatorship, a dozen years of debilitating sanctions, and the prospect of a new, impending war, I get matched up with a husband.

It's February 2003, and I'm touring Babylon just five weeks before my country will bomb and occupy Iraq.

Babylon's walled fortress was built twenty-two centuries ago, a city straight out of my early catechism days, a city that until today had seemed more mythical than real. Fingering its weathered yellow bricks, walking its worn pathways, standing in the shadow of the blindingly blue gates of Ishtar, I realize that Saddam Hussein's nearby palace puts this ancient fortress at Ground Zero. In an instant, an errant bomb could reduce twenty-two centuries of history to rubble.

The destruction of the Tower of Babel in 482 B.C. is one of the few biblical stories I remember. Its destruction scattered people to the far corners of the world, mutating their language while maintaining an ancient common thread. It's a childhood story that still challenges me to discover dreams I have in common with people who seem so foreign.

Our translator, our common thread, is a forty-four-year-old Iraqi woman who is married to a Japanese man and lives in Dallas. Amira has arranged for us to visit her mother, brothers, and sisters in Hilla, near Babylon. Her family, like most Iraqis I have met, is warm and welcoming. I find it remarkable that we have encountered no anti-American sentiment. In what I consider an extraordinary show of tolerance, people automatically separate us from our government. Perhaps it's because they feel their own government does not reflect them.

Immediately we are embraced by Amira's family and ushered into the dining room decked out with a meal lavish enough to feed twice our group. Two long, banquet-style tables overflow with a feast of platters heaped with every possible permutation of vegetables and chicken over steaming beds of rice. Huge rolls line the perimeter of the table, interspersed with bottles of the ubiquitous Furat water.

I am honored and embarrassed: during the time of my prewar visit, 16 million of the 26 million Iraqis rely solely on monthly government rations. Even the richest families spend three-quarters of their income on food. In spite of these hardships, the Iraqis I meet are generous, resilient, joyous, and eager to feed me.

Amira has nine remaining siblings; one brother is still missing from the Iraq-Iran War of the mid-eighties, another brother died during the Gulf War. At first Amira, with her long, flowing hair and Western cut jeans, appears as foreign as the rest of us, in contrast to her sisters in their traditional coats and scarved hair. But she clearly belongs here and enters easily into conversational routine as if she'd never left.

I bond with the women in the kitchen, not by cooking, but by dishwashing. Ascertaining that I am the only eligible woman in our group and a darn good dishwasher to boot, Amira's sisters immediately set me up as a match for their older, widowed brother.

I don't quite understand all the hilariously assertive gestures and enthusiastic, high-pitched "la-la-la-la-las," but I go along with what I hope is a joke. We're on war time, so we dispense with the flirting and courtship and move straight to the mock marriage ceremony. War time or not, I refuse to forgo a wedding ring, and the ladies understand when I point in horror to my empty ring finger. One of Amira's sisters produces wedding *earrings,* straight from a JCPenney box.

My makeshift wedding takes place in the dining room. Fake roses adorned with birthday candles complete my trousseau. Another delegate steps up as wife number two, and our husband-to-be praises Allah for his impending good fortune. The entire family gets in on the act, clapping and clowning.

He speaks only Arabic. I speak only English. He pantomimes a proposal, and I order him to peel my wedding apple. Sitting in this ancient fertile crescent, fourteen hundred years after the prophet Mohammed inhaled eternal life through the fragrance of an angel-sent apple just before he died, I share an apple with my new Iraqi "husband," hoping its enduring powers will protect him and this lovely, lively family.

Now connected to Amira's family by our sidesplitting antics, I realize on the road back to Baghdad what they surely know: initial war scenarios involve isolating Baghdad. Such action will serve to cut off outlying areas, like Babylon, from

Baghdad's stockpiles of food and medical supplies. In the early stages of a new war, an estimated five hundred thousand people will need trauma care, overwhelming the already-overburdened medical system.

Back in Baghdad, we hear that Secretary of State Colin Powell addressed the United Nations, declaring that the search for weapons of mass destruction has been inadequate. President Bush declares, "The game is over."

War is imminent.

The day we leave, workers at our hotel begin duct-taping the picture windows and welding protective barriers. On the street, people scurry, stockpiling food and water. Women stop me and desperately clutch my elbow, imploring me to go home and ask President Bush not to bomb them. These are women who know war.

Our farewell lingers for hours on the sidewalk outside our hotel. Over the intermittent din of the welding, Iraqis we have befriended, barely met, and never met come by for a final photo, as if compelled to document their existence.

A policeman we have never seen before today leaves his post on the corner to flash a friendly grin. A salesman carrying an open tray of doughy rolls on his head insists on a photo he will never see. The workers at the hotel wave and flash peace signs at my flashing camera.

Hassan, the entrepreneurial boy who has stationed himself outside our hotel, offers a filmy shoeshine in exchange for a few dinars or coveted PowerBars as he mugs for our cameras. He is either five or seven, depending on which day I ask, but his memory for which of us carries candy is flawless. Before the first Gulf War, nearly all Iraqi children were schooled. Now, before this war and after twelve years of sanctions, almost a quarter of the children are instead on the streets, earning meager money to help support their families. I'm too numb to let myself think what Hassan's life will become after another war.

From the neighboring Palestine Hotel, where he has a second job as a gardener, our waiter Abdullah brings me a bouquet of dusty marigolds and promises to stay in touch. He does, initially sending hopeful e-mails gushing with enthusiasm for his country's promising democracy, then bitter pleas to help him and his family flee their country's lawlessness. His last e-mail from the Palestine Hotel is a photo of a shredded garden buried in broken glass.

The last time I saw my "husband," he came to our hotel in Baghdad to bid us farewell. Still complaining about the lack of a wedding ring, I joke and laugh and try to postpone the inevitable. I tuck one of Abdullah's marigold's in his lapel, a shock of orange over the heart of his grim, gray suit.

When the bombs started falling, I wasn't there. The United States dropped ninety thousand tons of explosives on the entire country of Iraq during the first Gulf War's forty-two days of relentless bombing. We dropped ten times that amount on just the first day of bombing Baghdad in March 2003. I listened live on National Public Radio from the safety of my car half a world away, clutching my steering wheel on Santa Monica Boulevard, while honking cars angrily passed me, going about their self-important day.

Later, I waited anxiously for news of my new Babylonian family. In Texas, Amira initially heard that everyone was okay—shaken, scared, edgy, angry, but alive. Over months we hear of the deaths.

First, Amira's elderly mother died when she couldn't get her medication.

Then I hear my "husband" has died. The strain of the constant gunfire, the never-ending fear, took its toll on his heart.

I eat an apple in his honor, hoping that in death, he finds our common dream: peace.

KELLY HAYES-RAITT visited Iraq five weeks before the war and nine weeks after "mission accomplished." She expanded her observations into a forthcoming book, Keeping the Faith, *which includes this story and "Tongue-Tied" (page 144). The book follows her experiences helping Palestinian schoolchildren through armed checkpoints, interviewing Filipino women whose relatives have been kidnapped by the Philippine army, comforting Palestinian widows of the Lebanese Sabra and Shatila massacres, and assisting Iraqi refugees in Damascus. Kelly blogs at www.PeacePATH Foundation.org.*

Connecting to Raymond

Sally Brown

For weeks I struggled to encourage Raymond to read a short passage in a book, three grade levels below his class placement. His reluctance was palpable.

Raymond was a quiet ten-year-old boy, small in stature and shy in demeanor. Twice a week I hopped on a bus in Greenwich Village and slowly wended my way through bustling midtown Manhattan to Harlem, all the while thinking about how to reach my hesitant pupil. I sat quietly and watched the bus passengers shift from primarily white students, to white business people, to almost entirely African-Americans heading to their homes.

As I got off the bus and walked up the street, I felt a rush of anticipation laced with a little fear, aware of the stares of the store owners and shoppers. By the time I reached the towering high-rise apartment building where Raymond and his family lived, I was ready.

Raymond's parents were lovely, gracious, and appreciative

people, thrilled that this eager, young, educated white woman would try to help their young son learn to read.

Raymond and I would sit at the kitchen table in their clean and sparsely furnished apartment, and I would try to help him make sense of the words in front of him. He tried, but his halting, fumbling reading embarrassed him. He made little eye contact, preferring to look down at the table or floor, and he rarely smiled. I tried to make him feel all right about his struggles and to encourage him when he did well. It was uncomfortable for both of us.

For some reason that I can no longer recall, Raymond and I went ice-skating one afternoon. When we got to the rink, he quickly laced up his skates and was off. He loved to ice-skate, and he was good at it. He sped around the rink gracefully and competently, easily losing himself in the rhythms and movements.

I struggled to get the skates on. Then, reluctantly and hesitantly, I stepped out onto the ice. I am not a skater. I had skated some as a child, but not enough to become comfortable or confident; I move around the ice slowly, clumsily, and remain upright only with serious effort and concentration.

When I pushed off and skated awkwardly toward Raymond, he circled back with a big smile on his face. He encouraged me, gave me tips, laughed kindly when I fell, and reached out his hand to help me up. We skated around for what seemed like hours to me and minutes to him. Raymond's joy was evident.

There was no reading lesson that afternoon; but as we headed toward his home, there was a bounce in his step. He beamed and talked eagerly and proudly. We were comfortable.

The next time I came to Raymond's home, we settled in at

the kitchen table. As I pulled out the books, Raymond didn't look at the floor. He looked straight at me, smiled, and began to read.

SALLY BROWN, an avid learner and people person, lives in St. Paul, Minnesota. From the time she was very young, she enjoyed reading about people's lives. In high school, her family hosted a French exchange student. A few years later she lived with the student's family in France. Throughout her life, Sally has sought experiences that connect her with others: in her field of special education, in the Peace Corps, in community leadership and youth development, and through volunteer experiences in cultures different from her own. The things she treasures most are moments of authentic connection with others.

Mom and Trader Joe's

Jo Giese

Dear Customer Relations:

Last week I had a fabulous experience in your Westlake Village, California, store.

It was a sweltering hot day, and I wanted to take an ice cream out to my mom, who was waiting in the car. Since your store had only large packages of ice cream, I asked the nearest Trader Joe's employee if they didn't have anything smaller.

Jonathan Maylard pointed toward the pint containers. I said that was still too big. I explained that my eighty-nine-year-old mom was in the car, she was ill, and this was her first outing in a long time. I wanted to bring out something cool for her while I continued shopping.

He showed me the packages of ice cream bars. "Would she like one of these?" he asked.

"Sure," I said.

"Vanilla or chocolate?"

"Chocolate's her favorite."

He ripped open the carton and handed me an ice cream sandwich for my mom and another for me.

I told him, "You don't know how much this means."

As I was heading out of the store, he rushed up. "I've got something else for your mom!"

He had a bouquet of red roses.

He was about to give them to me when I explained that Mom had so little interaction with people these days that it would be nice if he could give them to her directly.

Before we approached the car, I warned him, "She'll probably cry."

In her pink nightgown she was reclining on pillows in the passenger seat, the only position where her shingles hurt less. The door was open to catch a breeze. I handed her the ice cream and explained it was a gift from Jonathan and Trader Joe's. I introduced her to Jonathan, and he handed her the roses. She cried.

I hugged Jonathan and thanked him for making our day. And I thank *you* for running a humane operation that allows people to shine in their work!

Best, Jo Giese

JO GIESE, a radio journalist, has been a special correspondent to Marketplace, *public radio's daily business program. She lost her husband in 2004 ("Doctoring the Doctor," a thirty-minute documentary about caring for her husband in his last year, aired on* This American Life*), and she has been finishing a book about recovering from loss,* Fumbling Towards Ecstasy. *No longer fumbling, she now lives with her new husband, Ed Warren, in Malibu, California, and Bozeman, Montana. Visit Jo's website at www.jogiese.com.*

My Call of the Wild

Barbara Ludwig

Wanted: Housekeeper, Help w/sled dogs, Remote,
Alcohol/Drug Free   Call 378-XXXX

The ad leapt off the page of the Fairbanks (Alaska) *Daily Miner*
as I sat in the diner washing down blueberry sourdough pan-
cakes with my morning coffee. I had arrived in Fairbanks two
days earlier, free, jobless, and looking for adventure. I couldn't
resist.

Since first reading Jack London's *Call of the Wild* in the
fifth grade more than thirty years earlier, I too had felt the call;
but I'd been putting off that Alaska trip for years. Finally I had
run out of excuses—no dogs, no children, and no men to hold
me back. I boarded the ferry in Bellingham, Washington, and
now I was dialing the number in the ad.

A rugged male voice answered.

Having been warned that "job" postings were not an un-
common way for Alaska men to secure mates, I quickly cut to

the chase and asked him if he was looking for a bed-warmer for the winter months.

His response: "I couldn't put that in the ad."

We both laughed, and since I have always admired honesty and a sense of humor, the interview continued. We agreed to meet on the Parks Highway. I did exercise some caution. I called my friend Janet and gave her his cell phone number and let her know all the details of the meeting place.

His concern was whether I would actually show up, because he had to hike out three miles from his forty-acre homestead and then drive another couple of miles of rough roads to the rendezvous spot. I assured him that I was a person of my word.

Our initial meeting dissolved both of our concerns. As he shouldered my backpack for the hike in, I couldn't help but grin to myself that this was exactly what I was looking for. He was a gen-you-ine Alaskan homesteader.

What a workout! It wasn't easy hiking on boggy moss and lichen.

We were loudly greeted by his thirty-three sled dogs, and he gave me the full tour. This remarkable man had been homesteading his property for twenty years, and his spread included a warm, cozy log house, a greenhouse, and a barn (he raised chickens, geese, and pigeons), all powered by a combination of solar panels, wind turbines, and a generator!

Oh, I forgot to mention that on the way in, he shot two grouse, which he prepared for dinner. That man made a killer brown gravy! A well-read, articulate, witty individual, he told me that his way of life was disappearing and that if I wanted to learn the ropes, I could find no better teacher. If I had any desire to end up with a sled-dog team and a handcrafted dogsled, that could be a possibility as well.

Aaah, the road less traveled has always been my choice. But since his offer included sharing his double bed, I found myself reluctant to hitch my wagon to that particular star. I decided to strike out on my own. After all, if *this* was my first job offer (okay, even if it was an unpaid "position"), I wondered what else Alaska had to offer. Was it a wise decision? You bet! Little did I know then that traveling solo would lead me to managing a remote Alaskan lodge, fishing on Bristol Bay, cooking in the bush for the Iditarod, seeing a Kodiak Island grizzly, and becoming the 2007 Women's Team Crosscut Saw Champion.

BARBARA LUDWIG, aka Blue Bus Barb, has been a traveler without an agenda since the early '80s and was encouraged by friends to put her stories on paper. She works on community building wherever she travels. Since leaving Alaska in 2009, she has become involved in building sustainable communities in northwestern Ontario, Canada. Interested? Intrigued? Contact Barbara at whfeather@hotmail.com.

 Charred Sugar-Crusted Salmon

Adapted from www.alaskaseafood.org

SERVES 4 TO 6

Dry Rub

    4 tablespoons sugar (2 brown and 2 white)
    2 tablespoons chili powder
    1 tablespoon ground cumin
    1 tablespoon paprika

¾ to I tablespoon sea salt
2 teaspoons freshly ground black pepper
½ teaspoon dry mustard
¼ teaspoon cinnamon

Combine all the ingredients in a small bowl. The amount of dry rub here is more than you need for the recipe. Store the extra in a tightly closed container. Not only is the rub delicious on salmon fillets, it can also be used on beef before grilling.

4 to 6 skinless salmon fillets (4 to 6 ounces each)
⅓ to ½ cup Dijon-style mustard
I tablespoon vegetable oil
lemon or lime wedges

Brush one side of the salmon fillets with mustard.

Pat on a generous amount of rub.

Heat the oil in a cast-iron skillet or a heavy-duty pan on high heat.

Cook, seasoned side down, for 2 minutes until charred.

If desired, smear a little more of the coating on the uncoated side. Turn the fillets over, reduce the heat to medium, and continue cooking 4 to 6 minutes more, until the fish is done the way you like it.

Serve with lemon or lime wedges.

The salmon can be served as a main course or cut into pieces with a sharp knife and served as an appetizer on tooth-picks. The fillets can also be cooked under a very hot broiler. Put them on aluminum foil, and set the broiler tray 2 inches from the flame. Cook without turning. The rub becomes crusty and blackened. —ma

My Opinel on the Camino

Ardyn Masterman

The Camino de Santiago is a 770-kilometer ancient pilgrimage path that begins in the Pyrenees in France, runs westward across the top of Spain, and finishes in Santiago de Compostela, the site of the remains of Saint James.

My Camino began in Burgos in 2004. I had been attending a month-long colloquium of Montessori teachers from all over the world. When I discovered that Burgos was on the Camino route, I decided to walk the trail. I repacked my backpack and sent the excess back to Australia. I kept my Opinel knife, which was like my trusted friend. It had been on many an adventure with me, and I had branded it with a distinctive yellow stripe.

At the statue of a gigantic *peregrine* or pilgrim in Astorga, I met Simone from Italy. Together we trailed the market square looking for warm jackets, as the high country was cold this time of year. We found two matching warm suede shirts, and I enjoyed *café con leche* in the busy marketplace.

We found our way out of town following the intermittent

yellow arrows. As the town receded, I looked to the far-off hills on the distant horizon and seriously wondered what on earth I was doing, thinking I could walk that far, let alone to the other side of Spain. As Simone and I walked together, sharing songs and laughter and life stories, the heat, the blisters, and the distant hills seemed far less overwhelming. Big old oaks punctuated the harvested fields. Massive wind turbines were silhouetted along the range to our north.

That night we reached Villa Franca in those distant hills and camped at the *Albergue Rabanal del Camino,* at 1,156 meters. We shared a meal with fellow travelers: a Russian, a German, and a Frenchman. The Frenchman was a young idealist determined to live out the spirit of the Camino by traveling without money, surviving on the generosity and goodwill of others. We shared fresh bread, tomatoes, and basil. Even some beers, as Simone was on a mission to find romance on the Camino. Unfortunately lights-out at 10 P.M. put a damper on the party. Little did I know that in the hurried cleanup in the dark, my trusty Opinel knife went into someone else's pack.

The next day I missed my knife, but by then I was dealing with a more imposing issue. Simone and I had different walking paces, so we separated. I suddenly felt very alone on my trek through a foreign land. But as I kept pushing forward through my fears, I met other people and made more friends. I felt reinvigorated by the adventure and spirit of the Camino.

I walked and sang for twelve days. In Galicia I met a man carrying a three-meter hardwood cross. Finally I walked into Santiago with an elated "tribe" from many nations, united in our accomplishment.

We were treated to a special holy-year viewing of relics and experienced the mass for the *peregrinos,* with the abbots hauling on the ropes of the giant swinging incense ball. Our tribe's elder suggested a "communion dinner," and we each shared something from our own Camino. I brought along my most recent walking stick, decorated with dried flowers and herbs, and I talked about nature being my solace and my rejuvenation. We rested for a day overlooking the ancient cathedral.

I bused on to Finisterre on the coast. As I walked into the albergue, I couldn't believe my eyes. On the table was my trusty Opinel knife with its telltale yellow stripe. It had done its own Camino without me! I asked who had been carrying it and suddenly recognized the French guy I'd met at Villa Franca. I was so pleased that my knife had turned up and had helped this brave and trusting soul on his journey. He had lived out the spirit of faith, friendship, and generosity, which encapsulated the Camino. He thanked me and said it had been invaluable, as many times he had used it to garner meals from crops in the fields.

With a sense of everything falling into place, I walked on to the tip of the headland at the very endpoint of the Camino amid a crackling thunderstorm, trying to keep up with a sprightly eighty-year-old German grandmother. I re-met fellow *peregrinos*. Even Simone arrived, flushed with romance. (She had found her Camino "husband" for the trip.) As we sat by a roaring fire, looking out to the last of the sunset beneath black flash-lit clouds and the wild sea below, I tingled with the elation of the moment, the place, and my personal achievement.

ARDYN MASTERMAN, who resides in Australia, was born into a life of adventure and travel. She feels most alive and inspired when on the move, exploring and living in new destinations, experiencing and adapting to different places and cultures. She is passionate about life, learning, and growing, and she loves sharing adventures and healing with others. She walks on pilgrimages to soothe her soul, climbs mountains to feel uplifted, sails to remote places on forays into wilderness, and hitches rides on light aircraft to get home. Along the way she is inspired to grow, dance, draw, paint, and write. Visit Ardyn's travel blog at www.adventureposs .wordpress.com.

Breakfast in Malacca

Wendy Lewis

It was our first day of a month-long trip to Malaysia. My friend and I had landed in Singapore the day before and caught the bus up the Malay Peninsula to the weathered Portuguese trading port of Malacca.

After staying the night in an old Chinese hotel, we went out looking for a place to eat breakfast. The street was full of small family-owned restaurants and stands selling delicious-looking and sumptuous-smelling food.

We finally decided on a place. As we entered the small corner restaurant, we saw a Malaysian woman sitting inside enjoying a plate of sizzling-hot fresh seafood on top of what looked like wide noodles. We wished her good morning and asked for the name of the dish she was eating. She told us, and we ordered it.

Later, as we were enjoying our rather unusual but delicious breakfast of shrimp, fish, squid, vegetables, and noodles cooked in pungent Asian spices, the lady finished her meal and came over to talk to us.

She asked us if we were enjoying the dish and how long we were going to be visiting Malaysia. We chatted for a few minutes, and she left wishing us a happy vacation and hoping we would enjoy our visit to her country.

We finished and waddled to the counter to find out how much we owed. The owner said, "Oh, nothing. That lady who was eating here before has paid for you."

What a beautiful gesture and welcome to our wonderful month in Malaysia.

WENDY LEWIS was born and raised in England and always dreamed of traveling to the faraway places she learned of in geography classes. After moving to the United States and raising two children, Wendy's dream came true, and during a ten-year period she traveled extensively throughout the world. She now lives in central Mexico and continues to travel.

Sharing Laundry

Clare Beckingham

After traveling forty kilometers outside of Danang in Vietnam, we arrived in the small village of Dai Loc. We were two Western volunteers who were there to help out in an orphanage.

My plan had been to use arts and crafts to teach English and build confidence, but I found out they were expecting a full-fledged English teacher. This came as quite a shock to me—and would've been equally shocking to my old English teacher!

I was absolutely petrified. As much as I wanted to be there, the thought of dealing with the cultural differences was overwhelming. I would have to discard my Western way of being in control of everything around me. But even more scary was the fact that the people at the orphanage and I didn't even share a language.

Sitting outside the orphanage a few hours after I arrived, I was shaking. Everyone else appeared nervous as well. My friend and I had never been to Vietnam before, and the staff had never had Western volunteers.

Soon a moped arrived balancing two mattresses on the back. The mattresses turned out to be twice the size of the bedframes. I had to convince the staff not to saw them in half.

Providing mattresses was the only bit of special treatment that was given to us, and that was fine by me. I wanted the real deal and I got it, but I don't think I could've coped on wooden slats.

As I'd been traveling before I arrived in Vietnam, I was desperately short of clean clothes. I communicated this to one of the mothers. (The five staff looking after the children were called mothers.) She took me by the arm, and we strode off to the "laundry," which was a room with the floor at a slight angle and a hole in the corner for drainage. The room was used for washing clothes, food, and anything else that needed a good hose-down. There were two cold-water taps and various bowls and pails.

I am of the press-a-button-and-stand-back school of washing, but I showed that I could muck in with the best by squatting—somewhat difficult with Western thighs—and scrubbing. Watching me brought smiles to the Vietnamese women, who couldn't resist taking over and showing me how it really should be done. I tried to join the scrubbing at various intervals, but they wouldn't hear of it.

Fascinated by the size of my clothes, the head mother skipped around the room in various ensembles of my wet clothes. The others were all rolling about, laughing. I realized that I appeared an extremely large woman to them. Somewhat amazed there could be a chest to fill a bra *that* size, the head mother was aghast at my Marks & Spencer B-cup!

We mimed jokes and together roared with laughter. We connected with our eyes and deep smiles.

A very strong bond was created that night over my dirty clothes. The staff had been worried about our arrival, and I had been worried about being there. But this special night proved we had nothing to worry about. The memory of that experience will remain with me forever.

I met many Vietnamese women who had an inner sparkle and strength. But one in particular, the head mother of the orphanage, was raising thirty children with the most wonderful compassion, love, and care I'd ever seen. And all in her stride. We did share the same language after all.

CLARE BECKINGHAM'S inquisitive mind and zest for life has led her to explore the world in many different ways. Inspired by a trip to New Zealand, she left a sensible job, went back to college, and hatched a plan to work from anywhere in the world. A year in Christchurch, New Zealand, ignited a passion for glaciers, leading to a failed attempt to get to Antarctica. On the return journey home to the United Kingdom she volunteered in a Vietnam orphanage, an experience that touched her deeply. She is still trying to get to Antarctica. Contact Clare at hello@clarebeckingham.com.

Kava and Trauma on Waya Island

Danielle Richards

Waya Island is one of more than three hundred South Pacific islands that make up Fiji. My experience there was definitely not what I had expected. From the moment we arrived at the village where my friend and I were staying, we realized that old customs still prevailed.

Each night of our visit we participated in the kava ceremony. Made traditionally, the kava root is chewed into a pulp, then water is added. It's then served from a large homemade coconut bowl. We would sit cross-legged in a circle inside the *bure* (a traditional thatched hut) as Septi, the chief of the village, filled smaller, individual coconut bowls. When we received our bowl, we would say "Bula," drink it down in one gulp, then clap twice. Universally used to say "hello," or "welcome," *Bula* means "life" and is a way of wishing good health and fortune to the recipient.

Sharing this kava drink is believed to allow friendships to flourish. When you are drinking it for hours, it has a relaxing and numbing effect. Kava ceremonies started off formal and energetic and always ended with voices merging, as the men played slow beautiful Fijian love songs on their ukuleles, and we sang along.

During one of these ceremonies, Septi asked me if I would like a "Fiji friend" to "tell stories with." Misunderstanding his meaning, I naïvely agreed. Moments later a boy named Andrew was presented to me. I was told, "He speaks good English and can play rugby!" Upon learning the meaning of this arrangement, and specifically what "telling stories" was (it didn't involve talking), I declined the offer of a "Fiji friend."

At breakfast the next morning, groggy from the ceremony the night before, I accidentally poured boiling water for tea on my hand. Not realizing the pain that would come, I decided to join the villagers on a hike to the next village.

As we were walking, my hand suddenly felt as if it were on fire. When we arrived, Andrew took me to see a woman who had lived with a tribe that was known for walking on fire. She clasped my hand in hers, said many things in Fijian I didn't understand, and called for Colgate!

For the rest of the afternoon everything from toothpaste, raw fish, butter, and goat fur was rubbed on my hand. As evening approached, most of the group headed back. Before I knew it, it was dark. "Fiji time," or the slow-paced lack of schedule that characterizes Fiji life, had gotten hold of me.

Waya Island had no cars, no roads, no electricity, and lots of rocky terrain. The walk back seemed daunting. Andrew held my uninjured hand and led me through the brush in the dark with extreme patience.

Our last night there was surreal. During a kava ceremony/going-away party for my friend and me, I got sick. Later I found out that I was suffering from dysentery, but at the time, the mixture of kava, laughter, and fun had me so elated, I thought it was nothing. The ladies insisted on walking me to the bathroom each time I had to go, which seemed like every five minutes. This was so telling of the generosity of spirit that existed there.

When I woke up the next morning, I headed for the bathroom but didn't make it in time. I changed into something else and was carrying my dirty pants when I rushed off to meet the boat that would take me back to the main island. The rest of the details are blurry, but I remember holding these pants while receiving a marriage proposal from Andrew and promises of breadfruit and biscuits.

Moments later, wishing Andrew well, I boarded the boat. During the ride I felt tingles inside my head and stomach, the kind you feel when your foot falls asleep. These tingles spread throughout my body. I remember my fingers not being able to move, fixed in a clawlike position. My jaw, too, was locked; I was talking through my teeth. Literally, I was stuck.

The men on the boat massaged my limbs to try to bring feeling back. I was sure I was going to die right there in the middle of the South Pacific Ocean. I still don't know what happened to me on that boat. Maybe it was fear, or maybe it was dehydration. The only water I had drunk for days was mixed with the kava. I knew I should have been drinking bottled water, but there wasn't any available on the island.

What I do know is that on my trip to Waya Island I had some unexpected adventures. Although I experienced a painful burn, a failed marriage proposal, dysentery, and the obvious consequences of traveling without being prepared, I found out how extremely comforting the warmth of unfamiliar people could be.

DANIELLE RICHARDS *has been traveling since she was in the womb. Having learned about the joys of travel from her parents, she loves exploring new places and having adventures. She was a founding teacher of the first solar-powered charter school in the United States and currently attends Northern Arizona University, where she is pursuing her second master's degree. Contact Danielle at danielle_haka@hotmail.com.*

An Awakening

Kim Bass

Immaculate was not! The white ants, red ants, sugar ants, crickets, cicadas, moths, butterflies, and mice were winning. Immaculate was our cook and housekeeper. She was a good cook, considering what little she had to work with. Most Ugandans eat high-starch foods to fill their bellies; they have no money for spices to make them flavorful. She was not an immaculate housekeeper, which was why the ants and mice were winning.

I had just started my second week working in the Learning Empowers Uganda Medical Clinic in Soroti, registering patients. The job was so much more than clerical work; its impact is still with me today, four years later.

Each day before 7:30 A.M. a representative from one of the internal displacement camps would sign up people who wanted to come to the clinic. (The civil wars had forced thirteen thousand residents off of their own lands where they farmed or ranched, mostly in northern Uganda and Sudan.) Patients had to walk to our clinic, some as much as thirty minutes in the throes of their illness. And when they got there, they had to wait patiently, sometimes for hours, usually sitting or lying on grass mats.

Most of the patients had malaria, urinary tract infections (not much water here), dehydration, AIDS, typhoid, or dysentery. One day I met a seventeen-year-old woman who was dying of cancer. She had known she was dying for four years. She had come to us for pain medication, but we had run out. Imagine being seventeen and living with the fact that you are dying. Or being the mother and feeling the frustration of not being able to get pain medication for your daughter.

Volunteering there was a challenge for me, unlike any I have ever faced. What agony to look this mother and child in the eyes and tell them we could not help. And to face all the others who were beyond help. There is enough painkiller in the world. There is enough water and food. Why can't we help?

During my six weeks in Uganda my emotions were often uncontrollable and unrecognizable to me. One day early in my journey, Philip, my new Ugandan friend, took me to see the Atcholi Quarter, where BeadForLife was helping people create new lives for themselves. I saw very old women and very young children, maybe five or six years old, hammering rocks the size of basketballs into pea gravel. They hammered all day to make one or two cubic yards of gravel (think of a bag of mulch) for just under one dollar a day. They all looked older than they were, yet they had a special spirit and winning smiles.

I stood on top of a hill in the Atcholi Quarter of Kampala and cried. No, it was a deeper feeling, almost an uncontrollable moaning from deep within. Philip asked me if I needed time for myself or if I would like someone to cry with me. Having someone offer to cry with me was a new experience.

I was beginning to realize that in this culture, people did not bear pain and suffering alone. Tribal togetherness was intense, and in keeping with tradition, even the wants and needs and desires of visitors were everyone's concerns.

Philip's considerate offer reminded me of the strong sense of community that we in Western cultures typically experience only in our biological families. Here in Uganda, when one member of the community suffers, everyone suffers.

I was amazed and joyous at the people and the support I felt, but I also felt shame for my good fortune in life, and for my ignorance of the suffering in so many other parts of the world.

I cried alone. As much as I wanted to respect the culture, I was used to dealing with my deepest feelings of pain and sorrow alone, especially when I was in new emotional territory.

A big sigh to release a bit of my anger about the unfairness of it all . . .

KIM BASS has traveled to Africa to help with the Soroti Clinic and www.BeadForLife.com, and to the Caribbean and Central and South America to work in orphanages and on other projects. At home in Sarasota, Florida, she is a real estate investor, an artist, an ardent AIDS and women's rights advocate, and a cancer survivor. Contact Kim at kabelement@aol.com.

Mixed Messages

The Beauty Contest

Rita Golden Gelman

Not being able to ask questions is always the hardest part—for me, anyway—of living in a culture where I don't speak the language. I can help with the cooking, giggle with babies, sing with kids, and laugh and mime my way through most days. I can connect through touch and a smile and sometimes through tears. But I can't ask questions.

In Thailand I became very close to the family who owned the bungalows where I stayed. No one spoke more than twenty words of English. One evening Fon, the daughter of the owner, knocked on my door. "Come," she said.

I couldn't ask where, so I slipped on my sandals and followed her to the pickup. Family kids filled the open back of the truck. Fon motioned for me to sit in the cabin with her. We drove (silently) for about ten minutes and then followed a road lit by many colored lights to a parking lot. As we all walked toward a big school building, we passed stands selling chicken on skewers, noodles, and other tastes of Thailand. Music filled the air. There were game booths and drinks and trinkets. But Fon didn't stop. We followed her into the building.

It turned out she was taking us to a beauty contest. Hundreds of people sat on folding chairs in a huge gymnasium with a stage in the front. The judging had already begun. Contestant number four, dressed in a soft blue, full-length nylon tulle gown, a diaphanous scarf that seemed to billow with each step, and a sparkling tiara, entered from stage right and walked to the freestanding stairway in the center of the stage. Each contestant had to climb up the stairs and down—in very high heels—demonstrating gracefulness, ease, and fluidity.

Then the contestants were interviewed. Some were obviously nervous, while others were relaxed, engaging both the judges and the audience with their smiles and their sparkling eyes. I didn't understand a word, but I loved the musicality of their voices and the flowing gestures of their hands and arms.

The tiny-waisted contestants posed and walked and curtsied. Then they walked, posed, and curtsied some more. They were all beautiful; I didn't envy the judges. It wasn't going to be easy to decide who should be crowned the winner.

People in the audience could vote by buying a bouquet of flowers for their favorite contestant. The contestants received the bouquets as they exited the stage. Shortly after the contestant left, the bouquets were brought back to the table and sold again.

After about fifteen minutes I poked Fon and indicated that my choice was number six. Fon smiled but didn't tell me her favorite.

Upon seeing a few more contestants, she poked me and spoke. "Boys, no girls."

It took me a couple of minutes. I looked up at the stage,

at the spectacularly beautiful contestants, and found it impossible to believe. The contestants, in their elaborate gowns, with their exquisite figures, their graceful movements, and their grand curtsies were all male transvestites.

 Larb Gai

Adapted from a traditional recipe

SERVES 6 AS AN APPETIZER

---

*T*his Thai dish makes a great appetizer or light lunch and is very refreshing on a hot day. It sounds complicated but it's really easy. If some of the ingredients are not available locally, go to www.amazon.com/grocery and they will send you to a mail-order company. You will find Kaffir lime leaves, lemongrass, and palm sugar as well as other ingredients used in international dishes. —rgg

2 tablespoons uncooked jasmine rice

1 pound kale or 2 pounds spinach, heavy stems stripped off

1 pound boneless chicken

1 tablespoon vegetable oil

2 tablespoons fish sauce, plus more to taste

6 tablespoons coarsely chopped shallots

3 tablespoons coarsely chopped mint leaves

3 tablespoons coarsely chopped cilantro leaves

2 tablespoons paper-thin-sliced lemongrass, white part only

2 tablespoons needle-thin-sliced Kaffir lime leaves, about ½ inch long

1 tablespoon palm sugar (or granulated if palm is not available)

3 tablespoons lime juice, plus more to taste

In a dry heavy pan, fry the uncooked rice, stirring constantly, until it is brown. Remove from heat.

Pound the rice in a mortar or grind it until it's the consistency of large breadcrumbs. (A clean coffee grinder works well.) Set aside.

Barely cook the kale or spinach in about ½ inch of water in a covered pot. As soon as it wilts, take it off the fire. Drain it, let it cool, squeeze out the water, and pat it dry. Set aside.

Mince the chicken using a food processor or chef's knife. Sometimes a butcher will do it for you. (You can usually buy chicken already minced in Asian markets.)

Heat the oil. Add the minced chicken and cook it over high heat until fully cooked. As it cooks, add 1 tablespoon fish sauce. Let it cool, and break up the clumps with your fingers.

Put the room-temperature chicken into a medium bowl. Add the shallots, mint, cilantro, lemongrass, and lime leaves.

Mix the sugar with the lime juice and 1 tablespoon fish sauce, and add to the bowl, thoroughly combining the ingredients. (If the palm sugar is not liquid, you may have to dissolve it in a little water or put a chunk in the microwave to liquefy it.)

Add 1 tablespoon ground rice, and mix it in.

Serve as appetizer on individual plates over a bed of barely cooked kale or spinach.

Sprinkle a little ground rice on top of each just before serving.

....

*Shredded fresh lettuce can be used instead of kale or spinach. And I always make extra browned ground rice (*khao khur*) and keep it with my spices. It's great in salads and on vegetables . . . stays crunchy. —rgg*

....

A Long Walk

Laura Fellman

It was said that she lived in a northwestern state. She was, above all, adventurous. Challenging herself was critical to her self-identity, and she dreamed big.

Charlie Nokes was another story. He'd spent four years as a World War II prisoner of war. Later he was a pharmacist and then a vice president at a large investment firm, enjoying adventure in other forms. When he was older, he loved to escape the summer desert heat by retreating north to the Idaho Rockies. It was Charlie who told me about the adventurous young woman.

In his escapes north Charlie volunteered as the camp host at Caribou-Targhee National Forest in Idaho. One day he was driving out of this secluded park, up a steep road, when he saw a young woman walking out of the mountains toward him. She was wearing overalls, a checkered blouse, and a straw hat; she was leading a heavily laden burro. Her large dog frisked around her. Astonished at the movie-set scene before him, Charlie stopped to talk to her and learned she was walking the length of the Continental Divide, from northern border to southern coast, alone.

Being a kind man and wanting to hear more, Charlie invited the woman to his motor home for a meal. After dinner he took out some photos of the area to show her. Noticing she was holding them just inches from her face, he asked her why.

She replied, "I'm blind."

LAURA FELLMAN, while living as unstructured a life as possible, keeps herself open to the new awareness that the exploration of desire and fear can bring. She is a student of the inward life, with increasing detachment from all that is transient. She travels often to do a North American, modern-age, nomadic version of retreating to a cave . . . the cave being her car: wandering while exploring the mind and its many false images and tricks. Contact Laura at laurafellman@shaw.ca.

Pickup in a Bar

Jacquie

Traveling by myself was not natural. Even though I had been divorced five years, traveling alone did not appeal to me. But I knew it was way past time for me to move on. I resolved to be a freer spirit. A massage therapist conference in Kansas City was a start.

I needed to define the woman hidden underneath the heartbreaks and the constant struggles of my life. My friends thought it was time for me to have a sexual "relationship." Was that really the solution? Perhaps in Kansas City I would find out.

I arrived at my hotel at ten in the evening. I hadn't eaten dinner. I was starving. But by the time I checked in and deposited my baggage in my room, the restaurant had closed. I thought about ordering room service, but what about my new-found resolve?

I went down to the lobby, where a cheerful hotel employee told me the bar was open until midnight and had pretty good sandwiches. Again, my old self considered going back upstairs and ordering room service, but that newfound-spirit thing had me moving gracefully toward the bar.

When I surveyed the bar, I saw lots of tables, a soccer game on the television, and an athletic-looking man about my age sitting at the bar, watching the game. My old self considered a quiet table by myself, but that "spirit" eased me over to the barstool right next to the man at the bar.

The conversation that ensued covered his love for biking, my experiences running marathons, his home in California, and mine in Arkansas. I inherited a gift for getting strangers to open up their lives to me from my mother, God rest her soul. During our pleasurable conversation, I ordered a glass of wine and a sandwich, and I began to see myself through his eyes: an attractive and available woman talking to a man in a bar. I was holding my own. Maybe sex was the answer to the opening of my heart? I was so absorbed in the conversation that I barely noticed when another man took a seat on the other side of me and ordered a beer.

Soon the three of us were talking about everything and nothing, laughing and reflecting. More than once I found myself thinking, *Is this really me sitting here between these two men, in this bar, at 11 P.M. in Kansas City?* It wasn't long before the first man got up, said goodnight, and left me sitting there with the second man. I began to look more closely at this gentleman.

He was a little older than I, nice-looking, with clothes and an accent that were indicative of a rural lifestyle. We chatted about his dogs and his work as a salesman. When my wine was gone, he asked if he could buy me another. He asked awkwardly if I frequented bars at hotels in the late-evening hours, and he touched my leg, more than once. Not in a "coming on to you" way, but rather in the natural course of the conversation. Well, at least that was how I chose to think of it.

A little later he got the meal he had ordered from room service. It came on a huge tray, with soup, a salad, steak and baked potato, a dessert, and a pitcher of iced tea. This man was hungry.

That hungry man's dinner was still sitting on the tray next to him at midnight when the bartender, who had been observing our connection, announced last call. Earlier, I had refused the man's offer to buy me a second glass of wine. At that point he stopped touching my leg. But our conversation, the smiling, the flirting, and the wondering were certainly still there.

I had not yet made a decision about whether I wanted to see the inside of his room and more. I offered to help him carry his huge food tray up to his room. He seemed embarrassed, but as we got up from the bar, I grabbed the pitcher of tea. He took his tray. As we walked through the lobby, the employee who had directed me to the bar earlier smiled very knowingly at us and asked the man if he intended to share his dinner with me for "helping him upstairs with the tray." Neither of us replied. On the way up in the elevator, he told me I had great legs.

By the time we made it to his floor, I was very surprised at how relaxed I was feeling. As we stood there at the threshold of his door, I knew it would take only a few words from me, and he would be more than happy to end my sexual repression. I could see myself in his arms, in his bed. I could taste his kiss, feel his tenderness. It had been such a long time. He was a gentleman, and he was obviously having a hard time reading me. Hell, I was having a hard time reading me!

I shook his hand and thanked him for the conversation, and we said goodnight. I was still formulating the words that could have changed everything: *Can I come in? So, are you going to share your dinner with me? I'm not really ready to end the evening.*

By the time I made it two floors down and crawled into my own bed, I was wondering why those words and a simple one-night stand could be so easy for so many and so difficult for me.

But I also had an inner sense, a sort of peace, knowing that someday, somehow, I'd know why I slept alone that night. It would be three years before I knew. His name is Larry. He is my husband.

JACQUIE WAS MARRIED for sixteen years, single for seven, and recently celebrated her third wedding anniversary with Larry. They enjoy life with their blended family. She achieved balance and tremendously strengthened her spirituality during a decade of heartbreaks, challenges, and loss by working 12-step programs of recovery, one day at a time. She encourages women to keep in mind that what may seem like an ending can very well be a beginning and suggests that if you have trouble finding a purpose in life, try finding a purpose for each new day—or each new hour! Contact Jacquie at lemwin@sbcglobal.net.

Curry Calamity

Karen van der Zee

I did not always know how to cook. When I married my Peace Corps Volunteer husband in a ten-minute ceremony in Kenya, I did not know how to boil a potato. Fortunately I was able to read and follow directions. With the help of Fannie Farmer's cookbook, I managed to produce edible meals—spaghetti, meat loaf, beef stew.

More interesting things began to develop when I ventured away from Fannie Farmer into the unknown realms of Indian cuisine. Many Indians reside in Kenya; on several occasions I had the opportunity to eat curry with them, usually chicken or beef. Curry was a strange and exotic flavor to me, coming as I did from meat-and-potato Holland. But being a lover of things adventurous, I embraced this new culinary experience with enthusiasm. Curry was different. It was hot. It was spicy. It brought tears to your eyes. It was magic!

Then one day in Nyeri I discovered a can of curry powder on a grocery store shelf. Although imported from England, it proclaimed itself to be an authentic Indian product. It was very yellow, which should have been a warning, but what did I know? I hurried home full of excitement. I could now make my own beef curry! Having mastered the art of making a halfway decent beef stew, I was confident that all I needed to do to make beef curry was to add the missing ingredient: curry powder.

That very afternoon I set to work in my kitchen, a tiny shed built as an afterthought onto our ramshackle little house with its lovely lemon tree in front.

Fannie Farmer in hand, I produced the stew and then carefully measured a teaspoon of yellow curry powder into it and stirred. I tasted the result.

Nothing.

I stirred in increasingly greater amounts, becoming more and more desperate when the stew turned a sickly greenish-yellow without tasting like anything resembling beef curry.

It was something else, something altogether unique. When the famous gourmet Jean Anthelme Brillat-Savarin stated that the discovery of a new dish does more for the happiness of the human race than the discovery of a star, this was not the dish he had in mind.

To tell you the painful and embarrassing truth, it was revolting.

But the ravaged stew was the only food available for dinner that night, and my man ate it. But then, he loved me.

The next day I went to the Indian grocery store and asked the owner what magic was needed to make a good curry. He gave me a pitying look, as if he had no hope for me in the curry department. He said to come back the next day, and his wife would give me the spices.

Spices? Plural?

Intrigued, I returned the next morning. Swathed in a

colorful sari, a diamond in her nose and a lovely smile on her face, the owner's wife gave me a lengthy explanation of the secrets of making a "simple" beef curry. It wasn't quite like Fannie Farmer's stew. She handed me an assortment of individually wrapped, freshly ground spices. It was a moment of great discovery: Curry is not a spice.

Not one to let ignorance defeat me, I set out further along the path of culinary knowledge, cheered on by my food-loving husband. This was a good thing since I was destined to have three children, many guests, and a long career in the kitchen.

And one day I may create a dish that will change the world.

HAILING FROM THE NETHERLANDS, Karen van der Zee is an expatriate writer not living in paradise. She's not remodeling an old farmhouse in Italy and does not drink wine from her own grapes. She has, however, seen her Palestinian butcher's bedroom in Ramallah, dined on fertility goat sausage in Kenya, and attended a traditional bride-price ceremony in Ghana. She is finishing a book about her expat (mis)adventures and excerpts are posted on her blog www.lifeintheexpatlane.blogspot.com. She is the author of thirty-five romance novels. Her nonfiction has appeared in The Washington Post *and other publications. Visit Karen's website at www.karenvanderzee.com.*

Curry refers to an entire category of dishes, rather than to a single spice or mixture of spices. No recipe for beef curry is set in stone, as there is no set recipe for spaghetti sauce or beef stew. Every woman worth her spices has created her own version or learned the secrets from her mother or grandmother. —kvdz

Beef (or Lamb) Curry

Adapted by Karen van der Zee

SERVES 4 TO 6

---

2 tablespoons salted butter or ghee (clarified butter)

2 large onions, chopped

2 cloves garlic, minced

2 tablespoons minced fresh ginger root

2 tablespoons ground coriander

2 teaspoons ground cumin

1 teaspoon ground turmeric

1 to 3 teaspoons cayenne pepper (you might want to start
   with half a teaspoon)

1 teaspoon salt

½ teaspoon freshly ground black pepper

2 tomatoes, peeled and chopped (or a generous cup of
   drained, canned Italian tomatoes)

2½ cups boiling water

2 pounds stew beef (or lamb), in 1-inch cubes

1 teaspoon garam masala (if not available locally, go to www
   .amazon.com/grocery)

Fresh cilantro leaves, for garnish

Heat the butter or ghee in a Dutch oven or heavy pot with a
tight-fitting lid, and sauté the chopped onion for a few minutes on high heat until it turns light golden.

Lower the heat slightly. Add the minced garlic and ginger, and
sauté about 2 minutes longer. Do not allow the garlic to
burn.

Add the dry spices and chopped tomatoes, and sauté for another minute or so until the fragrance of the spices comes out.

Add the boiling water, then the cubes of meat. Simmer on low heat for 2 hours (about 1 hour for lamb) until the meat is fork-tender and the sauce has thickened.

Transfer to a serving dish. Sprinkle with garam masala, and garnish with cilantro leaves. Serve with rice and chutney of your choice.

If you really want to impress your guests, serve this curry as they do in restaurants in Kenya, with as many side dishes of chopped fruits, nuts, and vegetables as you can think of, which you then pile on top of the curry. The result is a feast of color and utterly delicious. Here are some of the foods you can use, diced where necessary: tomatoes, red onion, green onion, hot chiles, cucumber, green or red sweet pepper, mangoes, peaches, bananas, peanuts, raisins, coconut.

Have on hand some thick, plain yogurt or clabbered milk, which cools the mouth and enhances the flavor of the curry, and enjoy. —kvdz

My Airport Pal

Rita Golden Gelman

It was 1995. I had a flight out of Bali to the United States for
the Christmas holidays. I checked two big bags full of sculpted
gods, carved lovers, rolled batik paintings, *ikat* fabrics, and
cotton sarongs to give away to family and friends. Once in the
passenger area, I bought a few magazines, a chocolate bar, and
USA Today, and then I headed for a seat. I was an hour early.

As I walked toward the waiting area, there was an an-
nouncement. For no apparent reason, all the flights on Garuda,
the Indonesian airline, were delayed by at least two hours. The
weather was bright and sunny, the airport was only moderately
crowded, and terrorism wasn't yet on the docket. Hmmm. I
wasn't in a hurry. My only concern was what I would do during that three-hour wait. I looked around for some unsuspect-
ing, interesting-looking soul.

He was fiftyish with a scraggly beard, a long, thin face,
and a light brown ponytail topped with a baseball hat. His
lanky legs were sprawled in front of him, forcing other passengers to step around them with their rolling carry-ons. A

ton of earrings and hoops hung from assorted piercings, and about ten silver chains dangled from his neck: delicate ones, heavy-linked ones, and twisted, braided ones, some reaching nearly to his waist. His short-sleeved shirt revealed two wrists full of bangles and wide Balinese bracelets. Three and a half decades away from the '60s, and it looked like he had never moved on. I decided that he'd probably be interesting. I sat down next to him.

Jeff was from Oregon and had already made nine trips to Bali. He was deeply involved in a serious love affair with the magical island. (I understood completely.) He told me that he spent six months out of every year in Bali, buying jewelry and artwork. The other six months he spent in the Pacific North-west, selling his wares—at flea markets, neighborhood fairs, and in the living rooms of acquaintances—for at least four times what he'd paid.

The United States charged an import duty on jewelry meant for resale, but it was okay to bring in a certain amount of used personal items without paying taxes on them. That explained the baubles and chains and earrings that were deco-rating his body.

We chatted until the plane took off; I didn't see him again until we reached Los Angeles. We walked together toward customs pushing our baggage in carts, the ones that were free every place in the world except the United States.

"They always stop me," he said. "Just watch."

I did, and they did. A woman in uniform tapped him on the shoulder and told him to come with her. I slowed down and stood next to him to see what would happen next.

"Are you with him?" she asked.

"Sort of," I answered.

She hesitated, looked at him, looked at me, and then, visibly disappointed, told him, "Oh, okay. Go on through." And she walked away.

We both had a couple of hours before our connecting flights took off.

"I owe you a drink," he said when we were finished in customs. We sat down on stools at one of the airport bars.

"Thanks," he said when the drinks arrived. He tapped my glass of wine with his. "If it hadn't been for you, I could have been in a lot of trouble."

"Oh? What kind of trouble?"

"I've got two bags of marijuana in the lining of my suitcase."

A Wet Shoe Story

Carolyn Soucy

In May 2005 seven members of the New Hampshire Master Chorale took a two-week trip to Vietnam. We were collaborating with the Vietnamese National Opera and Ballet for a concert series in Hanoi and Halong Bay.

When we arrived in Hanoi, we were informed that our home-stay families would be parents of children in the youth choir. I met Minh Hoa and her five-year-old daughter, Cat Phuong, at the Hanoi Opera House, and they whisked me away on a very long cab ride to their apartment.

It hadn't occurred to me, until I was in the cab, that I might not be entirely welcome in their home. After all, this was North Vietnam. True, Minh Hoa had agreed to house me, but during our conversation at the Opera House, she mentioned she shared her home with her parents. Unlike Minh Hoa, her parents were old enough to remember the war, and I was worried they might not be enthusiastic about hosting an American. Although Minh Hoa herself was friendly and kind, I was completely at the mercy of this family. If they harbored feelings of resentment, I wouldn't know until I arrived, and I had no idea where I was going or how I could contact anyone else in my group.

Once we arrived, I realized I had been foolish to worry. Minh Hoa's family welcomed me into their home with the utmost grace and warmth. Her parents smiled at me and showed me to my room, which was probably theirs, as it was the largest bedroom and opened to a balcony overlooking the street. They were keen to ensure I was comfortable and well fed. At the midday meal they insisted on filling my bowl every time it was empty despite my protests. Minh Hoa was the only person in the house who spoke English and just a small amount at that. With Minh Hoa translating, her mother said after lunch, "You should rest now. It is good for you," and I was happy to oblige. It was clear there were no feelings of anger toward me, even though the United States had been on the other side of the war in Vietnam.

On the second day of my stay with them, it started to rain in the afternoon. It began as a light shower and turned into a torrential downpour that lasted over an hour. The crowded city streets quickly flooded with four inches of dirty water, and traffic came to a halt.

At 6:30 P.M. Minh Hoa called for a cab to take us to the Hanoi Opera House for our concert. By 7:00 the cab had still not arrived, which was not surprising, considering the depth of water in the street. Every time a vehicle dared to drive by, water flowed into the kitchen. At 7:30 the cab finally arrived, and we all headed for the door.

Minh Hoa's father carried Cat Phuong to the car so she wouldn't get her feet wet. I readied myself for a wade. But before I stepped off the curb, Minh Hoa's mother stood below me in the street and motioned for me to get on her back. I would estimate her mother at sixty-years-old, five foot two, and 115 pounds. I was a twenty-six-year-old, five foot six, 175-pound *moose* compared to this petite woman. And she wanted me to get on her back!

I do not speak Vietnamese except for a few important phrases, and "I am not getting on your back" was not one of them.

She argued with me in Vietnamese, and I argued right back in English, our arms waving frantically. Ignoring my protests, she turned her back to me, and with her feet planted in the newly formed lake in the street, she enthusiastically patted her shoulders. When I tried to step around her, she moved from side to side, blocking my path. It was clear she didn't understand that I was saying no, but I kept objecting anyway. Even though she couldn't see me because her back was turned, I waved my arms and exclaimed loudly, "*No!* Please!"

She turned around then, and the look on my face of astonishment and stubborn refusal must have been enough for her to change tactics. As I again tried to step off the curb, she grabbed my arm and held out her hand, motioning for me to wait. She rushed into the apartment and returned with a pair of her best slip-on shoes and then helped me out of my own dress shoes and into hers. She handed me my shoes and smiled as I stepped into the muddy water. I could hardly believe it. This kind woman, who barely knew me, gave me her best shoes so that mine would not be ruined by the water. I was instantly filled with respect and love for these gracious and caring people.

CAROLYN SOUCY'S travel adventures began at the age of seven. In recent years she has participated in choral tours to South Korea,

Vietnam, Brazil, and Peru. Upon completion of her M.A. in Arts Administration and Cultural Policy, she plans to combine her two passions, music and travel, and to champion quality arts programming worldwide. A New Hampshire native, she currently resides in London. Visit the New Hampshire Master Chorale at www .nhmasterchorale.org.

Million-Dollar Moment

Bonnie Worthen

Michael, my husband-to-be, is a procrastinating dreamer who had been putting off a trip to Peru for thirty-five years. I'm impetuous. The day Michael told me of his dream, I booked flights for a two-week trip to Cuzco.

Many of our friends were concerned that we were going to such a dangerous country; there had been guerrilla warfare in the Peruvian jungles for many years. The train that we were planning to take between Cuzco and Machu Picchu had been robbed several times. Nonetheless, our excitement eclipsed any fears we had.

A month after booking, we boarded our flight. Twelve hours later we deplaned in Cuzco. The air was crisp and clear, and the sky was an immaculate translucent blue.

We had been warned about taxis; I had read tales of tourists being cheated. And worse. A man at the airport approached us and asked if we needed a hotel or a taxi. He was well dressed and friendly and introduced himself as Carlos. Michael took a liking to him. Before I could show any alarm, Michael had loaded our baggage into the back of an old station wagon, and off we went. My adrenaline was running overtime.

Carlos told us that the hotel we had previously booked was far from the main plaza, and he suggested one much closer. In thirty minutes we were settled into a pleasant room, safe and sound. His recommendation was perfect.

We were eager to explore Cuzco, so off we went, bundled up in our heavy wool sweaters. Cuzco is at an altitude of 11,200 feet. We immediately got ruddy cheeks and had difficulty breathing, but we saw such fabulous new sights.

Everywhere we looked there were short, dark women wearing colorful hand-loomed skirts. Because of the almost-constant cold, it's common to wear six or seven skirts at once. The women also wear a Spanish version of a black British bowler hat.

Hand-loomed and hand-knitted sweaters, socks, and blankets were piled up for sale around the plaza. The colors and beautiful designs were from Peru's ancestral past. Some of the knits were made with baby vicuña yarn and were much more sumptuous and feathery to the touch than the finest cashmere from India.

Shoeshine boys were everywhere. Vendors sold hot potatoes from steaming pots. Men sat underneath big black umbrellas behind ancient typewriters, waiting for customers. These men would read letters, answer business correspondence, or even compose love notes.

Someone had left the cover off a manhole on one of the busiest streets in the center of town. We leaned against a wall waiting for the inevitable. A small car came by and got stuck. Three men, one a police officer, calmly strode over to the vehicle and picked it up as if it weighed twenty pounds. The driver thanked them and drove off.

White furry llamas walked down narrow, steep, cobbled lanes. These llamas were heavy-lidded with extravagantly lashed eyes that gave them an air of enticing innocence. Even though I knew they were famous for spitting when they got cranky, I felt compelled to pet one. Luckily it was a very happy llama.

On the way back to our hotel, we checked out a modern convenience store. As we searched the shelves, I discovered that one entire side-wall was made of beautiful, dark-gray Inca stones! We had flown all the way to Peru to see world-famous Inca stones at famous archaeological sites, and here they were in a convenience store! Some of the stones were massive, large as an elephant. Some were only half an inch in diameter, cut to precision and perfectly wedged together. The Incas had no metal tools and used no mortar. Archaeologists still cannot explain how such precise work was done.

Michael and I saw Carlos again that evening as we wandered about the plaza. He suggested that we take some tours around the countryside before our trip to Machu Picchu. I was still a bit leery; the guidebooks stressed that tours should be booked only with bona fide tour agencies. But my sweet, trusting companion agreed to meet Carlos back at our room later that night.

Carlos discussed different tours. We agreed on one of them, and Michael paid in cash. In cash! No receipt! Oh well, I thought. It wasn't a large amount of money.

Next morning Carlos was in the lobby with our tickets. He escorted us to the bus and waved goodbye. When we returned,

Carlos was waiting for us. He then suggested two more tours, plus a full day at Machu Picchu. This time Michael took out his money belt to pay for everything at once. The first bill he grabbed was a fake one-million-dollar bill I had given him as a joke several months before. It looked so genuine that I once confused a bank clerk in Florida with it.

Carlos's eyes opened wide. He mumbled that he had never seen one of these before. The room got very quiet. We had a very long and hairy-scary moment. During that moment Carlos's Peruvian color vanished. We wonder even today if his eyeballs ever got back in place. I envisioned us with our throats cut and Carlos trying to book first-class passage to Paris.

Then Michael laughed and told Carlos it was a fake and gave it to him. I sometimes wonder just how close we came that night to real danger.

After a few awkward moments, we agreed to some tours. Carlos left with over a hundred dollars for the package. Again, we had no receipt. Next morning he was patiently waiting for us, tickets in hand.

Even though my husband alarmed me ten years ago when I saw the fire in that Peruvian man's eyes as he gawked at that phony million-dollar bill, I have never doubted Michael's intuition about tricky people and sticky situations. He is a perfect traveling companion, my Million-Dollar Man.

BONNIE WORTHEN is a world traveler, artist, writer, gardener, and gourmet cook. She is retired now so she can spend her time spoiling her husband and daughter. Her first published book, Period, *is still in print, of which she is very proud.*

Peruvian Ceviche

From a traditional recipe

SERVES 6 TO 8

This dish is easy, healthy, and tasty. There are cevicherias all over Peru; ceviche is a national dish. The traditional fish, onion, and lime-juice recipe is still the most popular. —rgg

  1   pound halibut or other firm, white ocean fish

  1   pound medium shrimp

  ¼   medium red onion

  1   tiny hot chile (*ají limón* is traditional in Peru)

  ¾   teaspoon salt

 15 to 20 juicy key limes, or enough to make 2 cups of juice

      (use 10 regular limes if you can't find the little ones)

Juice of 1 lemon

  ½   cup loosely packed, roughly chopped cilantro

Wash and dry the fish.

Peel and devein the shrimp.

Boil 1 quart of water, and drop the shrimp in. When the shrimp turn pink, put in some cold water, then drain and dry.

Cut the fish and shrimp into ¾ inch pieces. Small shrimp can be used whole. Put them in a medium bowl.

Cut the onion into very thin slices. Add them to the fish-shrimp mixture.

Seed and slice the chile into thin rounds, big enough so they can be identified by the eater. Add to the bowl. Add salt.

Squeeze the limes until you have 2 cups of juice. Remove the seeds.

Squeeze the lemon. Remove the seeds.

Add the lemon and lime juice to the fish/shrimp mixture, and mix well.

Add the cilantro, and mix.

Marinate in the refrigerator for at least 2 hours. Longer is okay.

Pour off most of the liquid. The fish should not be swimming when you serve it.

OPTIONAL: Thin strips of jícama and cucumber, diced tomatoes, small chunks of avocado, ½ to 1 cup each, to taste.

OPTIONAL SERVING SUGGESTION: In Peru, ceviche is served with 1-inch chunks of cold cooked corn on the cob and cold slices of orange sweet potato, boiled and peeled but still firm. It can be served over lettuce and garnished with cilantro.

These days chefs are competing to add flourishes. My chef friend Jared Cohen tells me that he adds about ½ teaspoon of sugar to the mixture. It doesn't appear in the traditional recipes, but it does cut the acidity. He likes it better the next day; I like it anytime after two hours. You might want to play with it. FYI: It is said that the marinade, once the ceviche has been eaten, is good for hangovers. —rgg

The Trip That Changed My Life

Kelly Hayes-Raitt

I came home pregnant. Of course, I didn't know it until the laundry was done and the jet lag had lapsed. India had shaken my soul; now it had invaded my uterus.

India seeps into one's pores. This uncontainable country's smelly colors and infiltrating chaos shake one's very essence. I felt like one of those plastic snow domes with scattered fake snowflakes and happy figurines flicked off their perches. After India nothing lands in the same place; one either loves this, or hates this. India is not a place of ambiguity.

And I was going with teenagers.

This was my first time in India, and I was chaperoning nine American teenagers, handling their logistics in a country that defies logistics handling. To further complicate our lean-budgeted trip, I learned, just days before we left the comfortable land of Happy Meals, that our food kitty was short. I was expected to miraculously raise several hundred extra last-minute dollars. I shook my head, "This may be the first time in history starving children are taken *to* India."

I figured God or Vishnu or Somebody would multiply loaves for us. After all, we were on a peace mission. Our nine teens were meeting nine Indian teens to create a musical reflecting their shared dreams for a world at peace a hundred years from now. Daunting task: we Americans, righteous in our individuality, were unprepared for a culture that reveres conformity. In this country a third the size of the United States with nearly four times the population, people who go along, get along.

Just crossing India's streets was a lesson in going with the flow—except to my foreign eyes, there was no discernible flow. Motor scooters weaved precariously, dodging the ruts made by buses that bulldogged ahead with people dangling off them like Christmas tree ornaments. Taxis invented their own lanes, careening onto sidewalks or into oncoming traffic, whichever best suited their reflex to bypass the occasional cow, donkey, monkey, or elephant. Children, barefoot and open-handed, threaded the amorphous traffic lanes, their lonely pleas drowned by belligerent horns. The air was a bitter mixture of exhaust, shit, sweat, and spices. On the surface, India is a jumbled assault on the senses. Only on introspection does it calm and clarify.

Not even India, however, could stop our kids from doing what all American teens do—attempt to conform by rebelliously asserting their individuality—all in the context of figuring out their self-worth. They cross-dressed, the boys donning dresses for a skit, the girls wearing the boys' overalls and T-shirts. They flirted. They hugged. They hugged a lot. They tested boundaries—theirs, each other's, and mine.

We traveled from Delhi to Jaipur to Agra to Hyderabad to

Madras to Aurangabad to Bombay by bus, by train, by air, by elephant, nursing each other through "Delhi belly" and culture shock from which even the adults weren't immune. In my own adult act of teenage regression, I started smoking again. Not the demure menthol ultralights I had smoked fifteen years ago in high school, but the chunky, boyish Marlboros favored by the Indian men—and by one of our group's chaperones, a man whose attention I couldn't quite capture. His cigarette smoldered seductively in the ashtray, and I just picked it up and inhaled.

We spent most of our time in Hyderabad, sort of the Cleveland of India, where we interacted with the Indian teens and volunteered at an orphanage. I horrified the staff at our five-star hotel one day by inviting the underclass orphans to our swimming pool. I bought the children knockoff Donald Duck T-shirt and shorts sets to wear as bathing suits, negotiating hard for a bulk price from a sidewalk vendor. The kids squealed and splashed. I heard later that the staff drained the pool after we left.

One of the orphans, a silent, alert five-year-old girl with a quick laugh, fell asleep in my lap during the bus ride back to the orphanage. As I gathered her sleepy dead weight, her arms draped around my neck, my forearm supporting her butt, I expected her to instinctively wrap her strong legs around my hips. Instead, the girl clung to my neck, her legs thrust out ramrod stiff and clenched tightly together from the waist down, even in her sleep protecting the most vulnerable part of herself against the memory of a previous violation.

At the end of the trip, I deposited the American teens at the Bombay airport and found my way to a resort on an island off India's coast. Travel-weary and sleep-confused that first night, I opened my door to insistent 2:30 A.M. knocking. The resort's husky German manager, who just hours before had "island welcomed" me with a silly drum parade and lame punch in a frosty glass, now drunkenly forced his way into my room.

The same man earlier had inexplicably upgraded my room, bought me a drink at the bar, and invited me to an exclusive VIP dinner. Now he'd come for his payment, and for a foggy moment I believed I owed him—a nanosecond he quickly exploited before I was too overpowered to effectively fight back.

It took me longer to deal with the fact that I'd been raped than that I'd been impregnated. For months, sitting on the stoop outside my Santa Monica apartment, I smoked Marlboros and dissected my encounter, mining every moment for the exact instant I had subconsciously chosen to allow my body to be stolen. While I don't believe anyone "asks" to be violated, I do believe I draw experiences into my life specifically to provide myself with opportunities to change. I didn't want to repeat this particular "challenge." I was determined to understand why I had made myself vulnerable.

I sat in the dark wrapped in my fluffy bathrobe, my baby long since gone, rewinding the summer. I took an extra long drag when I thought of the little girl who instinctively avoided wrapping her legs around me and wondered at what blink of an instant we little girls learn our bodies are commodities to be taken or traded. Although I never consciously believed there is a quid pro quo between allowing a man to buy me dinner and sleeping with him, on a deeper level I didn't believe a man would have any other motive. It wasn't that I didn't know how to say no, I didn't know how to say yes. I didn't believe I was worthy of a man's attention.

Yes, India had invaded my uterus. And it had shaken my soul. I traveled halfway around the world to learn I would never again accept some man's price tag on my body.

I snuffed out my cigarette.

A Stitch in Time

Rita Golden Gelman

Ban Krud is a beach village on the east coast of Thailand, about four hours by car from Bangkok. I was there because I had asked a Thai friend to recommend a village where no one spoke English.

In two weeks I had not seen a single international tourist; apparently, no one I had met in the village spoke more than twenty words of English, including the family who owned Rim Haad, the modest bungalow resort where I was staying. I had gotten what I wanted, and it was both challenging and frustrating.

One evening I discovered that the shy young woman who worked as a maid in the resort had quit. The next morning a woman in her late forties, at least ten years younger than I, stocky and cheerful, arrived. The first time I saw her, she was wheeling a cart filled with sheets and cleaning supplies. I walked over and introduced myself, pointing to my chest and saying my name. She smiled back, tapped her chest, and said, "Won." Pronounced *one*. Then she went off to clean the bungalows.

It turned out that Won knew more English words than anyone I had met. Later that first day I sat down next to her while she was resting. She began the conversation by telling me that Manit, the owner of the resort, was her mother. When I questioned this (everyone had told me that Manit had only one daughter, Fon), she amended it by explaining that she had grown up in Manit's house.

Our conversation, characterized by one- and two-word sentences and her extraordinary talent for mime, moved on to the fact that Manit wore sunglasses all the time because she had lost an eye in an accident. Then Won told me that a year ago someone in the family had beaten up the mistress of one of Manit's sons in the market—in front of the whole village. I also learned that Won's husband was a car mechanic and he came home every day covered in grease. Often he was too tired to bathe, and Won had announced that without a bath, there was no way she would sleep with him.

For more than an hour Won filled me with gossip, about her marriage, about the family, about the village, using two-word sentences and mime. I was exhausted when she finished. Of course, I wasn't sure the tales were true, but Won's talent for storytelling and improvisation did spice things up for me.

The next afternoon I saw Won sitting on some steps, stitching a torn pillowcase. I was excited because I had this cotton shirt that I liked a lot, but it was a little snug, and the buttons down the front pulled open whenever I moved my shoulders back. I'd been wanting to stitch it permanently closed and just slip it on and off over my head, but I didn't have a needle and thread. And since I didn't speak the language, I couldn't ask for them.

Then suddenly there was Won with a needle and thread—

and enough English for me to make myself understood. And I just happened to be wearing the shirt.

"Won," I said. "Look."

I showed her how the shirt opened up when I moved. The fabric stretched and pulled, and the buttons popped open. Then I showed her what I wanted to do by pretending to stitch up the front of the shirt. I mimed how I would put it on over my head instead of using the buttons.

"I'm so happy! You have a needle and thread."

She understood. "Yes," she said. "I have."

Then she wrinkled her nose, cocked her head, looked at me, and said, "But you old. Nobody care."

And having offered her opinion, she went back to her sewing.

I never got that needle and thread.

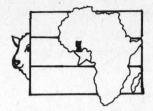

A Different Taste

Caroline Mailloux

Of all the things that frightened me about traveling alone to
Ghana at the age of twenty, food was not one of them. I had
enough to worry about: I was preparing to augment my aca-
demic experience by interning with a non-governmental organization (NGO) in rural Ghana to learn firsthand about rural
health care paradigms, development politics, and the adminis-
trative side of international nonprofits.

My home base was a small, humid, fertile cocoa-farming
village in southwestern Ghana. I lived in a concrete building
with sporadic electricity and no running water. In addition to
development issues at the grassroots level, my time in the village
exposed me to local agriculture practices and food-preparation
techniques, a struggling health infrastructure, a seemingly endless stream of Celine Dion blasting from the radios of faded,
run-down taxis, a variety of poisonous snakes, and an inspir-
ing sense of community. I had left the States expecting to learn
about local village life and development issues at the grassroots
level. My experience far surpassed my expectations.

What I didn't expect, however, was to experience the drastic impact of multinational corporations (MNCs) in this one tiny corner of the globe. Timber, gold, manganese, and bauxite companies with owners from South Africa, Lebanon, and Australia shaped the land, destroyed farmland, created jobs, and aided the Ghanaian economy in the short term by stripping the land of its natural resources. While these exports comprise a major source of foreign exchange and contribute to Ghana's economic stability, most of the profits are exported, along with the natural resources. Most Ghanaians earn their meager daily wages by subsistence agriculture. This duality raises the ever-pertinent question of unethical corporate conduct versus sustainable development. Yet somehow at the end of the day, the players on both sides of the debate are motivated by the need to feed their families.

Compared to the day-to-day realities of the MNC corporate culture and my own development work, enjoying the food of West Africa seemed like a guilt-free pleasure. However, I soon learned that my chances to learn about the diverse cuisines were linked to the exploitation of local populations and resources.

One of the largest MNCs in the region, a timber-exporting business, had a friendly long-term relationship with the Western interns in the region and often invited us to their gated community for lavish banquets and neighborhood dinner dances.

The parties helped me better understand the role that foreign companies play in Ghana's economic development—and their startling contrast to the NGO-supported grassroots health and education projects in the village. Nights of wine, hot running water, and scrumptious Lebanese food, and a glimpse at the BBC to reorient myself with the outside world, were always appreciated, even though I felt guilty about the rampant timber depletion that funded them. The families in the village where I lived labored all day in the fields just to harvest enough cassava and plantains to manually pound into balls of *fufu* for dinner.

Globalization politics aside, I enjoyed interacting with a melting pot of people. Three interns, including myself, were Americans. Another volunteer from our NGO was British. The timber company employed managers from all over the globe; their tech guy hailed from India, the head mechanical engineer from Romania, the head of security from Ghana, and the site manager from Syria. Several of the administrators' wives were born and raised in Yugoslavia and Russia, and the owner and many of the head production managers were from Lebanon.

At one such party in particular, spirits flew high all night. Expensive and delectable wines poured like water, energetic Middle Eastern music flung us to our feet, and the food—oh the delicious food! The company owner who sponsored the gala had spared no expense. The head cook expertly roasted a sheep on a spit and filled a table with tabbouleh, *fattoush,* baba ghanoush, kibbe, hummus, tahini sauce, *djaj mehshi, sha-warma djaj,* and *manakeesh bi zaatar,* which filled the room with exotic aromas.

After dinner and some dancing, our host, a very charming man, approached me in a friendly manner, holding a piece of meat from the table.

"Try it, it's nice," he coaxed.

I looked at the meat, my host, and back at the meat. I felt somewhat wary about ingesting it, as it appeared pink and raw. I had experienced enough digestive troubles abroad to know to take caution.

"What is it?" I asked as I closely examined it.

"I tell you when you're finished," he replied with a devilish smirk.

His charm won me over, and I opted to try it in appreciation for his generosity and in celebration of a new cultural experience. I popped the pink meat into my mouth and chewed a few times. The pink flesh didn't taste superb, but it was surely palatable. It had a distinctively rubbery texture. After swallowing the last bit, I glanced over at my host intrigued, ready for him to tell me the origin of the mystery meat.

"It's sheep ball," he announced flatly in his thick Arabic accent, and anxiously awaited my dramatic reaction.

A sigh of relief poured over me. I laughed and threw my arms enthusiastically in the air.

"Kamal! It's good! Don't worry! It's not the first time that I've ever had testicle in my mouth!"

Thunderous silence charged the room. I clasped my hands together and prayed I might disappear. My uncouth comment was inspired by a travel adventure in the Australian bush when I'd tried a bull testicle during a stay at a cattle ranch, and not by, well . . . err . . . you know. But the damage was done, and I fearfully awaited my social reprimand.

Rather than looking horrified, Kamal paused, grinned, belted out the most uproarious laugh, and then proceeded to converse in rapid Arabic with the other partygoers. Despite my embarrassment, my party faux pas had entertained my gracious and good-natured host. We all shared a hearty chuckle.

I will never forget my time in Ghana, and I will never forget that fateful night, nestled deep in the bush of Ghana's western region, when I ate sheep testicle. It was definitely worth a little embarrassment to connect a room full of people from all corners of the globe. I never did quite come to terms with the exploitative lumber industry and its effects on the region's grassroots development and health projects.

CAROLINE MAILLOUX studied global health politics at Brown University's development studies program. She is pursuing a career in international policy reform with the hope of channeling more U.S. foreign aid into horizontal, community-based, primary health care programs. She currently resides in Providence, Rhode Island, where she works at an occupational and environmental public health consulting firm. When not dreaming about West Africa's vibrant colors, unforgettable dining, and unparalleled hospitality, she enjoys exploring quirky Providence's restaurants and oddities shops and outdoor activities like cycling and skiing. Keep in touch with Caroline at caroline.mailloux@gmail.com.

✿ Curried Carrot Soup

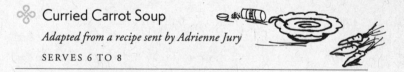

Adapted from a recipe sent by Adrienne Jury

SERVES 6 TO 8

*T**his soup is terrific. Whenever I make it I'm always sorry I didn't make more. So what does curried carrot soup have to do with an NGO in Ghana? To be honest—nothing! But we love this soup and it is a "Different Taste!" —ma*

- 2 medium onions, sliced
- 1 tablespoon salted butter
- 10 carrots, cut into ½-inch slices (about 6 cups sliced carrots)
- 1 to 2 tablespoons curry powder, to taste

2 tablespoons powdered chicken stock

Salt and freshly ground black pepper, to taste

2 tablespoons applesauce

2 tablespoons fresh dill, snipped

2 tablespoons fresh mint, chopped

½ cup low-fat sour cream

Sauté the onion in the butter for five minutes.

Add the carrot slices, curry powder, chicken stock, and 3 cups water.

Simmer until the carrots are soft.

Add more water if necessary in ½-cup increments. (Generally you will need 3 cups more.)

Add salt and pepper, and adjust for taste.

Blend. Put half the soup in a blender. Blend at medium speed for a few seconds. Add the rest of the soup and the applesauce. Blend until smooth.

Serve with fresh dill, mint, and sour cream.

....

Some powdered chicken stock is quite salty. Check ahead of time. The caldo de pollo *I use in Mexico often substitutes for salt. I use less than 2 tablespoons powder and add no additional salt. At one of the tastings Jean (Allen) made a batch of applesauce and set it out with the herbs and sour cream. People put big dollops of the applesauce in the soup. The curry and the applesauce provide a very different but wonderful taste. —ma*

....

Southern Hospitality

Leslie Berkower

It was 1994, before the prevalence of cell phones. I was a single mother living in San Antonio, Texas, and working as a district manager for World Book Encyclopedia. My best friend Marlene and her husband Jerry were out of town, and I had offered to care for their houseplants and backyard while they were away. They lived in a gated, exclusive subdivision, where the land sprawled and the homes were spread out.

One day I was on a tight schedule. I had a sales appointment thirty miles from their home and just an hour to do the chores and get to my appointment.

After watering the houseplants, I proceeded to the backyard through the kitchen door. When I finished watering outside, I attempted to reenter the house through the same kitchen door. It was locked. I panicked!

There was no other way into the house; their security system was like Fort Knox. My purse and car keys were locked in the house, but my sales materials and agenda were in my unlocked car in the driveway.

The clock was ticking. I knew I needed a locksmith, but I had no phone and didn't know any of the neighbors. It was the middle of a scorching Texas afternoon, and the neighborhood looked deserted.

Knowing my only hope was to find a telephone, I ventured out onto the streets looking for someone, anyone, whose phone I could use. After walking a ways, I noticed a man in his front yard. I approached him reluctantly and explained what had happened and asked if I could use his phone.

"Sure," he said. "Come on in. I'm John,"

I called the locksmith and then asked John if I could also call to cancel my appointment.

"Why don't you take my wife's car? She's using mine today, and I'm sure she won't mind. I'll go to your friend's house and wait for the locksmith for you."

He pointed to the brand-new Mercedes in the garage and handed me a key.

I was stunned.

Being a single parent and a motivated sales person, I gratefully accepted his offer. I drove the thirty miles to my appointment praying that all other vehicles on the road would keep their distance. I arrived safely, made a very profitable sale, and drove back to John's house, strictly obeying every traffic regulation. I was very nervous, but thankfully, I made it safely back through the gates of the subdivision. I drove into John's driveway, relieved that the ordeal was almost over. Now all I had left to do was negotiate my way between the concrete posts in his three-car garage. I thought I had cleared the posts when I heard the crunch.

The post on the left made an accordion of the driver-side

door. Now I was really panicked. This was the worst moment of my life.

I was standing inside the garage of this kind stranger who had loaned me his wife's new Mercedes, and I had to go in the house and tell him I had just made a musical instrument of her car door.

I considered running, but there was nowhere to go; he had my purse and car keys.

So I mustered up every last nerve and, with my head hung low, went inside and revealed the ugly story. We went out to the garage where John assessed the damage.

"Ah," he said. "Don't worry about it. I have a cousin who owns a body shop. He'll take care of it. You'll only have to pay for the parts. He won't charge me labor."

I didn't know how to react to his kindness. I gushed apologies and thank-you's and told him I would give him a set of *Childcraft* encyclopedias for his two-year-old grandson.

"Ah," he said. "It's okay."

Then his wife came home.

Picture it: a strange woman in your kitchen with your husband who had loaned the strange woman your brand-new Mercedes which she crashed.

John's wife somehow kept her cool, but I could tell she was smoldering inside. I chanted apologies again, ate some humble pie, and took my leave.

The car repair cost less than $100. I delivered the set of *Childcraft* as promised. I later heard that the story made the rounds among the men of the golf club. I remain forever touched and grateful for the kindness of this fine man, whom I never saw again.

LESLIE BERKOWER was born and raised in the suburbs of New York and has lived on both coasts as well as in the Midwest and Colorado. A child of the '60s, Berkower lived in a teepee and miner's cabin, worked in a vegetarian co-op, and became a single parent at twenty-four. She has spent most of her career in sales and has had many adventures and mishaps, much like the one told here. Berkower now resides in Philadelphia, Pennsylvania, and makes frequent jaunts to visit her two-year-old grandson in Brooklyn, New York. Contact Leslie at lberkower@yahoo.com.

Wild for Worms

Karen van der Zee

I had planned to eat worms tonight, but instead I'm facing a hamburger and fries. I am not amused.

I live in Ghana with my spouse, but at this moment we're visitors in a country with the exotic and lyrical name of Zimbabwe, land of the fabled Shona chiefs. And here we are sitting in a restaurant called the Silver Spur, decorated with images of an American Indian chief in full feather regalia—on the wall, on the menus, and on the placemats. Our waiter is a handsome black kid wearing jeans and a black T-shirt sporting, yes, an Indian chief. "My name is Steve, and I am your waiter tonight," he says, greeting us cheerily.

The menu offers no worms, but there are steaks and hamburgers and "surf and turf" and a Tex-Mex dish and more familiar foods. And let me not forget the salad bar.

I'm here with three men: GD (my husband) and two American consultants with whom he'll be writing a foreign aid project proposal. We discussed dinner plans earlier. The men were not interested in worms. They wanted steak, red-blooded Americans that they are.

I pointed out that *mopane* worms have three times as much protein as beef.

They gave me a look.

I gave up.

So here we are at the Silver Spur. We eat and drink beer. The men talk about the project proposal that has brought them to Harare, and about economics and politics. The situation is not good in Zimbabwe, and it will get a lot worse, but we don't know this yet.

I think of worms while chewing my hamburger.

Mopane worms, also called *madora* or *macimbi,* are not worms at all but caterpillars that make their home in the *mopane* trees. Sun-dried and stewed, they're considered a delicacy, and who am I to disagree if I have not tried them? Even just one? Just so I can gross out my family and friends with my tale of gastronomic daring.

But it is not to be tonight. I'm in exotic Zimbabwe, and I'm eating a hamburger served by Steve. It's enough to make me want to cry. GD, being a good guy, squeezes my hand and promises me that tomorrow we will try and find worms.

From our hotel room the next day, *Fodor's* in hand like a real tourist, I make my phone calls. The guidebook says *mopane* worms are served in the Komba Hari restaurant in—I kid you not—the Sheraton Hotel. I call several times, but nobody answers.

We'll just go there and see.

After GD arrives back from a day of meetings, we get in a taxi and commence our quest.

The Sheraton is a very luxurious place indeed. We follow

the signs to the restaurants. There are several, one of them a Japanese eatery. Through the wall of glass we see the customers seated along the U-shaped tables and the cook standing in the middle doing his fast and fancy cooking show on the grill in front of the diners. We've come to the end of the hall, to the last restaurant, which we take to be the one we are looking for. An elegant Zimbabwean hostess at the entrance smiles at us and invites us in. It looks very ritzy. Everything gleams and glitters and wonderful aromas permeate the air.

"Do you serve worms?" I ask.

She stares at me.

"*Mopane* worms," I elaborate.

She frowns. "We have a buffet," she says, gesturing at the tables laden with food.

"African food?" I ask hopefully, and she looks puzzled now. I tell her that the *Fodor* guidebook says that the Komba Hari serves local delicacies such as pumpkin leaves, *sadza, kapenta,* and *mopane* worms.

She points at the restaurant next door. "That is the Komba Hari," she informs us.

"That is Japanese," GD states.

"Yes," she says.

My mate and I look at each other. So much for *Fodor's.*

We thank the elegant Zimbabwean lady and get out of there.

There are no worms at the Sheraton.

The doorman gets us a taxi. "To the Ramambo Lodge," GD tells the driver, "in the BB building."

The Ramambo is our backup restaurant, this one from the *Lonely Planet.* It offers wild game dishes featuring eland, crocodile, ostrich, warthog, and more. However, no *mopane* worms. But if we can't have worms, we'll try crocodile. We're still in the Sheraton driveway when the taxi begins to make death-rattle noises, but it keeps moving and manages to deliver us to the Ramambo without expiring.

As we climb out of the decrepit vehicle, a frightening apparition leaps out of the shadows—an enormous African in a cheetah-print shirt wielding a huge shield and a wild-looking headdress. For a moment I think we are dealing with a madman until I realize he is the welcoming committee.

What can I say? Tourism brings in money. Give 'em what they want.

As the name suggests, the place looks like a game lodge with heavy log furniture, a rustic wooden floor, split bamboo walls, and a slanted beamed ceiling. Traditional Shona stone carvings are displayed everywhere. A podium sports a marimba band of four cheerful and energetic musicians, singing and dancing, creating a wonderful festive atmosphere. Just, you know, to make you feel you're experiencing the Real Africa.

Our table is tastefully set with all the necessary eating utensils and graced with pretty flowers. I settle in for an eating experience. A waiter, also in a cheetah-print shirt, asks for our drink order, and we select a Zimbabwean chardonnay.

We study the dinner menu, which offers intriguing dishes featuring various wild game meats, as well as more standard Western fare for the weak-hearted. For a first course we decide to share an order of crocodile tail: *delicious tender white meat, sautéed and served with garlic butter,* says the menu. I select warthog as my meat of choice for the main course, mostly because warthog is really ugly and I have no tender feelings toward the beast. Granted, it too is one of God's creatures, but having seen warthog in Kenya, I respectfully judge it to be one of His mistakes. We should all be eating it.

The warthog dish is described as follows: *tender strips marinated with ginger, stir-fried with spring onions and served with fresh pasta.* Just the way the villagers in the bush prepare it, I am sure.

GD goes for the Truly Authentic Zimbabwean food by the name of *dovi,* a traditional dish of eland *biltong* (dried) served in a peanut sauce accompanied by *sadza. Biltong* is the South African word for jerky and can be made with any kind of meat. *Sadza* is a thick porridge made from white maize, sort of like cooked grits minus the salt, and stodgier. We ate it when we lived in Kenya, where it is also a staple food, known as *ugali.*

We are sipping our chardonnay when the crocodile arrives, a pretty cross-slice of tail, irregularly roundish and almost flowerlike, with its small round bone in the center and several thin bones radiating out. It has been sautéed to a rich golden color, and the garlic is clearly in evidence. Taking knife and fork, I cut a morsel of the meat and eat it.

If anyone ever tells you that crocodile tastes like chicken, he's lying.

It tastes like pork.

Apart from the flavor, the meat also has the texture of a pork chop and is quite delicious. I consume all of my share to the tune of "The Lion Sleeps Tonight" from the marimba band.

Soon we are looking at our respective plates filled with another taste sensation. My pasta resembles something you'd find in an Italian restaurant, except that the strips of meat are warthog. I spear a piece on my fork and try it. I am expecting it to taste like some sort of gamey pork, the creature being related to the pig and living in the wilds of Africa. I am wrong. No, it does not taste like chicken. You could have told me it was beef, and I would have believed it. Needless to say, there is no challenge in polishing off my warthog, but I leave some of the pasta simply because there is too much.

Meanwhile, my spouse is savoring his peanutty eland *biltong.* I sample some but find the meat a bit dry and chewy, not surprisingly, and the peanut sauce overpowers the flavor. However, the sauce does wonders for the starchy *sadza,* which is as bland and tasteless as food can possibly be.

Finished, we decline dessert, and with a wave of thanks for the band, we leave and walk the short distance back to our hotel, where we collapse into bed.

The next day, our last in Zimbabwe, I am exploring Harare in a taxi. On one of the streets I see several cardboard boxes stacked up in the shade of a big tree. WORMS FOR SALE, reads a big handwritten sign.

Worms!

I turn to the taxi driver and point at the boxes. "Are these for eating?" I ask.

He gives me a blank look. "No," says he, "they're for fishing."

Clearly, I'm not going to have my worms this time around.

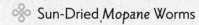 Sun-Dried Mopane Worms

ried worms can be stored for a long time.

Harvest fat, mature caterpillars from *mopane* trees, or buy them.

Taking several in each hand, squeeze out the slimy yellow guts. Boil the caterpillars in salted water for about 30 minutes, then dry them in the sun. Eat as a snack, or use in soups and stews.

Language

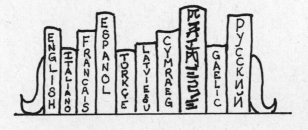

Patīkami What?

Maria Altobelli

There has to be a way my husband Paul will pay for this.

Suddenly we need to go to a country where my stock of foreign languages are of absolutely no use. Now instead of saying "*Prazer*" or "*Mucho gusto*" or "*Piacere*" when meeting someone, I'm expected to wrap my tongue around the likes of "*Patīkami iepazīties.*" I have to hope I pronounce it correctly so as not to sound like I'm making a rude noise in public or telling people I'm lusting after their teenage son.

Patīkami iepazīties is Latvian and spoken by only one and a half million people in the world. Twelve of those people live in Skujas, and those twelve constitute the entire population of this tiny hamlet in southern Latvia where we are headed to meet Paul's Aunt Angela.

Latvia has had a turbulent and oppressive history, and Paul's aunt has seen some of the country's worst years. At eighty-something, Aunt Angela is one tough cookie. Today she lives in the same rustic log cabin her parents built. I later found it also to be home to a large group of mice that were there for us all, and a smaller but more persistent group of fleas that were there just for me. Despite the fact that water is hauled from the well, heat comes from a cooking stove, and the bathroom is an outhouse, Aunt Angela feels she's living well on her $120 monthly pension. Then there's the added pleasure of being reunited with Paul, her long-lost nephew.

Looking at how she has filled the two simple rooms with vases of cosmos, dahlias, delphiniums, multicolored zinnias, varieties of chrysanthemums, sprays of wispy greens, and boughs with the vividly colored leaves of fall, I wish I had studied harder. It's hard to express gratitude and tell how beautiful a place looks with a meager thirty-six Latvian words.

I had tried to learn more, but Latvian isn't easy. My first teacher tried valiantly for fifteen minutes to get me to pronounce her four-letter name correctly. My second teacher shook her head with disgust when I failed to speak fluently at the end of our first one-on-one lesson. I confess to giving up on tapes that insisted I say "What are the ramifications of the upcoming proposal changes for the future of the project under consideration?" after only one repetition. In the first lesson! "What ever happened to *Who, what, why? Where's the bathroom?* That kind of stuff?" I asked Paul.

"Latvians have high expectations."

My thirty-six words are actually less of a handicap than my nationality. Latvians, no matter where they live, are expected to marry other Latvians. Strike one against me. The other problem is Skujas's proximity to Aglona, where an event at Aglona's basilica checkered the locals' opinion of outsiders forever. The massive white spires of this impressive church and the painting of the Black Madonna housed inside have drawn pilgrims to the area by the busloads. For years, a native Aglonian priest, a rising star in the church hierarchy, said daily mass. That is, until the day he absconded with a ravishing pilgrim whose last name ended in the same vowel as mine. Italians have not been very popular in the area since then.

My father gave me that treacherous last name, but the other half of my genetic code saved the day. Nowhere in the world are potatoes so revered as they are in Latvia, surpassing even the fervor of my mother's native Ireland. Tears well up in Aunt Angela's eyes at the mere mention of *kartupeli*. We arrive in Skujas in late summer, when Latvians are out in the fields, bent double with their hands in the soil, trying to find the tubers tractors or pitchforks have uncovered.

Paul and I have grown scads of potatoes for years, but in our present rental house in Mexico, it is not an option. I miss the thrill of unearthing tuber after tuber, so for two glorious days I am out helping Aunt Angela with the harvest. Paul pitches in for a while but bows out early, using the excuse of Latvian lessons. Aunt Angela later informs him that he has earned maybe one *lat* (a little under two dollars) for his effort in the field, but that my salary should be at least five *lats*.

Aunt Angela and I make a team, she with the pitchfork and me scurrying about like a crab on the loamy ground, retrieving the potatoes and depositing them in burlap sacks. At one point she straightens up, rubs her stomach, and says, "Yum, yum." This I could understand. We are going to eat; I follow her kerchief and rubber boots toward the house.

My stomach is growling, and I am looking forward to a big meal. Or maybe the Latvian specialty, *pīrāgi*. While we were in the beautiful capital Riga, I had pigged out on these two-bite morsels. Instead, Aunt Angela yanks a bunch of fat carrots out of her garden, gives them a swirl in water from the rain barrel, and carries them to the porch. She sits down, pats the bench opposite her, and begins to speak to me in Latvian. Instead of nodding my head and smiling stupidly as I have been doing since we arrived, I decide the time has come to take an active part in the dialogue. When she pauses and waits for a response, I answer her in Spanish. The Spanish has a nice flow, distinctly different from the few hackneyed Latvian phrases I have belabored endlessly up to this point.

When there is a pause in my Spanish, Aunt Angela continues in Latvian.

After all the bending in the field, the sun shining through the porch glass provides welcome warmth on my back. The carrots are sweet, fresh, and crunchy and fill the void in my stomach. We accompany our words with much gesticulating and exaggerated facial expressions until Paul gets up from the table outside where he has been practicing his verbs, sticks his head in the door, and asks if he is needed as translator. Aunt Angela shoos him away with a torrent of words, and we resume our bizarre scenario.

Paul later informs me that Aunt Angela told him to go away because "your wife and I are having a very good conversation and would rather not be disturbed."

Latvian *Pīrāgi*

Adapted from a traditional recipe

MAKES 50 *PĪRĀGI* (OR MORE, IF YOU MAKE THEM SMALL)

*P*reparing these habit-forming tidbits gives the term *"labor intensive"* a new meaning. *Pīrāgi are best done as a communal activity. The cook can prepare the dough and the fillings (if more than the traditional bacon filling is used) and wait for helping hands to roll out the circles and form the turnovers.*

Dough

1	teaspoon sugar
¼	cup warm water
1	package dry yeast
1	cup milk, scalded
2	tablespoons oil
1	tablespoon sugar
1	teaspoon salt
1	large egg, lightly beaten
¼	cup sour cream
4	to 4 ½ cups all-purpose flour

In a small bowl, mix 1 teaspoon sugar and warm water, and sprinkle the yeast on top. Set aside in a warm place for 10 to 15 minutes or until the mixture begins to bubble and rise.

Combine the scalded milk with the oil, 1 tablespoon of sugar, and salt in a large bowl, and mix well.

In a separate small bowl, mix the egg and sour cream. When the milk has cooled, add the egg mixture.

Add the yeast mixture and 1 cup of flour. Beat thoroughly with an electric mixer. Add another cup of flour, and continue beating.

Add the rest of the flour in ½-cup increments, mixing with a wooden spoon. The dough should be somewhat sticky, the same as for a sweet bread recipe.

Turn the dough out on a lightly floured board, and knead gently for 5 minutes.

Place the dough in a large clean bowl that has been lightly coated with oil. Cover the bowl with a clean, damp dish towel or a plastic bag, and set it aside to rise in a warm, draft-free place, 1 to 2 hours.

Shape and fill as directed below.

Traditional Bacon Filling

    1   pound thick, *lean* bacon, diced (a high-quality lean bacon is
        the key)
    ½   pound sliced ham, diced
    2   onions, minced
    Freshly ground black pepper to taste

Sauté the bacon on fairly high heat, stirring it often so it cooks down but doesn't brown too much. Add the ham, and sauté a couple minutes more, stirring from time to time. Lower the heat, and add the onions. Continue to stir off and on until the onions soften and become translucent. Add freshly ground pepper to taste. Cool.

SHAPING PĪRĀGI

Preheat oven to 400°F.

Pull off a baseball-size piece of dough. Working on a lightly-floured surface, roll the dough into a log 2 inches in diameter. Cut the log into half-inch slices. Lightly roll each slice into a circle a quarter-inch thick.

Put a tablespoon of the filling on half the circle. Dip a finger in
a bit of warm water and run it lightly around the edge of the
circle. Fold the dough in half, and seal the edges securely.

Gently roll the *pīrāgi* between your palms to make an oval
shape. The *pīrāgi* will be smaller than an egg and have a fat
middle with rounded ends.

Place the *pīrāgi* on a lightly greased baking sheet. Brush each
one with a beaten egg and pierce the dough with a fork.
Bake for 10 to 15 minutes or until brown.

The *pīrāgi* are best eaten right out of the oven, but they are
also good at room temperature. They freeze well. To serve,
unthaw, place the *pīrāgi* in a single layer on a sheet of aluminum foil, and seal the foil around them. Reheat in the oven
at 350°F until warm.

*Besides the traditional bacon filling, you might want to ex-
periment. Mashed potatoes mixed with half the amount
of sharp cheese work great. So do mashed potatoes and cabbage
cooked with onions.*

The dough can be used for various other appetizers.

*Jean Allen made these for a fancy party with a number of wait
staff and other help. She noticed the waiter seriously eyeballing the
pīrāgi as she placed them on his tray. She told him to try one. He
popped one in his mouth, smiled, and proceeded to serve each of
the wait staff, the kitchen help, and the bartender before bringing
the tray around to the waiting guests. —ma*

A Desert Garden

Tim Amsden

Our new home in the high desert of rural New Mexico had no garden. My wife Lucia and I needed help with the scraped, bare, compacted earth. Through mutual friends we met Mary Anne and Jones. They worked most of a summer to transform our hardscrabble yard into something of deep beauty.

Mary Anne was a gift; she was an attractive woman in her early forties, with an encyclopedic knowledge of plants. She loved things that grow. And she loved soil and rocks, and she brought them all together to create beautiful and spiritual places. Jones was a handsome young Navajo with a face that lit up when he was joyful. He had a deep respect for the earth, and he particularly liked working with stones.

Over three months the two of them created our living yard. The ground was so hard before they started, I could not even drive a spike into it with a hammer. In order to put a small iron bird-feeder pole in the ground, I had to use a drill. The first thing they did was work the soil intensively, breaking it up with a pickax. Then they added composted sheep manure and other good things. By the time they had the soil as they wanted it, we could sink six inches when we walked on it.

Next they laid out walks and areas for planting with low stone borders. They brought in plants and seeds and small trees and put in flowerbeds and a fire pit. They hauled lichen-covered stones from high Navajo country to make benches and contours and to give the garden texture and beauty. They created a wonder.

We still talk about the times Mary Anne and Jones pulled into the yard, truck loaded down with rocks and plants they had collected from high up in the hills. In went cactus and yucca, sage and desert rose, grasses and flowers; almost all of it leafed and bloomed the next year. Then came bulbs and seeds and plants Mary Anne brought back from a visit to her family in Maryland. Next were a plum tree and Russian sage and an herb garden that included chocolate mint, then irises and hollyhocks and tulips, hibiscus and larkspurs and columbines, ground junipers, a Rocky Mountain juniper, and a variety of ground cover. There were succulents and aromatics till every inch was filled with life.

Over the summer we came to be good friends. On occasion they would still be working even after the sun had set, and we would build a fire in the pit and sit and talk. Our strongest images of the two of them are Mary Anne barefooted and ankle deep in rich soil, her strong arms and shoulders moving and planting and caressing, and Jones, small of build but very strong, bare to the waist and wielding the pickax to break up the hardpan.

In late fall of 1998 we had a dinner to celebrate the completion of Mary Anne's and Jones's work, and to show how much we meant to each other. Mary Anne, Jones, and Jones's mother came, as did Mary Anne's brother Jay and his friend Joe, who were visiting from Baltimore. Mary Anne brought a big pot of *mole,* Jones's mother made fry-bread, and my wife Lucia made all the other fixings, trimmings, and dessert. Before dinner Jones offered a blessing in Navajo and passed around a glass of water so we could all sprinkle ourselves and ask for a personal blessing.

After dinner we all went out into the cold, clear night to sit around the fire pit and talk. Lucia suggested that we all speak of what we were grateful for, and surprisingly, even though the night was intended to celebrate the completion of the garden, the garden was not much mentioned. Everyone spoke of our gratitude for each other's friendship, and of the gifts we had given each other. We reminisced about images and moments we held dear. It was a magic, open-hearted evening, spiced with wild country and exotic tastes, a rich cultural mix, and deep sharing, grounded in the soil and fire and starry night air.

TIM AMSDEN grew up in Wichita, Kansas, collected a few degrees, and worked twenty-five years for the Environmental Protection Agency. He and Lucia now live outside Ramah, New Mexico, where they both indulge their compulsions to write. Among other places, Tim's work has appeared in Pudding Magazine, Poetry Ireland Review, Potpourri, Out of Line, Rockhurst Review, New Mexico Magazine, Arabesques Review, contemporary verse2, Istanbul Literature Review, *a Pima Press poetry anthology titled* Lasting: Poems on Aging, *and a Pudding House anthology titled* Hunger Enough: Living Spiritually in a Consumer Society.

Train to Tithorea

Jan Gelman

"Tithorea," I repeated to the concierge of an Athens hotel. He shrugged his shoulders. So did his coworker. "It's a small town about two hours outside of Athens." I was due to arrive that evening to visit a young Greek woman I had met on the island of Milos, my home for the past month.

"That's okay," I finally said in frustration. "I'll just go to the train station and figure it out from there."

"Tithorea? Why you go there?" The Greek train conductor took my ticket and shook his head. "Greek boyfriend?"

"*Ochi,*" I said. No.

His smile widened. "No boyfriend?"

Wrong answer. "*Ney, ney.* Yes. Boyfriend in America." Nine months into my year of traveling alone around the world, I knew my imaginary boyfriend quite well. "Where is Tithorea?" I asked.

"Little. Very little," he said. "I tell you when we there." He smiled and winked. "I'm Jorgos."

I smiled. "I'm Jan."

I looked around the train car and realized I was the only non-Greek there. An older woman across the aisle smiled and offered me a piece of gum. I smiled back and accepted. I dug out my book and thought about Johanna, the woman I was visiting. We had met at a restaurant on Milos and hit it off immediately. She spoke only a little English, and my Greek was far worse, but somehow we communicated and ended up hanging out a few days together. When she left, she invited me to visit her home.

We pulled into the first stop, one whitewashed structure no bigger than a newsstand, with no visible name sign. The stop was more like a hesitation, and we were moving again. I opened my map to try to figure out where we were.

"No problem." Jorgos leaned on the armrest of the empty seat next to me. "I'll tell you where Tithorea is."

"Are you sure?" I asked as we passed through another tiny, no-name station.

"No problem."

Jorgos came by to tell me that we would be arriving in Tithorea in a half-hour. "But don't worry," he assured me. "I'll come get you before we get there."

We passed through several towns, even a few with signs. I started getting excited to see Johanna, meet her family, and see another side to Greece other than the islands.

Then it happened. Jorgos was running back through the train, waving his arms in the air. He skidded to a stop in front of me. "Why you not get off? Why you not get off?"

"I thought you were going to tell me when we got there?"

"Tithorea!" He said and pointed behind us. "We just passed Tithorea!"

I stared at him in disbelief. "What do I do? I need to get off!"

"You can't get off!" he said. Everyone in the train was staring.

"When do we get to the next stop?"

"Forty-five minutes," he said.

It was nearly eight o'clock and almost dark.

"Is there a train that goes back?"

"No."

I shook my head. "What do you mean, no?"

"You find a ride or a hotel there," he said.

"No," I persisted. "I have a friend expecting me."

"*Ella, ella!*" he shouted. Come, come.

We practically galloped from car to car. I struggled and stumbled, hitting innocent passengers in the arms and heads with my overstuffed pack. We finally made it to the front, where the engineer sat in his little compartment driving this train farther and farther away from Tithorea.

The two men bantered back and forth, glancing at me and waving their hands. I stood there feeling my heart pounding. "Who is your friend?" Jorgos asked.

"Johanna," I said, and the engineer started banging on something that resembled a radio. He rattled off Greek, but I heard just static in answer. Again he repeated something, and a muffled voice broke through the static. I waited. The banter continued from Jorgos to the engineer to the voice to the engineer to Jorgos and back to me. I imagined they were trying to call the Tithorea station to find Johanna.

"No find," said Jorgos.

"Now what?" I asked.

Banter again. I looked out the window at the lush, endless

tobacco fields and then turned back to the chattering men. Suddenly the engineer shouted something, and the train skidded to a screeching halt. I flew forward into Jorgos. Passengers yelled, and the engineer yelled back. Then the engineer bolted from the controls and flung open the engine-room door.

Outside were green fields and a small dirt road. The engineer motioned to me. *"Ella! Ella!"* he called.

I looked out the open door and saw a car driving toward the train down the dirt road. The engineer was waving at it. The car stopped, and the engineer jumped off the train and Jorgos followed. They talked to the driver in the car, and they started waving at me. *"Ella! Ella!"*

I readjusted my backpack and jumped off the train. "Tithorea!" the engineer chanted. "Tithorea! Tithorea!"

"They take you," said Jorgos, and he helped me into the car.

The train pulled away, and Jorgos waved at me. The engineer blew the horn. The passengers were leaning out the windows cheering and waving as they passed by.

I was in shock. I looked up at the couple sitting in the front seat. *"Yasou,"* I said. Hello.

They smiled and greeted me back. Then we drove away.

"English?" I asked.

"Ochi," said the man. The young woman shook her head.

"Tithorea?" I asked.

"Ney," they said in unison, beaming from ear to ear.

And off we drove along tobacco fields and the train track. I used up all my Greek in three minutes, so we just smiled and laughed about nothing in particular. About twenty minutes later we arrived in a village, and the driver stopped and asked directions. Then he weaved in and out of tiny streets until we came to the train station.

"Tithorea," he announced with a grin.

I pointed to the couple and put my hands together in a sleep motion. "Live here?" I asked.

They shook their heads and pointed to where we came from. It was then that I realized that they were never even going in this direction. They had just come here to drop me off. *What amazing people,* I thought, as I thanked them profusely and got out of the car. They drove away waving.

My friend was not there. A woman let me use a phone in the station. Johanna's English wasn't good enough for me to explain over the phone what had happened. I just told her I was at the station. She said something that I didn't understand and hung up.

I walked to the parking lot and waited.

Five minutes later a dark-haired, handsome man drove up on a motorcycle. He started talking to me in Greek and gesturing with his arms. I had no idea what he wanted. And then I looked more closely. He looked just like Johanna, and I knew she had an older brother.

"Johanna?" I asked. He nodded furiously, smiled, and motioned for me to get on the back of his motorcycle. I pointed to my pack, knowing there was no way I would fit with it. He nodded and drove off, leaving me in what was now a familiar state of confusion.

I waited. And waited. And waited.

Finally a taxi pulled up with Johanna's brother tailing it on his bike. They both stopped in front of me, and the brother picked up my pack and put it in the car. Then he told the driver something, and I followed his directions to get in the taxi. We drove off. Johanna's brother waved and went the other way.

The taxi wound its way through town and up into the hills. I laughed out loud as I thought of the last hour's events. As we headed farther up a mountain, I looked back at the small buildings and vast tobacco fields surrounding the village.

Then the taxi driver stopped. Another taxi was flying toward us down the narrow road. It stopped when it reached us. And finally there was Johanna. Her arms were up in the air, and she was laughing. She hopped out of her cab and jumped in mine.

"We'll go to my house," she said cheerfully. "How was your train ride?"

"Great. Just a typical day of travel."

WITH RITA AS her mother, Jan Gelman was surely born with a travel gene. One highlight from her many journeys was a year-long solo trip around the world in her twenties that included this experience in Tithorea. Jan and her husband, Bill Smith, live in Seattle, Washington, with their dog, Roxy, and are always looking for travel adventures together. In her work as a leadership coach, consultant, and facilitator, Jan also brings her global lens into focus by keeping an eye out for how cultural differences impact business relationships and performance. Visit Jan's website, www .jangelman.com.

Vegetarian *Dolmades*

Adapted from a recipe in the Time-Life Foods of the World *series*

MAKES 30 *DOLMADES*

---

*T*he toughest part of this is getting the leaves out of the jar. Do it thoughtfully and carefully. It's also fun and quick if there are two or three people rolling.

- 1 jar of preserved grape leaves (If possible, choose one with leaves with thin veins. You will need 45 leaves to make 30 *dolmades*.)
- 6 tablespoons olive oil
- 1 cup finely chopped onions
- ⅓ cup uncooked long- or medium-grain white rice
- ½ teaspoon salt
- Freshly ground black pepper
- 2 tablespoons pine nuts
- 2 tablespoons dried currants
- ½ cup cold water
- Lemon wedges, one per person.

LEAVES

Bring 2 quarts of water to a boil.

Remove the leaves from the jar. (This is tricky. Do it carefully, tearing as few leaves as possible.)

Unroll the leaves, and drop them into boiling water. (At this point you do not have to separate them.) Turn off the heat, and let them soak for 5 minutes.

Drain and put them into a bowl of cold water to cool. Then carefully separate the leaves and spread them on towels to dry, dull side up.

FILLING

Heat 3 tablespoons of olive oil in a heavy 12-inch skillet over moderate heat.

Add the onions, and stir for 5 minutes until soft and translucent, not brown.

Add the rice, and stir constantly for 2 to 3 minutes. Do not let the rice brown.

Add ¾ cup water, salt, and pepper, and bring to a boil over high heat.

Reduce heat, cover, and cook 15 minutes or until the rice is cooked and the liquid is absorbed.

In a small skillet, heat 1 tablespoon olive oil and brown the pine nuts.

Add the pine nuts and currants to the rice.

STUFFING AND ROLLING

Prepare a 10- to 11-inch heavy skillet (with a tight-fitting lid) by placing 15 leaves on the bottom of the pan, layered on top of each other. (Here's where you use the torn leaves.)

Place a leaf on a plate, and snip off the stem and the thick bottom of the veins.

Spoon a tablespoonful of filling on the dull side of the leaf just above the place where you cut off the stem, leaving room on both sides.

Fold the two flaps up over the filling. Fold in the sides. Roll the wrapped filling carefully from bottom to top of the leaf. Place the roll in the skillet, seam side down.

Repeat until there is no more stuffing.

Stack the rolls side by side as tightly as possible to make sure they won't unwrap while cooking.

COOKING

Sprinkle the *dolmades* with two tablespoons of olive oil and pour in ½ cup cold water. Set the skillet on high heat until the water boils. Then reduce the heat to low and simmer, tightly covered, for 50 minutes. You may need to add another ½ cup water after 20 minutes.

Uncover and cool.

Serve on a large platter or individual plates, and garnish with lemon wedges.

Harry, our Bulgarian engineer who learned English from porn movies and rap music, grabbed the whole platter of dolmades and ate every one but the two I tasted in the galley. His exact words after tasting the first one were "This is good shit." He is requesting that I make more tomorrow. —ma

Tongue-Tied

Kelly Hayes-Raitt

The one I wanted to wrap in my arms and bring home was Nebras.

I didn't even know her name when I went back to Iraq, shortly after the assault on Baghdad. I was armed only with a photo of a beggar touching her nose with her tongue.

I'd met her a few months before, when I'd traveled to Iraq with a women's delegation, just five weeks before the U.S. bombings and invasion. Unfazed by impending disaster, the little girl, old enough to be in primary school, had begged for handouts in a popular market. I taught her to touch her nose with her tongue. Clearly she wasn't used to an adult making faces at her and delighting in her company. She followed me around the *souk* nearly swallowing her tongue in laughter as she imitated my nose-touching stunt.

She was cold. The dirty scarf wrapped loosely around her neck neither protected her from the chill nor hid her calcu-lating ability to work the shoppers. Without a translator, the most I gathered was a photo of a gleeful girl with laughing eyes and an incredibly acrobatic tongue.

When I return to Iraq five months later to find how war had touched the people who had so deeply touched me, translators are reluctant to take me to the *souk*. The mood in Baghdad has shifted. Gunfire is heard nightly, and no one wants to be responsible for my harm. Finally, the day before I am to leave, I convince one translator to take me "shopping." I canvass the cluttered shops for hours, flashing the little girl's photo.

"Yes, that's Nebras." Finally, a shopkeeper gives a name to the girl whose deep, brown eyes had humanized the smoldering CNN newscasts that absorbed my life back home. "But I haven't seen her in a while. Not since before the war."

I catch my breath. I have just learned Nebras's name. She can't be one of the thousands of nameless Iraqis we dismissively call "collateral damage." I step out into the bright sunlight, and my translator catches my arm.

"We need to leave," he insists. The equally insistent gunfire across the river rattles my nerve. I feel conspicuous in the *souk*'s crowded, narrow alleys. People dart, avoiding eye contact. Shops close prematurely. Barricaded soldiers seem hyperalert in the edgy heat.

As we worm our way back to our car, I stifle my creeping panic. Behind me, a commotion erupts, and I turn around to see a crowd of men shoving toward me. I freeze. The shopkeepers part, revealing the terrified eyes of a familiar elfish girl they are dragging to me by the scruff of her T-shirt.

Nebras doesn't recognize me at first. Not until I show her photos of herself does she smile. Backed against a shop facing a tight crowd of curious men, Nebras retreats shyly, studying her photo intently. I shoo back the men who had treated this beggar only as a nuisance and, kneeling before her, I ask the interpreter to tell her I have come from America to see her.

Without warning, the overwhelmed girl lunges forward and kisses me on the lips.

We buy her an ice cream from a passing vendor. She unwraps it and holds it out to me. My defenses melt. After two weeks of rigorous attention to all food and water that passed my lips, I lick the sweet street fare, sacrificing my intestines to this little girl's pleasure at hosting a visitor with all she can offer.

She's an only child who doesn't know her age. It was particularly ironic that we had met outside the Al Mustanseria University, the world's oldest science college, built in 1233. This schoolless girl's only education has been in navigating the streets outside the university's ancient walls.

I empty my purse of dinars, stuffing the oily bills into her plastic purse. She gleefully buys another ice cream for us to share.

Military helicopters zigzag overhead. Rumors that the American troops have closed bridges and jammed traffic make us jittery. Nebras escorts me out of the dicey *souk*, grabbing my hand and expertly keeping my skirt from being snagged by the ubiquitous wartime razor wire.

As we pass a store being repainted, she mentions it had been hit during the war's initial attacks. She had spent the long nights of the early bombings in a nearby mosque.

I hug her harder than I intend. I feel her wiry hair against my cheek, her grungy T-shirt against my shoulder, her warm, open heart so willing to accept mine.

And then I'm gone.

A Boat Ride

Laurice Haney

It was one of those rare days in Paraguay, a cloudless sky and a sun peering down between the trees. The air was cool with the promise of enough warmth without becoming hot. The port on the Paraguayan River was bustling with people, crew, and passengers anxious to board the supply boat.

My fiancé Kevin and I stood to one side, tickets in hand, waiting for the signal that we could board. We had taken time off from our Peace Corps posts to travel, and we now had to return. As usual, we were short of cash, with only enough money for the boat ride to the port of Rosario, the bus fare to Itacurubi del Rosario where I was stationed, and a cheap lunch.

Once we were under way, Kevin sought out the captain and explained that we would be disembarking at Rosario and asked that he let us know when we got there. I had been to the port before but was afraid I might not recognize it. After a short chat, Kevin gave the captain a cigar, with the hope that it would help him remember us.

Periodically we walked around the boat; each time we

passed the captain, Kevin called out, "Don't forget us," and supplied him with another cigar.

As so often happens in Paraguay, the boat was running behind schedule, and we still hadn't reached Rosario by sundown.

The boat pulled into another port, and Kevin and I stood on the deck above as we watched the men unload several crates of fruits and vegetables. The captain was shouting orders in Guaraní. After about twenty minutes, the boat was again on its way.

Within ten minutes I spotted Rosario. I said to Kevin, "There it is, but we aren't stopping!" We immediately ran to the captain, who, upon seeing us, slapped his forehead with his hand.

"That is not the *port* of Rosario," he said. "You were supposed to get off where we were unloading back there. I completely forgot about you." Then he grinned widely. "Don't worry. I know a family downriver. I will go with you to their house and explain what happened. You can spend the night with them. Tomorrow morning you can catch the boat back to Rosario."

"But," we explained, "we have only enough money to take the bus from Rosario to Itacurubi."

"*Tranquilo.*" The stock answer in Paraguay was his reply.

By this time it was pitch dark, and there was no electricity in this part of the country. The boat pulled to the bank, and the deckhands lowered two narrow planks, side by side, making a shaky walkway to the mud.

The captain held my hand as I attempted to get my balance on the top of the ramp, holding my red American Tourister overnight bag in my right hand. I managed my way down without falling off. Kevin came next. We turned to watch the captain make his way down, but instead, the men were hauling in the planks, and the boat was pulling away from shore.

"I thought you were coming with us!" I shouted.

"Don't worry," he said. "The house is back there among the trees. Tell them I sent you."

I felt around for my flashlight. We heard the sound of a barking dog from the house that we presumed was in the near distance. Cautiously we made our way toward the sound, aware not only of the dog but also of the fact that many Paraguayan men own handguns to protect their families.

We saw the outline of a house. Soon a man appeared at the cracked door with his wife behind him and two children looking out between his legs. He shushed the dog.

Kevin had mastered Guaraní during his time in Paraguay, a language that I found mystifying. This was a useful skill in the remote parts of the country since many people there don't speak Spanish. He explained our predicament, including the fact that we didn't have any money to pay for their hospitality. The man swung the door open and invited us in.

Since the sun was down and there was no way to see anything, the family had already retired for the night. Their house was unusually large for the countryside, with the sleeping quarters on the second floor. Below, a hard-packed-dirt floor was used for the kitchen and daytime living area. There was a makeshift bed with rawhide lacing on the bottom, supported by three posts. The couple gave us fleece blankets which provided welcome warmth against a cold night.

We fell asleep quickly and woke with the sun. The family was up and the woman already at work preparing breakfast. She served us *bife al caballo,* a boneless slab of beef, fried with salt, pepper, and garlic, then topped with a fried egg. Since our last meal had been a meager lunch the day before, it was a tasty and much-appreciated treat.

We asked what time the boat would be returning. "Oh, the boat won't be back for another three days" was the reply. We were aghast. We both had meetings to conduct and couldn't possibly be away that long. Plus the painful fact that we didn't have money loomed over us.

"Can't we walk to Rosario?" I asked. "It's only fifteen or twenty minutes by boat. It shouldn't take that long through the jungle."

"We don't have roads here," said our host. "I have an idea, though. We have a neighbor who is a fisherman. If he has a big enough catch, he rows up to Rosario to sell his fish in the market. I will send my son to his house to see if he plans to go today." After what seemed an eternity, the boy returned and said that the neighbor would be glad to take us.

Sometime later, a very small rowboat pulled up to the bank. The fisherman was a short, stocky fellow wearing only a pair of shorts. He had no hair and no teeth, but his bronzed skin covered powerful muscles. Kevin explained our predicament, including the fact that we had no money. The fisherman shrugged his shoulders and invited us to board his boat.

We said our goodbyes and thank-yous and climbed into the boat. There were only two fish in the boat. The fisherman pulled out into the river, and I started calculating that we would probably get to Rosario in one or two hours.

Two hours stretched to three, then to four. The fisherman rowed steadily upstream. I sat on the long bench of the stern, red American Tourister by my side, bailing out the water that was quickly leaking into the boat. Kevin kept up a steady stream of Guaraní, frequently complimenting the man on the beauty of his catch. He also offered to help row, but each time the man refused.

As the day wore on, the fisherman asked if we minded if he stopped on an island for a break. By this time he had been rowing for about five hours, nonstop. The current was so strong that any lapse in his work would have meant swiftly flowing downstream. We had had no idea before setting out what a sacrifice this man would be making for two strangers.

At sundown we reached Rosario. The fisherman rowed us in, stern first, so that I could get out without having to walk across the boat. The three of us stood on shore, and the fisherman shook hands with us. We offered our deepest gratitude. Our new friend offered us one of the fish. We tried to refuse, already feeling enormously guilty for having hitched a ride at his expense without being able to compensate him. He insisted, so we accepted with more gratitude.

The last leg of the journey went without incident. We had enough bus fare, and we arrived in Itacurubi del Rosario, my home base, within the hour. The next day, Renita, the woman who ran the *pensión* where I ate my meals, made a fine fish soup.

LAURICE HANEY started her travels as a Peace Corps Volunteer in Paraguay in 1975. Her favorite locations are the most remote, including Belize, the Amazon and Pantanal in Brazil, and Oaxaca and Chiapas in Mexico. Her husband, Beau, joined in the journey in 1993. They get away as often as possible. Their favorite experiences have been where they have made friends and enjoyed cross-cultural interactions. Their dream is to board a plane in Atlanta, with only passports and toothbrushes in hand, and travel the world. In the meantime, they have a travel website at www.quantumnetworktravel.com so they can share their passion.

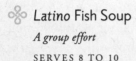

Latino Fish Soup

A group effort

SERVES 8 TO 10

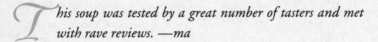

This soup was tested by a great number of tasters and met with rave reviews. —ma

- 2 tablespoons vegetable or olive oil
- 1 large onion, chopped
- 5 to 6 cloves garlic, crushed
- 5 tomatoes, diced small
- 1 teaspoon sea salt
- 2 large green peppers or poblano chiles, chopped in 1-inch chunks
- 1 large sweet potato, peeled and cut in 1-inch cubes
- ½ teaspoon red pepper flakes
- 1 teaspoon dried thyme (or 2 teaspoons fresh)
- 2 pounds firm-fleshed white fish fillets
- 2 tablespoons vegetable oil
- 1 plantain, cut in ½ inch circles (optional) (Use fairly ripe plantains that are just beginning to go black.)
- 1 can (400 ml) coconut milk
- ½ cup cilantro, chopped
- 2 to 3 limes, cut in wedges

½ cup crushed peanuts
Hot sauce (optional)

Heat the oil in a large, heavy-duty pot over medium heat. Add
the onion. Cook 2 minutes, stirring occasionally.

Add the crushed garlic. Lower heat. Cook 3 minutes or until
the onions are soft, stirring occasionally. Make sure the garlic does not brown.

Add the diced tomatoes and ½ teaspoon sea salt.

Cook 30 minutes over medium heat, stirring occasionally, until
the water has evaporated and the tomatoes have darkened to
a rust color. This step develops the flavor of the soup and
should not be rushed. As the mixture dries out, stir more
frequently to prevent burning.

Add 6 cups of water, the peppers, sweet potato, red pepper
flakes, thyme, and ½ teaspoon sea salt. Once the water comes
to a boil, turn down the heat and simmer 30 minutes over
low heat, or until the sweet potato is cooked.

Meanwhile sauté the fish in medium-hot oil until it is almost
done and liquid comes from the fish. This step removes the
strong fish taste and gives the soup a more mellow taste.

Remove the fish from the pan and drain. Cut the fish in
medium-size pieces.

Add the fish and the plantain circles (if used) to the soup. Simmer 3 minutes.

Add coconut milk. Simmer an additional 3 minutes, or until
the fish is tender.

Add the cilantro. Taste and adjust seasonings.

Serve the soup with lime wedges, crushed peanuts, and optional hot sauce.

*If a thicker soup is desired, cut the fish fillets in medium
pieces, shake them in a bag with ¼ cup all-purpose flour seasoned with salt and pepper, and sauté them in 2 tablespoons of oil
until golden. Fry in two batches over medium-high heat (adding
more oil if necessary).*

*If coconut milk is not available, the tomato stock is delicious
on its own. If the soup is too thick at the end when the coconut
milk would be added, thin with water. The type of pepper can be
varied. If sweet potato is not available, use orange camote. —ma*

A Great Mix of People

Rita Golden Gelman

"Go to Suriname," said the man. "It's my favorite place in the world." I didn't even know where it was.

The next day I went to the library. Suriname is one of three tiny countries in the northeastern corner of South America. Until independence in 1975, it was the colony of Dutch Guyana.

It didn't take a lot of research to figure out what's so interesting about Suriname. It's the people. They're an incredible multicultural mix of colors, ancestry, traditions, languages, and physical characteristics.

At first there were the native Indians. Then the Dutch came along and colonized the region and brought over 45,000 African slaves to work their sugar plantations. Some of those slaves ran away and built small African villages up Amazonian rivers in the interior. (Their descendants, called Maroons, are still there.) When the slaves were freed in 1861, the Dutch brought in indentured servants from India, Java, and China. A community of Portuguese-speaking Jews came up from Brazil, started their own sugar plantations, and built a synagogue that's still being used; it's just down the street from a mosque.

The descendants of all these people are still there, coexisting peacefully: Hindustani, 37 percent; Creole (mixed black and white), 31 percent; Javanese, 15 percent; and Maroons, 10 percent. The remaining 6 percent are native Indians, Chinese, Dutch, and Jews.

The first language in Suriname is still Dutch, though most of the Dutch people went back to the Netherlands after independence. There's also a common language that everyone speaks, a kind of Creole-Dutch-English that's called *sranang tongo*. *Sweety Krisnati* is "Merry Christmas." *Mi denki so* is "I think so." Fun language.

The more I researched Suriname, the more I knew that I had to go. I checked out the Servas (see "My Favorite Organization Ever," page 17) host book for Suriname and found that nineteen families were looking for international guests. I wrote to all of them and said that I was coming down and would like to meet them all. But first, I hoped they would help me find a place to rent for a few months. I heard back from the national secretary.

"Come straight to my house from the airport," she wrote. "I'll help you find a home."

Within four hours of my arrival, I had an apartment. My three months in Suriname were amazing. I loved the people I met, the foods I ate, and the experiences I had.

One of those experiences was a trip up the Saramacca River to visit a Maroon village. I went with two city people who had served as cooks for missionary groups who were "doing their thing" in the villages. Jenny, Rudy, and I took a bus and then a small power-driven boat up the river, which was low and spotted with rocks.

Maroon life revolves around the river. Early in the morning, before school, boys were leaping from rock to rock in the water. Bathing, chasing each other, playing games, teasing the girls. Beautiful shiny black bodies against the dark sparkling water. From early morning until afternoon, women were washing clothes and themselves. Each morning I sat with Jenny up to my neck in the water, for more than an hour, talking, scrubbing, watching, washing, and smiling.

We slept in our hammocks at night in a special guest house. Jenny cooked. During the days we talked to a lot of friendly people.

After four days in the village, we got back on a boat and then the bus, heading for home in the capital city of Paramaribo. There were only five of us on the bus: myself, the driver, his assistant, Jenny, and Rudy. After about fifteen minutes, the driver stopped the bus in the middle of the road. (There were no other vehicles.) He opened the door and walked over to a table that was selling bloody meat in see-through plastic bags. He returned with one of the packages. Then the assistant jumped off and bought another one of the bloody bags.

"What is it?" I asked Jenny. She didn't know the name of the animal in English, but when she and Rudy left the bus to buy their bags, I went too and bought mine.

"Okay. Tell me what you do with it?" I asked.

"Cook it like a stew. You know, carrots, potatoes, that sort of thing."

When I got to my apartment, I dumped the contents into the sink and washed off the blood to see what was there.

I had in my sink the back quarter of an armadillo, overlapping segments of armor and all.

Somewhat squeamishly I cut the meat out of the hardened shell, removed the bones, and threw the bloody bits into a pot with water, carrots, potatoes, cabbage, and a lot of Indian curry spices. I figured it was a good idea to go heavy on the spices.

I was right. Two hours later I dutifully ate a bowlful of armadillo stew. Two hours and ten minutes later, I gave the rest to my landlady's dog.

French Confusion

Michael Worthen

When I was in French class in high school, many years ago, the teacher said, "Now class, when you go to France, you must remember that the French are very formal. You must greet them politely, or they will consider you rude. *Bonjour Monsieur/Madame, Comment allez-vous? S'il vous plaît,* and *Merci* are the basic necessities of the French language. Every casual conversation, no matter how insignificant, must begin with these formalities."

With this simple lesson in greetings and politeness, I have plodded my way through France for over forty years using my fractured high school language skills, and no French person has ever been rude to me. A perfect example of the necessity of formality was my experience at the very crowded and hectic Nice post office.

My wife, who speaks much better French than I, asked me to mail an important letter. Usually I depended on her to deal with the post office because there always seems to be some issue, minor or major, that requires more French than I know. Nevertheless, I was brave and went by myself.

After arriving at the post office, finding the right window for an international letter, and getting a ticket out of the machine that dispenses numbers for the next person to be served, I sat for twenty minutes waiting for my number to be flashed on one of the many electronic screens. Heaven forbid if I wasn't watching carefully and missed my turn; I might have to start over because any explanation as to why I didn't respond on time, in English, wouldn't be taken seriously. That would be one of the "minor problems" I worried about.

So I sat staring at all of the screens and listening for the lovely chime that accompanied the change of numbers. Number 789 flashed on the screen. I was next!

In my clumsy French I bought one postage stamp and one extra stamp that made it international; I also received one free stamp that made it *Par Avion*. Wow, three stamps for one letter.

I found a spot at one of the few work tables and applied the stamps. Then I had to find the proper slot to post the letter. There it was, "International." I deposited the letter, and it slid down the chute into the basement of the post office. Oh no! I still had one of the necessary stamps in my hand. Now I had a "major problem."

Terrified that the check to pay a bill would go nowhere, I rushed through a nearby door into a workroom for *employees only*. Oh dear, now I was trespassing in France!

Three postal employees looked at me as if I was trespassing not only in France but worse yet, trespassing in their postal workroom. I was frantic to communicate and tempted to blurt out my problem as quickly as possible.

Then I remembered the French etiquette lesson of long ago and said, *"Bonjour, Monsieur. S'il vous plaît, parlez-vous anglais?"*

"*Non,*" came the quick but friendly reply and the typical French shrug of his shoulders. I looked sadly toward the others. They echoed "*Non*" and shrugged their shoulders.

I then quickly blurted out, in my best French, what my problem was, while waving my stamp frantically in the air. All three began to chuckle. The chuckle soon turned into a roar of laughter. When they were through laughing, rolling their eyes, and gesturing with their hands, one of the men happily took the stamp I was waving at him and told me, in perfect English, "It would be my pleasure to assist you." He then rushed off in the direction of my deficient letter.

Later, I returned to our apartment and told my wife what had happened. We checked our French-English dictionary to figure out why I had gotten such a comical reaction. We finally figured out that what I had told the men in the workroom was "I threw the postman down the waterfall without a bell."

Vive la France!

MICHAEL WORTHEN was an archaeologist and kitchen designer. He is now very happily retired. He spends his time working in the garden and enjoying his wife's gourmet kitchen activities.

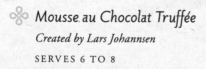 Mousse au Chocolat Truffée

Created by Lars Johannsen

SERVES 6 TO 8

T his is Rita's favorite dessert when she visits Lars and Nirin in Nantes, France. Lars says it doesn't last long. It's guaranteed to make even the most disgruntled postal employee smile. —ma

½ pound dark chocolate (70 percent cocoa)
5½ ounces salted butter (about 10 tablespoons)
1½ tablespoons strong coffee
1½ tablespoons rum or cognac
6 room-temperature, large farm-fresh eggs
4 tablespoons thick crème fraîche (or Mexican crema)
1½ tablespoons sugar

Melt the chocolate and butter with the coffee in a microwave. Stir until well mixed. Or set the chocolate, butter, and coffee in the top of a double boiler and melt over low heat. Add the rum or cognac.

Separate the egg yolks and whites.

Pour the warm chocolate mixture into the egg yolks while whisking them to a thick but soft sauce. (This is the secret of its consistency.) This procedure can also be done in the double boiler. Add the crème fraîche.

With an electric mixer, beat the egg whites with the sugar until they form soft peaks. Add the egg whites softly and little by little to the chocolate with a dough scraper.

The mousse will be better if left (covered) all night in the refrigerator before serving.

....

If you enjoy the slightly bitter flavor of dark chocolate, this will become a regular dish when friends visit. Serve it with a liqueur and perhaps cheese after an Italian or French meal. The mousse is best served in small portions as it's an extremely rich and satisfying dessert but is surprisingly easy to make.

If you are worried about using raw eggs in the mousse, buy pasteurized shell eggs that are safe for uncooked recipes.

Either (or both) the coffee or the rum/cognac can be increased to 2 tablespoons. —ma

Turkish Delight

Kay Moody

At the age of fifteen, our son Henry lived in Istanbul, Turkey, for a year as an exchange student. Later he majored in Turkish studies in college. While living in Turkey, he stayed with a family who had a son, Mustafa. We made it a true exchange when we invited Mustafa to come to our home to spend a year going to school in America. Our invitation of one year turned out to be ten years. After Mustafa graduated from our local high school, he got his bachelor's degree at our state university and his MBA from Loyola. He began working in Chicago. That's when his parents informed their only child that it was time for him to return to his home in Istanbul. When Mustafa returned to Turkey, he met the love of his life. Our family went to our Turkish son's wedding and met his parents and his beautiful bride.

Before we left, we shopped for souvenirs to bring back home. And of course we spent a day at the world-famous Grand Bazaar in Istanbul. We had a long list of items: silk scarves, leather bags, Russian caviar, teas and spices, painted pottery. The list was endless. You cannot buy anything in the bazaar without bargaining.

We spent a long time in one shop. Each time the shopkeepers had a price for us, we added one more jar of caviar, another scarf, or more spices. And every time we added something, they conferred with each other to recompute a price to include our latest addition.

My husband, daughter, and I kept haggling over the price, and although the shopkeepers were fluent in English, they chatted back and forth in Turkish while we decided on our purchases. After a very long time, still unable to agree on a reasonable price for all our items, one of the men looked at Henry and said, "You're their son, aren't you? Why are you so quiet?" In perfect Turkish, Henry replied, "Because it's more fun to listen. And yes, my sister's red hair is natural, and she is happily married and not available to go home with you; and I agree, my father is too fat and doesn't need another can of caviar!"

The shopkeepers were shocked to hear a young American speak flawless Turkish, but they appreciated the joke that was played on them, and we all laughed together. As Henry knew, Turks have a wonderful sense of humor.

KAY MOODY and her husband, James T. Moody, have been married for almost fifty years. Although they are in their seventies, both continue to work full time, Jim as a U.S. district court judge in the Northern District of Indiana, and Kay as an owner, administrator, and instructor at the College of Court Reporting in Hobart, Indiana. Kay is presently writing her sixth court reporting textbook for online students. Visit Kay's website at www.ccr.edu.

A Rose and a Kiss

Maria Altobelli

"Back from Italy with great recipes, eggplant, and a hand kissed by an Italian."

The postcard taunted me. I had Italian blood coursing through my veins and had never seen Italy.

My husband Paul and I set off from Mexico City's Benito Juarez airport in September 2002. Before we left, I had heard repeatedly, "Don't bother studying Italian. All Italians speak English."

Instead of listening, I had sweated over language tapes for a year before the trip. From the moment we stepped off the plane in our rumpled travel clothes and white tennis shoes, I saw that Italians actually do speak Italian—a lot of Italian. The year of study was not enough time to achieve fluency, but it was better than nothing. Too bad I hadn't boned up on European fashion tips as well.

My linguistic ability increased rapidly, however, since Paul insisted I question each and every person on Italian soil.

His favorite line was *Fa una domanda*. During the month, he would ask me something I couldn't possibly know. (After all, it was the first time in Italy for both of us.) I'd shake my head or shrug my shoulders, and he would counter with *Fa una domanda*.

The one person I did not want to question was the only other passenger in our nonsmoking first-class compartment. Tall and drop-dead gorgeous, he had thick, wavy hair that fell past the collar of his cotton shirt, his eyes obscured by wrap-around sunglasses.

"No way I'm asking him anything."

"So how do we make the connection from Verona to Rome? Do you see anyone else around to ask?"

Damn the logic of German-born men. I got up and made my way down the aisle. In a country devoted to fashion, he sat in a rumpled shirt, jeans, and tennis shoes. As he heard my greeting, he slipped off his sunglasses. *Oh, geez.*

I took a deep breath and started my litany of questions. My queries received elaborate and gracious answers. He even added questions of his own to make sure he'd given me the right advice.

He was on his way from making someone very happy or off to Verona to do the same. Perhaps it was a case of both the former and the latter. His only luggage consisted of a massive bouquet of long-stemmed roses a lush, earthy tone I had never seen before. Even though I had exhausted my linguistic skills and most likely his patience asking directions, I couldn't resist murdering Dante's language a little more by making a comment about the flowers.

We were getting ready to get off the train when I heard the

word "*Posso?*" (May I?) repeated several times. I turned to see the young man gesturing toward a rather confused Paul with one of the roses. The fellow kept repeating "*Posso?*" Averting my face, I whispered, "*Yes!* Say yes! Just nod your head."

It wasn't an eggplant, but I was given a beautiful rose whose petals unfolded to display the color of a miniature radicchio.

The drying petals of that rose sustained me through many a verbal blunder on our way south. We were heading to Campania. Naples is the province's best-known city, but we didn't stay there. Instead we took the train inland to Benevento and then bused to Montefalcone di Val Fortore, the birthplace of my paternal grandparents.

After that first visit, we kept returning to Italy like swallows to Capistrano. We always went south. One day Paul and I got on a rickety train filled with rowdy schoolkids and one nattily dressed gentleman. The fellow started a conversation. "But why do you come to southern Italy? Tourists usually go north."

I explained the Montefalcone connection.

"Ah. Montefalcone di Val Fortore." He pronounced the name of this tiny mountainous hamlet in the tone normally reserved for Florence or Venice or Rome.

We parted at the Lecce train station. He shook Paul's hand vigorously. With a slight flourish, he gently lifted my fingers, bowed his head gracefully, and lightly passed his lips over the back of my hand.

"Enjoy Italy," he said. "You are home."

I've always had the recipes and the eggplant. After all, I've been cooking seriously since I was twelve. But now I have a rose and a hand kissed by an Italian.

Roasted Pepper Casserole

SERVES 6 TO 8

---

*E*very time we go to Italy now, I think of my first Servas visit to Genoa in 2004. It was my third time in the country and the first time I had such an excellent, in-depth view, all due to Servas. The organization has always had a very active group in Italy, and Genoa was no exception. After spending a day on a walking tour with a very knowledgeable day host, I wanted to take her out to eat, but we had walked our way past the three o'clock closing time for the trattorias. She suggested we go to her apartment but apologized that she had only pasta and some peppers. Sounded great to me. And what peppers! This is one of those "on the road" recipes. You confirm the ingredients used and then go home and experiment with measurements.

6   sweet red bell peppers or a mixture of red, orange, and yellow
2   small onions, chopped
2   to 4 tablespoons olive oil
4   garlic cloves, minced
1   cup coarsely chopped Italian (flat leaf) parsley
½   cup chopped tomatoes, peeled
2   tablespoons capers, rinsed and chopped
2   to 4 anchovies, rinsed and chopped (optional)
1   cup black or pimento-stuffed green olives or a mixture of both
1   cup fresh breadcrumbs from good bread
½   cup grated parmesan cheese
⅓   cup olive oil

Preheat oven to 350°F.

Roast, peel, and seed the peppers. (See "Roasting Peppers" on page 170.)

Cut the peppers into strips and put in a bowl.

In a medium frying pan, sauté the onions in oil until transparent. Add the garlic, being careful not to brown it. Add the parsley, tomatoes, capers, and anchovies (if used).

Add the contents of the frying pan to the peppers, and mix gently. Add the olives.

Pour the pepper mixture into an oven-proof pan. Cover with the breadcrumbs mixed with parmesan. Drizzle with olive oil.

Bake for about 15 minutes. Set under the broiler to brown the breadcrumb topping, if desired.

ROASTING PEPPERS

Peppers can be roasted by setting them on the burners of a gas stove. Adjust the flame so the skin blisters. Keep turning the peppers to char them lightly all over.

Or cut the peppers in half, flatten the halves with the palm of your hand, and roast them under the broiler until they char, checking them often. You might want to get the peppers closer to the fire by setting them on a pie tin.

Once the peppers are blistered, put them in a bowl and cover it with sticky wrap, or put them in a clean plastic bag, secure the opening, and cover the bag with a kitchen towel.

After 30 minutes, the skin will have loosened so you can rub or peel it off. Remove the seeds, and if using poblano chiles, scrape out the veins with a teaspoon and be sure to remove the hard seed area under the stem.

Master Kim

Bonnie Betts

Master Kim was the first person to help disarm my travel fears. As a child, I grew up watching the Vietnam (or as the Vietnamese call it, the American) War on television. I recall countless times thinking, *What a sad thing to be happening in such a beautiful place.* I wanted to go there one day. At the age of forty-six, I felt it was time to realize my dream and take my solo journey to that "beautiful place" that still haunted me: Vietnam.

Many serendipitous incidents confirmed that this was my time to go, particularly one evening when I was trying to focus on meditating with my weekly group. As I was drifting off with thoughts of how to put my trip together and learn some of the language, I opened my eyes and noticed an Asian man in his sixties sitting in a chair in the lotus position, slightly apart from our group. He was later introduced as Master Kim, the new resident monk at the Vietnamese temple in Olympia, Washington, where I lived. I greeted him and told him of my plans.

"Come see me," he said. "I will teach you how to speak Vietnamese."

Master Kim spent generous hours helping me learn some basic sentences and polite words to say. He teased me and corrected me as I tried to pronounce the difficult words. He invited me to a ceremony where I observed him wearing a golden robe on stage while laypeople in their gray robes sat on the floor chanting back and forth with him; the sound was beautiful, almost familiar. Master Kim gave me a Vietnamese name, Bong Hoa (Beautiful Flower), and informed me he would be visiting family in Vietnam while I was there. We made plans to meet during my travels.

Four guidebooks later, my rucksack was packed and I put on an air of confidence as I landed in Vietnam. Sure, I had traveled to other countries, but the cultural difference and language barrier were so much more extreme here. It was Master Kim who helped me to feel secure as I finally stepped foot on Southeast Asian soil.

When it came time to take my flight to join Master Kim in Hue, I practiced the phrases I had memorized to say when meeting Master Kim's ailing ninety-year-old father. Upon landing, I found my way to their house via taxi and was surprised to see Master Kim, a monk who was always in long pants and robe, come out of his home to greet me in shorts and a T-shirt. I was so happy to see his familiar face in this strange land.

He led me inside and introduced me to the three generations of his family all living together in this small structure. I was instantly made to feel at home. I felt a warmth from his father that made me realize it didn't matter what came out of my mouth; it was the action of compassion that mattered. To my relief, however, I did say the right words, as I wanted Master Kim to be proud of my Vietnamese.

In the following days, dressed in his monk's attire, Master Kim led me, along with his twenty-year-old English-speaking niece, Lai, to monasteries, ancient temples, orphanages, and job-training centers. We rode rickety bikes through the chaotic traffic to our various destinations. I was gifted with a gray layperson's robe at an orphanage and felt honored to don it over my clothes despite the July heat. The children sang beautiful songs and practiced speaking English with me.

"Which child do you want?" teased Master Kim.

Nuns played with my long golden locks while Master Kim and Lai laughed, explaining that these women wanted to shave my head and make me a nun. As I smiled and pulled my hair protectively into my hand, the sparkle in their eyes told me they were being playful.

We drank tea and had lunch with masters, monks, and nuns. I was able to sit on the floor in my gray robe and participate in a ceremony, catching Master Kim's eye on stage as I tried to chant and bask in the sounds I had been introduced to in Olympia.

At his house, I would always find Master Kim in shorts. On one occasion he had me sit next to him as we watched a movie, and we laughed together as ninjas flew through the air to defeat their enemy. Since Master Kim needed to spend much time with his father, I spent my free moments with his beautiful niece, Lai.

Lai quickly became my interpreter, my friend, my confidante. She pedaled me on the back of her bicycle to help me run errands and sightsee. I hung on to her seat and sang American songs in her ear ("Yankee Doodle," "Oh Susannah," etc.).

At her request, I helped teach her English class. I invited her to stay with me at night in my guest house, and she was happy to join me. We spoke candidly about the differences and similarities of our cultures, politics, and families. At times I had to remind myself where I was and that I was not just chatting with an old friend.

Having read that it is customary for friends in Vietnam to hold hands or walk arm in arm (even male friends), I went to link my arm with hers one day as we strolled down the street. I was taken aback when she pulled away.

"I just wanted you to know that I think of you as a good friend," I explained.

"People would think that we were gay since you are American," she countered with a grin, "and there is too much of an age difference for us to be friends."

"Then you will be my niece!" I declared, to which she smiled a big smile and started calling me Auntie Bonnie.

The day came too quickly when it was time to get on a bus and say goodbye to Hue and to those I had grown so fond of.

Back in Olympia, as Master Kim and I sat side by side viewing our photos of Hue, he laid his hand over mine. This gesture said more than words ever could; we had an unspoken bond strengthened by the time spent together in his customs and culture, and we now shared a mutual love for "our" niece, Lai.

BONNIE BETTS resides in Olympia, Washington, with her life partner, Jon Ewen, and their two cats. When she is not working as an occupational therapist in the public school system, she can be found climbing the Cascade Mountains, kayaking Puget Sound, or planning her next overseas adventure. Her motto: Don't dream your life, live your dreams! Contact Bonnie at bonbetts@msn.com.

Vietnamese Soft Spring Rolls

Adapted from a traditional recipe

MAKES 10 ROLLS

Fresh cilantro, heavy stems cut off, at least 40 snips with leaves

Fresh mint, at least 40 leaves

Fresh Thai basil, at least 40 leaves (You may have to order them online: www.amazon.com/grocery.)

Very thin, dry rice-stick noodles (enough to make two cups of softened noodles)

25   cooked shrimp, peeled, deveined, and cut in half into two crescent pieces

1   large carrot, cut into 2-inch matchstick-size pieces

1   small red bell pepper, cut into 2-inch matchstick-size pieces

1   cup romaine lettuce, shredded into long, thin strips

1   cup bean sprouts

15   circular rice-paper sheets (8 to 9 inches in diameter) (Have 5 extra sheets handy in case some tear.)

Wash and dry the cilantro, mint, and basil leaves.

Soften the rice-stick noodles according to directions.

Arrange on a large platter: noodles, shrimp, carrots, peppers, lettuce, sprouts, cilantro, mint, and basil.

ASSEMBLING THE ROLLS

Put ½ inch of warm water in a dish that is wider than the rice-paper sheets.

Spread a terrycloth towel next to the dish. Have available a light dish towel.

Put a single rice-paper sheet into the warm water for 20 to 30 seconds. (There will still be a little stiffness when you take it out.) Place the sheet on the big towel, and gently pat it dry with the smaller towel. Move the softened sheet to a plate.

In the bottom half of the rice sheet, place 2 or 3 half-shrimp in a row. Add whatever other ingredients you like. Shape the filling into a hot-dog shape, leaving 1 inch on each end of the "hot dog." Fold the sides over the ends of the filling, and roll tightly from the bottom to the top.

With a brief demonstration, guests can make their own.

The rolls can be made up to 6 hours before serving and stored in the refrigerator covered with damp paper towels and plastic wrap.

If serving as hors d'oeuvres, place the rolls on a tray, and cut them diagonally in half.

Serve with Dipping Sauces (recipes follow).

I love to have my guests make their own. Everyone enjoys the challenge. I change the cooled water for warm water from time to time. I have also included fried tofu strips and slivers of apple and cooked pork on the platter, even matchstick-cut broccoli stems. My latest addition to the platter is rice crackers, broken into pieces. They provide a nice crunch. —rgg

The pork and shrimp together make a very tasty combination. Like many who tasted this recipe, I personally prefer to use much more of the mint and basil leaves than the recipe calls for.

The added herbs give the rolls a fresh, zingy taste. I like to substitute curly endive or a mixture of other tart greens for the romaine. And Rita is right, even guests who were dubious about making the rolls loved it. The camaraderie of watching and commenting as people roll their own is a great icebreaker at a party. —ma

TWO DIPPING SAUCES

Lime Dip

- ½   cup lime juice
- 2   teaspoons palm or granulated sugar
- 1   teaspoon fish sauce

Mix the lime juice and sugar until the sugar is dissolved.
Add the fish sauce.
Adjust to taste.

Peanut Dip

- 5   tablespoons hoisin sauce
- 3   tablespoons plum sauce or sweet/sour sauce
- ⅓   cup very hot water (or more)
- ½   cup peanuts
- Few dashes of soy sauce
- Dash of hot pepper sauce, to taste
- Red pepper flakes (optional), to taste

Combine all the ingredients in a blender. The sauce should be the consistency of cream, so adjust the amount of water accordingly.

I don't usually make my own peanut sauce from scratch. In-donesian Bumbu Pecel *is fabulous and no work at all. If you have an Asian market nearby, see if they have it. The peanut sauce comes in a block, and you scrape what you need into a small amount of boiling water. Takes a couple of seconds, and it's delicious as a dip for the spring rolls. You can also buy it on www .amazon.com/grocery. —rgg*

Passion

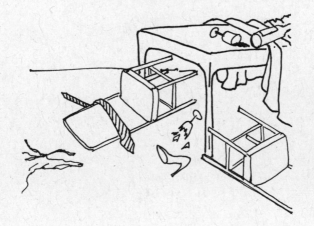

The Perfect Seatmate

Rita Golden Gelman

I had a window seat on my five-hour flight from New York to Los Angeles. The man in the seat next to mine arrived seconds after I did. I'm usually careful on airplanes. I know that some people hate talking to strangers, and I don't want to impose. But this guy was a talker.

Before the plane even took off, I knew that he was a lawyer, married with two children, living in Westchester County. Within minutes we knew all those little facts about each other that set the stage for deeper conversation. Before long we were both talking about the dreams we had when we were young college graduates, dreams I was living, dreams he knew he would never realize.

He talked about his dissatisfaction with his chosen career and his disillusionment with the fact that the law profession had very little to do with the basic concept of "justice." We talked about religions and spirituality and our shared belief that if there really was a God watching over us, He or She would have prevented things like the Holocaust and the ongoing deaths of innocent people. He shared his depth of feeling for his wife of many years, and the disappointments. We talked about our kids, our fears, our passions. By the time dinner was served (those were the days when they served meals on planes!), we had verbally probed places that neither of us had ever shared, even with our spouses. This was my kind of seatmate!

We barely stopped talking during dinner. The intimacy kept building, and the intensity of our words was overwhelming. Then, when the lights went out after dinner (for the movie), he reached over, took my hand, and said, "I don't want to stop talking, but may I hold your hand while we talk?"

My first thought was *Oh my God, I've known this man for two hours. How could I?* Then I thought again. What could happen? We were on an airplane, and my hand was hardly a body part that could be seriously violated. Why not? So I smiled and said yes.

And for the remaining three hours, as we talked, he literally made love to my hand. He never touched me above my wrist, but it was absolutely incredible. His fingers caressed my palm, my fingers, between my fingers, and the back of my hand. His touch was light and sensuous and then firm and strong. My whole body was aroused, my heart was pounding, my head flooded with fantasies. It wasn't long before I began returning the touch, the caress, the fondling. It was probably the strangest and most titillating sexual experience I have ever had, and it happened in full view of flight attendants, pregnant women on their way to the toilet, and toddlers racing up and down the aisle.

The next day he called me at my friend's house to tell me, "It wasn't just another one-flight stand."

Two years later I received an e-mail from him. He was

divorced and asked if we could meet somewhere. We did. It was a pleasant evening and a long, intimate night, but it paled in comparison to the passionate three hours of "hand love."

FINGER FOODS

So there's this sexy story about hand love and a suggestion from my friend Lars that it should be accompanied by recipes for finger foods. I loved the idea.

Obviously it had to be a sexy finger food. I mean, a piece of sausage on a toothpick with a grape tomato wouldn't do it. After hours of searching the Internet in vain, I wandered over to the supermarket and walked the aisles. Then I found it—in the freezer. Puff pastry! That flaky, melt-in-your mouth buttery layered crust. Elusive, seductive, sensuous, calling out to be filled with something wonderful. Oh, yesssss.

Pepperidge Farm makes it in strips you can fill and shape, and in mini-pastry shells that beckon. I caramelized shallots, mixed them with exotic mushrooms, spinach, and a touch of wine, and I spooned the filling into some of the shells. Fantastic. Then I combined the caramelized shallots with red pepper, goat cheese, and a bit of anchovy, and I filled a couple more. Oh, the things you can make! I'm going to stop here and throw out the challenge. Be creative. Only one tip: That puffed-up elusive crisp of pastry needs something with a strong, passionate personality. So play and have fun. —rgg

In Search of a Familiar Soul

Catherine Buchanan

When I was eight, I announced to my mother that I had a twin somewhere and that I was going to search the world over to find that person even if it took my whole life.

When I was thirty, I wrote and illustrated a children's book. I drew a frightened small person who built a tiny boat out of leaves, set sail for a tropical island, and found a large, fit man with long black hair throwing rocks into the sky all day because he didn't know how to cope with his anger. I did not know that I was drawing my future.

When I was forty, I took a trip to Samoa, where I stayed in a beach resort. One morning I gathered my sketch pad and pencil and set out to do some drawing. Mesmerizing shimmers threw the line between the sizzling white sand and the ultramarine sky out of focus. The air was so hot that my throat burned when I breathed. The intense equatorial sun could sear pie-dough-white skin to blisters, so I covered up my legs with a sarong.

I was wondering how to render the scene, pencil poised, when a young man on a sleek, chestnut horse appeared through the haze of the mirage. He was an image out of my most romantic fantasies. Horse and rider charged toward me at a full gallop. Riding bareback, half naked, with long black hair flying, he turned the horse skillfully into the surf without breaking stride. I had definitely been out in the sun too long.

The horse leapt through the breaking waves as the young man unbelievably stood on the animal's back. The man was a lovely golden color, the color pale people sweat under tanning lamps trying to achieve. Laughing, he dove off the swimming horse, giving a whoop of pure joy. The man and the horse swam together beyond the reef in the clear turquoise water. Then the man threw his tattooed legs over the horse's back, and as he hung on to its mane, they rode out of the ocean in one smooth motion, water streaming off their muscular bodies. They disappeared down the beach in the direction they had come. I was still wondering if I was imagining things.

I felt exposed and conspicuous, my heart racing, my pencil still frozen in the air, my sketch pad on my knees. In those couple of moments, the image of the athletic young man on the horse etched itself permanently into memory.

There was no way to know at the time that the man on the horse had doubled back and was watching me from the grove of palm trees just off the beach. I did not know that he wanted to talk to me, and I certainly did not know that years later I would meet him again and that we would both remember this day.

Several years elapsed before I returned to Samoa to visit friends; I decided to stay. At the time, there wasn't a thrift store on the island, and my friends and I decided to open one.

Another four years passed. The store was popular and success-ful; my paintings were displayed locally, and a few had sold. Bartering helped the business thrive, and I was always on the lookout for chances to trade services. I arranged to have bales of recycled clothes delivered with the goods for a hardware store. The trade-off was photographing the owner's daughter at the hotel where she performed traditional Samoan dances.

The evening of the performance I arrived just after the music started. All the seats were taken, so I slipped down in front and sat on the cement stairs with my back to the musi-cians. It was a good vantage point for photos of the girls danc-ing. The Samoan fire-knife dancers were the last act of the evening. They leapt on stage to wild, beating drums, spinning flaming machetes. It looked impossibly dangerous and from the burns and scars on their bodies, it clearly was. Sitting down in front, I felt the heat of the fire. Feats of acrobatic agility and ignited spinning weapons posed a photographic challenge. The men moved fast; fire illuminated the moving bodies and threw dark shadows. I concentrated on a face with white teeth flash-ing a smile in the middle of the flaming circle created by the spinning knife. My jaw dropped when I recognized the man.

I had seen him six years before on another island, gallop-ing on horseback down a beach. I felt a flush of excitement and hid my face behind the camera, but concentrating on tak-ing pictures was now out of the question. As I started to leave after the show, the overwhelming draw I felt for him slowed my steps. I wanted to talk to him, but I could not imagine he would feel the same. A quick glance around the audience was a clue as to the effect he had on women. I swear, even the nuns looked flushed, and it wasn't entirely the tropical heat. I felt starstruck and guilty, mostly because he had been in my dreams and fantasies for years, and here he was again in the flesh. He was even better-looking than I remembered.

That week he was on my mind most of the time. I had arranged to photograph the girl for three consecutive Thursdays for the price of my shipment. I knew I would see him again. Luckily I had taken a picture of him that focused on his face surrounded by flames and that illuminated the tattoos on his thighs. I had printed one to give him, by way of saying thank you without explaining why. I waited for him after the show. Women lined up to be photographed with him. A stunning young blond woman on vacation from Switzerland slipped him her room number on a piece of paper. I saw him toss it in the bushes after she walked away. When the crowd dispersed, I gave him the photo and was going to walk away, acting appropriately demure. But he picked me up off the ground with both arms and held me. He looked into my eyes and said, "You came back." Understandably, I was confused.

He described the day at the beach, how I had been sitting with a sarong over my legs and my drawing pad balanced on my knees. He told me he had circled back but could not find the nerve to talk to me. He said he had thought about me many times since. I couldn't quite admit how much I had been thinking about him.

He visited me often, dropping by my store, talking in his soft voice about his plans and dreams. I did my best to hide my feelings because of our age difference and because I was used to living alone and was not sure I could give up my solitude for a man with several hundred relatives. I imagined we could be friends, although my heart and my head were actively arguing the point. The days he came to visit were so much better than the days he didn't.

One morning he stopped by before the store was open and I asked if he wanted to go out for breakfast. He turned and disappeared out the door without saying a word. A few minutes later he came back with a paper bag from the grocery store with two bottles of Coke, two doughnuts, and two hard-boiled eggs. He laid them out on the desk. He had done exactly what I had asked, only it had not occurred to him that "to go out" meant to a restaurant.

I didn't see him again for a long time after that, and I missed him. I decided the next time I saw him I would tell him how I felt about him, but I didn't get that chance. When he did come back, months later, from working on another island, he burst into the store looking somewhat frantic. He explained that he had been holding all of his feelings in, that he was in love with me, and he had to say so. I nodded, and he kissed me. He whispered, "You're mine now," but I already was.

I closed the store early that day. We drove back to my house after a long walk on the beach. The pretense of separation was gone. We walked with my hand surrounded by his. I had barely been able to admit to myself how much I wanted to touch him. We stopped at a grocery store since there wasn't much to eat at my house. Beyond Coke, eggs, and doughnuts, I didn't know what he liked to eat. Given a choice of all the things in the store, he picked red-hot chiles, ramen noodles, mayonnaise, and a jar of sour green pickles.

He boiled water, cooked the noodles, added the hot peppers, and spooned a huge glob of mayonnaise on top. The pickles were served on the side. He handed me a bowl and smiled slyly, as if he knew his creation would also fuel our lovemaking. The peppers burned my tongue, but the mayonnaise cut the pain. Maybe he was on to something, but I don't think we needed an aphrodisiac that first lovely night together.

There are two endings to finding the man I told my mother about when I was eight and drew when I was thirty. There's the ending where we build our own house and live happily together, which is the storybook version. And there is the unfortunate truth.

By the end of a year, my lover and friend lost his mind. He tried to kill me. He swung a long, heavy piece of metal off the table saw at my head. I ducked and ran to the neighbor's house. I had to have him arrested to save myself, which was the hardest, most heartbreaking thing I have ever done.

I don't know what happened to him; I still wonder. People suggested he was on drugs, but I never saw it. He went into jealous rages that made no sense. He was also sick, with painful stomach problems.

The last thing I saw him do was throw large rocks in an out-of-control rage, just like the drawings in my book from twenty years before. For two years I have wondered about him often and hope he has found some peace. I have had to work hard to find my own. I picked up the pieces of my life with help from friends and have made a new start in Hawaii.

CATHERINE BUCHANAN *describes her experiences in words and paintings. Friends and relatives can't decide if she is brave or uncommonly naïve. She sailed from Berkeley to New Zealand with inadequate charts and lived to write about it. For some, her writing inspires the pursuit of adventure; others are amused and glad they weren't there. She believes in magic but doesn't often admit it. She is thrilled by the unanticipated moments reserved for travelers. She paints the landscapes and people who inspire her along the way. Friendship is the best pursuit of all. Visit Catherine's website at www.catherinebuchanan.com or write to her at cb2c@ yahoo.com.*

Making the Move

C. J. MacLeod

I watched cowboy movies and cowboy TV shows from the time I was very young. *Hopalong Cassidy, The Cisco Kid, The Lone Ranger*—I wanted to live in that landscape. I wanted to be those guys. Never mind that I was female. I was eight years old, wishing myself down the rabbit hole, anywhere but where I was.

Family vacations, in a green Dodge pickup with a camper turtled onto the truck bed, took us to Canada. "Close that book!" Daddy yelled. "I'm not paying good money to drive all this way for you to read. You're missing the scenery!" Ours was a don't-talk-back family. I was thinking, *Yeah. Trees. Mountains. Trees. Mountains.* But I liked Canada. Vancouver. Nice and far away. When I was old enough, I moved there.

It was at a corner bookstore in Vancouver's Kitsilano district that I was handed the book that turned out to be the loose string I would use to pull myself out of the labyrinth of a writer-artist's life in which I inexplicably and consistently scored incompletes. The proprietor of the bookstore was Ruby, my landlady at a ramshackle, peeling-wood, shaky house that overlooked the ocean, for which I paid too much rent and was grateful to have. Her store was a store of women's books. I bought one on women painters.

Ruby thought I might like one of the new books that she was just unpacking. The white book she pulled out of the small cardboard carton dripped a rain of pink Styrofoam peanuts. It had blue and yellow letters on the cover. It was *Writing Down the Bones* by Natalie Goldberg. As I read the book and tried the exercises, I yearned. If only I could write in a café, like this Natalie does. If only I could have a friend to write with at a Rexall drugstore, with a marble counter and a soda fountain, or anywhere. A writing partner. I wished I could study with Natalie Goldberg. I wished I could go to Santa Fe.

A printmaker friend at the art store where I worked said, "You'd like Santa Fe. I went there last year. You'd fit right in."

I said I was afraid to go to Santa Fe because I would have to change my life (again) to move there, and I didn't want to do that. So I painted a Santa Fe series from photos of the New Mexico landscape culled from magazines at the library.

When the body of work was done, I snagged a show at a Vancouver café famous for its spicy New Mexico green chile stew. I put the paintings up. A month later I took the paintings down. The owners didn't do a mercy-buy of one of the smaller pieces. They didn't even give me a complimentary bowl of green chile stew. Nobody bought anything.

I didn't pull the ripcord offered me by Natalie Goldberg's *Bones* until ten more years went by. For my fiftieth birthday I booked a weeklong workshop with Natalie at the Mabel Dodge Luhan House in Taos, New Mexico. On the shuttle from Albuquerque to Taos, I found myself in the world of my cowboy imagination. I stared out the window and tried not to cry. The landscape was just as Georgia O'Keeffe had painted it. It wasn't gone. It wasn't paved up and built over. There was still rich red desert and sagebrush and piñon.

The other people in the shuttle were chattering about the workshop. I said nothing. My silence, a mask over fear. Here was where my dreams called me. And when the van stopped at the guest house, the air was clean and sweet. I let out a shaky sigh. "What will I do without a twenty-four-hour Kinko's?" I had come to depend on their copying, Internet, computer, and phone services.

But it was more than just the landscape. I'd also met my lost tribe: other women who write, paint, dance, sing, or make pottery, in various cells of isolation, some with families surrounding them, others, like me, really alone.

One year later I gave away my antique library table, my harp-backed chairs (lovingly restored from layers of junk-shop grime and careless paint), my tropical plants, the white mink coat I found on a wrought-iron fence, my microwave, my vacuum cleaner, my bookshelves, my bed—everything except my paints and books. And I moved to New Mexico.

By making the hard leap, I opened myself to magic. I self-published my novel, started writing a book, got a piece published in a literary magazine about leaving my abusive boyfriend, another in a book about working for poverty wages. I even had one of my yellow paintings hang in the Museum of Fine Arts on the plaza in Santa Fe.

I am writing this from a twenty-four-hour Kinko's (yes, there is one here), for I have never earned enough to afford my own computer. I'm sixty years old. I'm still working on it. But I did learn how to make a great green chile stew!

C. J. MacLEOD currently lives in Puerto Vallarta, Mexico, where she writes a weekly column for the Vallarta Tribune *called "Out of the Armchair." She has lived in two other countries and has been a writer-artist all her life. Her paintings may be seen on her website, www.santafekitchenstudio.com. Visit her blog about being an unknown painter at www.outofthearmchair.wordpress.com. Contact her at CJart@live.com. C. J. hopes to get gallery representation for her latest yellow wallpaper series, the tropical fruity paintings.*

 ## Green Chile Stew

Adapted from a traditional southwestern recipe

SERVES 4 TO 6

---

  4 slices thick, lean bacon, chopped
  1 pound pork, cut in 1-inch cubes
Salt and freshly ground pepper, to taste
  1 large onion, chopped (1½ cups)
  3 large garlic cloves, minced
  1 teaspoon ground cumin
  1 teaspoon dried oregano
  2 cups beef broth
  1 large russet potato, chopped, or 1 small can of corn, drained, or 1 cup cooked beans (navy, pinto, or black)
  1 to 2 pounds roasted poblano chiles (See "Roasting Peppers" on page 170)
  4 plum (Roma) tomatoes, peeled and chopped
  ¼ cup chopped cilantro
 12 flour tortillas

Fry the bacon in a Dutch oven or heavy pot until fairly crisp. If the bacon is very lean, use 1 tablespoon olive oil in the pan. Remove and set aside.

In the same pot, brown the cubed pork, seasoned with salt and pepper.

Add the onion, garlic, cumin, and oregano. Stir a few times. Add the beef broth. Bring to a boil, and reduce the heat. Simmer for 30 minutes.

Add the potato, corn, or beans. Simmer for an additional 45 minutes.

Roast the chiles, then peel and chop them.

At the end of the 45 minutes or when the meat is tender, add the chiles and tomatoes, and cook an additional 10 minutes.

Sprinkle the bacon and cilantro on top. Serve with flour tortillas.

George

Debra Unger

Just past sunrise the day after I arrived in Vero Beach, Florida, I walked from my motel to the beach across the street, eager for some light aerobic exercise. A few friendly fishermen were the only people I saw at that early-morning hour. I walked along the water's edge where the sand was wet and firm, stopping frequently to collect seashells.

After an hour I decided to walk back. Both of my hands were overflowing with seashells, and I had to stop occasionally to pick up the ones I dropped. I tried to resist the temptation to collect more.

The fishermen still had their lines cast in the water. One of them asked me to touch his fishing pole for good luck. He hadn't caught any fish yet, but his friend, George, had already caught two, a pompano and a permit, both still gasping for air in his small bucket. George asked me if I was Italian. I told him I wasn't but thought he was. He said he was Greek, from the island of Icaria. He wore a small gold cross around his neck. Our mutual attraction was instant and obvious.

We started to talk. He impressed me with stories about his worldly travels. He told me he had served in the British Royal Air Force (RAF) in Palestine after World War II and had seen most of the Middle East. Following his service in the RAF, he had joined the merchant marine and traveled throughout Africa, South America, Australia, and New Zealand. His father was Egyptian, from Alexandria.

I told George that I was Polish and Jewish, that I had spent time in Israel (in part to realize my father's dream of going there after his liberation from German concentration camps), and that I had also made a pilgrimage to those very camps in Poland, France, and Germany.

I regretted that I had to leave since we were eager to keep talking. George said he would be fishing again the next morning up until nine o'clock, and I said I would try to come back before nine. He gave me a small Ziploc bag for my seashells and a warm, engaging smile.

All the rest of the day I couldn't stop thinking about him. I even tried, unsuccessfully, to find his name and address in the phone book.

The next morning I set off early for the beach. George and his friend, John, were already there. George and I greeted each other with anxious excitement. He handed me two large seashells, the kind he said you can no longer find, and I gave him one I had chosen for him from my collection. He said he had thought about me a lot since our meeting the previous day. I admitted I had been wondering if he had been thinking about me as much as I was thinking about him. He was flattered that I had tried to find his name in the phone book.

He reached out to brush a speck of sand off my face and

seemed to tremble at the touch. Then he asked John if he had ever seen a woman with such beautiful lips and eyes.

"There are two types of people in the world," John said to me. "Beautiful women and lecherous Greek men."

George wasn't bare-chested as he was the day before, but below the hem of his bathing shorts, his tanned, muscular legs were pleasing to my eye.

We continued talking, filling in some of the gaps in each other's stories. He attended to his two fishing poles only when John spotted a tug or slack in one of his lines. George whispered to me that sometimes, when he'd been fortunate enough to catch the limit of six pompanos in one day, he would return to the beach later for more. "That's cheating," I said. "It doesn't hurt anyone," he replied. "Except the fish," I answered. He smiled.

Just before nine o'clock George began packing up his equipment. He appeared to be regretting his necessary departure.

"I'll give you a ride to your motel," he offered as we walked together. The motel was only a short distance from his car. I tried to decline his offer, but I surrendered to my desire to prolong our visit.

When we arrived at the motel, he said softly that he was feeling inspired to write poetry. I encouraged him to write a poem and send it to me. He made sure he had the address card I had given him, searching for it anxiously until he found it in his knapsack. We said sad goodbyes to each other and hugged tightly. He kissed me vigorously on the mouth, twice, maybe three times. I didn't want him to go.

In order to catch my 9:15 flight the next morning, I had to leave for the airport before George and John started fishing.

I woke early, walked to the beach in the dark, and found George's fishing spot.

A half-moon glowed in the dark, slightly cloudy sky, directly in front of where I stood. Several stars shone brightly. I gathered up a handful of shells and turned around. With the ocean and moon behind me now, I laid the shells in a circle on the sand. I placed two of them, partially touching, in the middle of the circle. Around the circle I formed a raised heart of sand. Then I turned to face the moon and imagined that someday I would stand on a beach on the island of Icaria and, gazing at the other side of the moon, send my love to George.

DEBRA UNGER feels most at home when she's traveling to places she's never been. In the course of her travels, she's learned to speak Hebrew in Israel, crossed the Egyptian desert by camel, floated down the Nile on a felucca, explored mountains and caves on Crete, rafted the Colorado River through the Grand Canyon, and pilgrimaged through Eastern and Western Europe. Originally from northern New Jersey, Debra currently lives in northern Colorado with her cat, Teddy Bear. Contact Debra at DUnger@fcgov.com.

Fairy Godmothers . . . Who Needs 'Em!

Sandra Hanks Benoiton

Fairy godmothers have never pounded a path to my door. I've always known that if I wanted to be invited to a ball, I would have to make it happen myself. As a flower-power '60s girl, balls were not my gig.

The man I thought was my Prince Charming and I were not getting along, so we agreed on a year-long separation. I decided to use my time traveling and turned my pumpkin into an around-the-world airline ticket.

I met Mark on my birthday during my last week of a stop in Seychelles, a small island nation in the Indian Ocean. *Love at first sight* is the romantic way to phrase my immediate reaction to him, but *recognition* is more accurate. On a level somewhere beyond the depths of my being, I knew him and realized I'd been looking for him for forty-two years without knowing I was searching. Our week together was astounding.

Then suddenly my husband was back in my life, having been given permission by one or more of his many girlfriends to meet me in Asia and travel with me for a month. It was a very long month.

I may have been with a six-foot-two blond advertising executive, but my thoughts and heart kept drifting back to Seychelles. Now that I knew Mark, song lyrics made sense. Always a cynic, these hokey emotions seemed false to me before, and I felt anyone touting them was either faking it or lying to themselves. Now it was different.

At the end of the month I told myself I would return to Seychelles if I could get a ticket for less than a thousand dollars. I wanted to know if this was a relationship of immense importance or a holiday fling that I'd blown out of proportion.

In 1993 the World Wide Web had not yet stretched its fibrous reach everywhere, so getting information, plotting travel, and buying tickets was a difficult process. None of the tiny travel agencies in Kuching, Malaysia, had ever heard of Seychelles, and although they could arrange a week's stay in a Stone Age longhouse, they had no way of getting me to Seychelles and back.

Maybe this was a good thing. Would Mark be happy to see me back? Would he even still be in Seychelles? He might have returned to his home in England rather than stay on for the monthlong holiday he'd planned. Was going back the dumbest thing I'd ever contemplated? How embarrassing would it be to show up again only to find I'd completely misunderstood the situation! But I had no way to evaluate any of this without actually flying back.

Mark was staying with his parents, and they had no phone. A letter was out of the question. *Do I? Don't I?* My toss of the dice was the plane ticket. Get it and I go; don't get it and I don't go.

I arrived in Singapore at eleven on a Friday morning. If a trip to Seychelles were going to happen, it had to be arranged within the next few hours. There was only one flight a week between Singapore and Seychelles: Saturday morning at 3 A.M. That was it. It was this night or never.

After throwing my bag into my hotel room, I took off down Orchard Road and began hitting the travel agencies. Who could sell me a ticket on Air Seychelles? Not this one, not that one. Sey*where*?

By three o'clock I realized I would get no help from any agency; I'd have to book directly through Air Seychelles. Unfortunately, no one had any idea where the office was, and Air Seychelles didn't answer the phone. After many frustrating stops in phone booths, I finally got through.

"We close at five."

Great.

The directions were complicated: the MRT to a stop way out of downtown. A bus for another few miles. A hike of many blocks, upstairs in a nondescript tower of flats set amongst a dozen just like it.

I walked into the office at ten minutes to five, just in time to see the workers packing up papers, combing their hair, and sticking lipstick tubes back into purses. One made eye contact, so I tackled her.

"I need to see about a ticket on tonight's flight."

"Sorry," she said, "but we only sell to travel agents."

I explained that I'd already been to a number of those, and none had been helpful. She clucked sympathetically while continuing to prepare to dash off for the weekend, managing to keep her eyes diverted from my desperate, imploring gaze.

Taking a deep breath, I plunged into my story, with the hope that this young woman had a romantic streak.

"But you see, there's this man . . ."

Within a few minutes the staff of the Air Seychelles Singapore office was gathered tightly around, listening to my tale of maybe love. By five o'clock I'd traded seven hundred dollars and a promise to send a postcard with the outcome of the trip in exchange for a round-trip ticket on that night's flight—return flight open.

I didn't sleep at all on the plane, even though I was completely exhausted. Nerves kept me wide awake and running to the toilet. As we touched down, I felt sick, and when I collected my backpack, I was shaking so badly that I was sure customs was going to be suspicious.

A taxi driver took issue with my destination. A banana stand in an obscure village was not acceptable. He spent the drive insisting that I really wanted a hotel. I left him shaking his head as he dropped me at the little tin shack at 5:30 A.M.

Now that this was done, out of my hands, left to the will of the gods, I relaxed. Propping my backpack against the wall, I fell immediately and deeply asleep. Mr. Moté, a shop owner I had met on my last visit, found me there an hour and a half later when he came to open his shop; others had passed quietly, noting my return and happily grasping the gossip fodder I'd provided.

In faltering Creole I tried to convey the reason for my unexpected reappearance and my apprehension regarding Mark's reaction. Would he be unhappy I was back after a month?

"*Pas possible,*" Mr. Moté said. Not possible.

That was reassuring.

A few minutes later Mark and his dad drove up. The smile on Mark's face as he jumped from the car let me know I had done exactly the right thing. Within an hour he arranged a house for us, a rustic place perched on the rocks just above one of the world's most beautiful beaches. We stayed there for three months, then I went east and he went west. We rearranged our worlds and married in September 1994, thirteen months after we met.

Even without the fairy godmother, we live happily ever after.

A SIZE NINE in itchy feet, Sandra Hanks Benoiton has been traveling for much of her life and living internationally since the early 1990s. A writer with a few books, hundreds of articles, and dozens of websites under her belt, her work ranges from her peregrinations to politics, from adventures to advocacy for children on the planet.

She lives in the Indian Ocean island nation of Seychelles, where she writes about the world from her veranda. Visit Sandra's personal blog, Paradise Preoccupied, *at http://sandrahanksbenoiton.wordpress.com.*

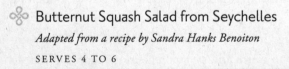

Butternut Squash Salad from Seychelles

Adapted from a recipe by Sandra Hanks Benoiton

SERVES 4 TO 6

Be careful not to overcook the squash. It's best if it still has a little bite to it. Serve with curries, roasts, steak—well, just about anything. —rgg

Marinade

- ⅓ cup olive oil
- ⅓ cup apple juice
- ⅓ cup white wine or rice vinegar
- 2 tablespoons sugar (or less, to taste)
- ½ teaspoon salt
- ¼ teaspoon pepper
- 1 medium sweet onion, sliced thin
- 1 medium butternut squash

Combine the olive oil, apple juice, wine or vinegar, sugar, salt, and pepper in a big bowl. Add the onion slices. Marinate overnight in the refrigerator.

Peel the butternut squash and cut it into 1-inch cubes. Place the squash in a saucepan, cover with water, and boil until just tender. Remove the squash from the hot water while it's still a little firm. Stop the cooking with cold water. Allow it to cool.

Drain the squash, and arrange it on a plate. Top with the marinated onion slices and pour half the marinade on the squash. Chill. Keeping it in the refrigerator overnight increases the flavor. Add the remaining dressing just before serving.

....

Butternut squash is simply not found in Mexico, so I replaced the squash with chayote, a wonderful staple in this part of the world. It worked great. I liked the dressing made with a little less sugar and found that the taste was enhanced by letting the squash sit overnight in the dressing in the refrigerator. If a stronger taste is desired, pour the dressing on the drained squash while it is still warm. —ma

....

Filipino Elvis Presley

Jessica Bryan

Since early morning, the man known as the Filipino Elvis Presley has been stirring the contents of a large pot over an open fire on the other side of the irrigation ditch. He was given this nickname because of the emotion that pours from his slight, angular frame when he sings, as if every cell of his body were lamenting his own, private Heartbreak Hotel. Although he is blind in one eye and has a large gap in the front of his mouth where he is missing two teeth, he is quite attractive.

I am distracted from thinking about Elvis when visitors arrive. Descending from several *jeepneys* parked in front of the church, they are dressed in their Sunday clothes, the children scrubbed until their faces shine. The adults are carrying packages and bedrolls bound with twine.

"Today we welcome our brothers and sisters from Maria Aurora," announces Mely. "They have traveled many hours to celebrate the Lord with us."

Soon everyone is drifting to the patio behind the church,

and the packages are piled on a table. The visiting women, who are wearing nylon stockings even in the stifling heat, sit and begin to fan themselves. They look like a bouquet of drooping flowers. Mely welcomes each person individually, and as usual, I do not understand most of the conversation. They are from an isolated, mountain province far to the east and do not speak English. I can only observe as Mely and Trinidad serve the guests tall glasses of sweet, lukewarm tea and cookies. After a while, the women retire to the house to begin cooking, and the children disappear in the direction of the basketball court.

My gaze begins to wander again across the irrigation ditch. Most of the men are sitting in a large circle, laughing and singing and passing a bottle around.

Drawn to their laughter, and to Elvis and his pot, I balance myself carefully on the log that crosses the ditch, inching my way slowly. When I arrive at the circle of men, they seem disconcerted by my presence. Perhaps a Filipino woman would never be so bold as to join in the camaraderie of men.

But then Joseph smiles. "Jessica, sit here with us," he says, motioning to a chair beside him. "I will give you a taste of *basi,* sugarcane wine."

This produces some snickering from the assembled men— perhaps they are aware of the attraction between Joseph and me. They watch closely as he pours some of the clear liquid into a small glass, their joking silenced. Taking a sip, I begin to choke violently. Gasping for breath, I nearly fall on the ground. *Basi* is as strong as vodka or tequila, but my "initiation" must be completed. I drink the rest of the wine quickly and without further difficulty. The men applaud and roar their approval.

As they return to their drinking and gossiping, my attention is drawn back to Elvis, who is a short distance away, still stirring. Unnoticed by the others, I quietly approach him.

"What are you cooking in your pot?"

"Ah, Jes-se-ka, this is *very* special. This soup is the head of the dog. It makes man very strong with woman."

He says this with great reverence as I gasp and recoil backward from him and the pot. My American love of pets stands in stark contradiction to the Filipino habit of eating just about anything. Consider *balut,* for example, fertilized eggs containing the partially formed bodies of ducks, which are boiled and eaten. (*Balut* are also believed to have aphrodisiac qualities.)

Unable to come to terms with eating the family dog or with the mystery of Filipino male virility, I decide it would be better to return to the more reasonable activity of cooking with the other women.

Late in the afternoon, when a feast has been spread out on long tables, everyone gathers together again for food and conversation. Soon night comes, and Elvis and the other musicians begin to make music. Everyone starts dancing: women with women, old with young. There are no social reservations in this large, extended family of "brothers and sisters," where all are loved and respected equally.

Satiated with dinner, consisting mostly of *lumpia* (similar to egg rolls) and *pancit* (fried noodles). I leave and wander toward the basketball court, where some of the men have begun to play ball. Many of them are still drinking, and they are all smoking cigarettes "to keep the mosquitos away."

Joseph picks up my guitar and begins to sing "Lovers' Moon," a song about two lovers who are a world apart. As he sings the mournful words about a moon shining over only one of the lovers, I wonder whether the song will be about us in some not-too-distant future.

Glancing over my shoulder, I see my young friend Luna standing behind me. She has the face of an angel. My breath catches in my throat because I have never seen anything so beautiful. She moves toward me and wraps herself around my back for warmth because it has become chilly. We sit together in perfect contentment and watch the players. They are moving shadows, illuminated by moonlight filtered through a fine, ethereal mist. The *tap tap tap* of the ball as it hits the cement, the squeaking of shoes, and Luna's soft breath in my ear are the only sounds to be heard, and it occurs to me: *Nothing* needs to be any different than it already is.

JESSICA BRYAN is a freelance book editor and the author of Psychic Surgery and Faith Healing: An Exploration of Multi-Dimensional Realities, Indigenous Healing, and Medical Miracles in the Philippine Lowlands *(2008) and of* Love is Ageless: Stories About Alzheimer's Disease *(2002). In addition to editing, writing, and traveling to the Philippines periodically, she is a spiritual medium and does clairvoyant readings and energy healing. She lives in southern Oregon with Tom Clunie, D.C. Write to Jessica at editor@mind.net. Read her blog at www .psychicsurgery.wordpress.com.*

What Happened for Chana

Jan Bayer

Each of the four holy cities of Israel represents one of the four elements, and Safat is air. I'm a Gemini—maybe that's why I felt so peaceful there.

A walking tour with my guide Shlomo, on my first morning in town, made the history of Safat come alive. He sent chills up my spine with legends about the ancient synagogues, rabbis, and battles, as he pointed out the bullet shells still embedded in the old city walls. I tried to hide the tears that welled up in my eyes from the overflow of emotion.

During the first four months of my six-month-long trip around the world, I visited Japan, China, Thailand, Bali, Singapore, and Egypt. Along the way I learned some of the history of each of the cultures, but no history had come so alive as the one I heard from Shlomo that morning in Safat. I realized in my traveled-out stupor that what I was learning now was personal: the story of my own people. My energy felt renewed.

Because Safat is an artists' colony, I was drawn there to visit fellow painters. After Shlomo's tour, I wandered through the galleries of this hill town built of stone. It was there that I met Chana. She radiated a peace and confidence that I admired. She was sitting in the doorway of the Hasidic (Orthodox) Art Gallery, and when I said hello, she answered in English. We began to chat and soon discovered we were both Americans. She invited me to sit next to her, and her story began to unfold.

Chana, who was thirty-seven years old, ran the gallery with her artist husband. In the tradition of married Orthodox Jewish women, she wore a wig to cover her hair in public. I saw a shiny new wedding band on her finger. Chana, as she now called herself, had grown up in a Christian family in Cleveland, Ohio. She confided she had always been drawn to Jewish friends but didn't realize until five years ago that she herself longed to be a Jew. She told me, "I was born with a Jewish soul but had to be raised in a non-Jewish family so I could make this journey of discovery." In Cleveland she began to study and convert but couldn't meet an Orthodox mate there with whom to share a religious life.

So two years before I met her, Chana decided to move to Jerusalem. With the help of the community there, she studied and worked. The matchmakers sent her to meet prospective spouses in different towns all over Israel. Eventually she was sent to Safat. When she met Yacov, her husband of four months, she knew at once that he was the one.

At dusk a few evenings after I met Chana, the town square was lit up like a stage set, and we were dancing to Israeli folk music. Afterward I ran into Chana and met her husband, a bearded man wearing a traditional black coat and hat. They said they were hoping to be blessed with a child soon. Later, over tea at Chana's home, I told her that I longed to remarry and was eager to find a life partner. I wondered how she'd had such fast results in finding a husband and a new life in Safat.

She said, "I knew exactly what I wanted and prayed to God for it." She added, "Here in Israel, especially in the holy city of Safat, one is closer to God than anywhere else on earth."

I believed her. Then she added that the most direct pipelines to God are from the Wall in Jerusalem and from the old cemetery on the hillside of Safat, where the most famous rabbis and scholars are buried.

"How morbid," I said.

"I know," she said. Chana then told me that when she was sent to Safat by the matchmakers, they told her she must go to the cemetery and pray. She had already met two men in Safat, but she wasn't interested in either of them. So under pressure from friends, she forced herself to go to the cemetery. She felt self-conscious—everyone knows what a single woman is doing in the cemetery.

Her prayer was apologetic. "I made sure to tell God that I wasn't so desperate to find a mate that I had to come to a cemetery to pray for a husband. I had only come to please my friends. I assured God that I knew He had already heard my prayers. It was all right to answer them in His own time. I could be patient."

Then Chana told me that two hours after this prayer, she was introduced to her future husband, Yacov!

I didn't sleep well that night. I woke up at seven, before the heat of the summer day set in, and followed my map down the hill on the rocky winding path to the old cemetery. My whole body was trembling. Near a secluded grave site I hid behind a tree and made my speech to God: "This is Jan here. Chana sent me. You answered her prayer so quickly. I want to pray for a husband too. But there's one difference between Chana and me. *I. . . . am desperate!*

That was many, many years ago. The question is, *Did it work?* The answer is, *No. Thank God. I'm happily single.*

JAN BAYER also tells of her travels through her vivid oil paintings. Grateful to have inherited both the travel gene and the artist gene, much of her creative inspiration has come from living, studying, and traveling around the planet. During her twenty-five years as a professional artist, Jan has sold her work through galleries on the East and West coasts. Now living in southern California, she can be found painting on the cliffs above the sea or indulging in another passion, eating burritos. View Jan's paintings at www .sdvag.net/B/JanBslide.htm or e-mail her at beingjb@gmail.com (please put "Chana" in subject line).

Dance Class

Maria Altobelli

Dancing was the kiss of death in my sheltered universe. As an only child, I spent most of my time in the imaginary world of characters from books and in the invented lives of my stuffed animals. Anything that forced me out of this safe cocoon sent me into spasms of overt timidity.

During my teen years, singing and dancing were popular with everyone else. In a group, it was always possible to mouth the words to songs, but it was extremely hard to feign movement without, well, moving. At high school dances and sock hops, the possibility of actually being asked to dance was far more mortifying than standing forlornly on the sidelines.

Somewhere between adolescence and middle age, a change occurred. I can't say that my first visit to Mexico in 1972 created an instant metamorphosis. It was just that in every subsequent trip, Mexico seeped more and more into my blood, and a sense of rhythm slowly crept into my body. There is something about a Latin rhythm danced in Mexico that is relaxing as opposed to dancing the same rhythm stateside. In the United

States the movement had to be *right*. In Mexico it could just be fun.

When my husband and I came to live full time in Mexico, I hit on the idea of taking dance classes in each new city we visited.

Mexico City always had the weirdest students. Conservative and very Catholic Puebla had, surprisingly, the best classes. The minute I walked into the class, it was easy to see this was a group composed of dedicated dancers: each one of them carried either a huge handkerchief or a small towel to mop away the serious sweat generated by several hours of frenzied movement.

The instructors made us change partners after each song ended. I would smile and say, "Okay, who gets to dance with the old lady now?" since invariably I was the oldest there.

The guys, at least the first time around, would try to hide the involuntary cringe, shrug their shoulders philosophically, and move into the dance position, one hand firmly in the small of my back, the other holding my hand at shoulder level. They took a few steps and would break into a grin. "But you can move! Gringos aren't supposed to know how to move."

Now it was my turn to shrug my shoulders. "Mexico can do that. Even to a gringo."

A while back I saw a feature on the evening news about a couple who, once they retired, performed a dance routine on the streets of Mexico City as a supplement to their meager pension. When the husband died, the woman continued a modified but quite energetic routine that she did alone. She went out almost every day despite the fact that she was close to eighty. In my shy life I would have been mortified to see someone dancing like that on a street corner. Today I'd be happy to join her.

Chiles en Nogada (Picadillo-Stuffed Chiles
in Walnut Sauce)

From Nancy Zaslavsky's book, A Cook's Tour of Mexico

MAKES 12 STUFFED CHILES

*J*ust as Mexico taught me to be passionate about dancing, she
taught me to be passionate about poblano chile peppers. The
*firm-fleshed, blue-green chiles add an exotic taste to food whether
chopped up fresh or roasted and peeled. When Paul and I moved to
the country in 1999, my criteria for a suitable place to live included
a location within one hour of good Parmesan cheese. I have since
amplified the criteria to include easy access to poblanos. Here is
Mexico's national dish. The colors of the Mexican flag—the red of
the pomegranate seeds, the green of the poblanos, and the white of
the fresh walnut and cream sauce—make it a natural to be served
during* Fiestas Patrias, *September 15 and 16. The dish is best served
at room temperature and is perfect for buffets. —ma*

Picadillo Stuffing

    2   tablespoons vegetable oil

    1   cup chopped white onion

    4   garlic cloves, minced

  1½   pounds lean ground beef chuck

    6   ripe plum tomatoes (fresh or canned), puréed and strained

    1   teaspoon sea or kosher salt

  12   grinds black pepper

   ½   teaspoon ground cayenne pepper

   ½   cup sliced almonds (with or without skins), toasted

   ½   cup chopped walnuts, toasted

   ½   cup raisins

½ cup candied fruit: chopped barrel cactus if available,
    dried mango or papaya from a health food store
    (no citrus)
½ teaspoon ground cinnamon
1 teaspoon dried oregano
½ teaspoon dried thyme

Heat the oil in a large skillet. Add the onion, and cook until transparent. Add the garlic, and cook until golden brown. Add the beef, stirring and breaking up lumps until thoroughly cooked.

Stir in the tomatoes. Season with salt, pepper, and cayenne.

Add nuts, raisins, candied fruit, cinnamon, and herbs. Reduce the heat, and simmer for 20 minutes.

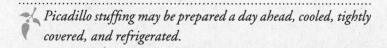

Picadillo stuffing may be prepared a day ahead, cooled, tightly covered, and refrigerated.

Chiles

12 plump, fresh poblano chiles

Roast the chiles. (See "Roasting Peppers" on page 170.)

Cool the chiles enough to handle. Peel carefully—do not tear them. Cut a slit down one side of each, vertically, from the stem almost to the pointed end. Remove all the seeds and any large veins, leaving the stem attached.

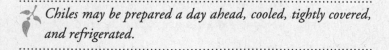

Chiles may be prepared a day ahead, cooled, tightly covered, and refrigerated.

Walnut Sauce

  1 cup finely chopped walnuts (Use fresh, not dried, walnuts if
     possible, for their slight bitterness.)
  2 garlic cloves, finely chopped
  2 cups Mexican crema, crème fraîche, or sour cream (whole
     milk or low fat)
  1 tablespoon Worchestershire sauce
  1 teaspoon Maggi seasoning sauce
 12 grinds black pepper
 ½ teaspoon sea or kosher salt

Blend all the ingredients in a processor or blender until the
sauce is well blended but not a smooth purée.

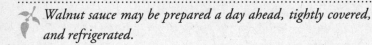

*Walnut sauce may be prepared a day ahead, tightly covered,
and refrigerated.*

Assembly and Garnish

  1 small head crunchy iceberg or romaine lettuce, shredded
 12 red radishes, thinly sliced
  1 fresh pomegranate, seeded (reserve the seeds)

Reheat the picadillo stuffing to warm (not hot), and fill the
chiles.

Cover a serving platter with the shredded lettuce, and decorate
with radish slices. Place the filled chiles on top of the lettuce
and radish slices.

Just before serving, cover the warm-to-room-temperature
chiles with the cool walnut sauce. Sprinkle with ruby-red
pomegranate seeds.

If the stuffing or chiles are hot, the sauce will separate.

For language buffs: Picadillo *is a traditional dish usually made with ground beef and other ingredients. The word comes from the Spanish* picar *which means to chop or mince. It comes in a lot of different varieties in many different countries, including the Philippines.* —rgg

The Drummer

Danielle Richards

I was in Serbia, staying with a Romany family. They had arranged for me to take *darabuka* lessons from a man named
Asmit. His bedroom doubled as our classroom due to lack of
space. After the first lesson, the windows needed to stay shut
because the neighbors had called the police about the noise.

We drummed in this room, which was over a hundred
degrees and filled with smoke from all the Monte Carlos he
would suck down. This man, who was rumored to have two
wives; this man with a visible history of his life written in the
tattoos on his chest and arms (his shirt would be off because of
the heat); this Turkish gypsy would drum with more passion
than I could comprehend.

Asmit was always a gentleman with me, never insinuating
even a hint of any suggestive action, but when he played that
drum, these feelings would well up in me. My throat would
tighten, and I could feel my heart beating against the skin over
my chest to the rhythm of the drum in double time. I could
cry and laugh and explode all at the same time. This emotion,

this fervor, would rise up through my entire being, making my skin quiver, quake, and vibrate. I wanted to stand up and dance, to shimmy all the shimmies I knew. But I didn't.

When I played the rhythms he taught me, he would sometimes sing lyrics in a language I didn't understand but that felt unexplainably beautiful and passionate. This music was so exhilarating, so overwhelming, that I couldn't even look in his direction.

This man could have scared me, but instead I was consumed with the desire to dance, to use my body, to express the purity of emotion and the essential beauty of my soul, which was more fully aroused than I ever imagined possible. All of these sessions took place with us speaking different languages. We didn't speak two words that were the same, but I learned, oh, how I learned, about passion.

The Sweet Life

Marcia L. Hannewald

I was twenty-four, bursting with wide-eyed curiosity and un-bridled idealism, and more than a little relieved to have sur-vived a grueling first year of law school. My reward for all the late nights, copious hours of note-taking, and unfamiliar self-doubt was a summer law program in Siena, Italy.

Trudging up the narrow cobblestone road leading to the ancient stone farmhouse I shared with my classmates, I marveled at the natural beauty surrounding me—heavy purple-tipped grapevines framing barnyards speckled with cackling charcoal hens, to the lipstick-red poppies whose lush blooms defied the stifling heat.

It was Palio time in Siena, and the sleepy tourist town had come alive with a pulsing energy. I was unprepared for the crowds, the noise, the pure frenzy, as the city center transformed itself into a medieval horse-racing track. My dog-eared copy of *Lonely Planet* explained that the festival originated in the eleventh century as a way to give thanks to the blessed Madonna.

As I walked, I was totally engrossed in the vivid Palio scene:

a young jockey nervously wiping visibly sweaty palms on his brilliant gold-trimmed feudal costume, a priest solemnly blessing a horse with the dip of a silver chalice, cheering throngs shouting out a cacophony of unintelligible phrases as a sea of colorful flags whipped madly overhead.

I was startled out of my reverie by a robust "*Ciao, bella!*" emanating from my left. I turned quickly to see a tall, smiling man with an unruly crop of curly black hair waving enthusiastically to me from the yard of a whitewashed stone cottage trimmed in bright pink roses. Ignoring my mother's telepathic warning that nice girls don't talk to strangers, I tentatively waved back.

Grinning broadly, the handsome stranger walked rapidly toward me, extending a chiseled arm in friendly greeting. "I am Nico," he explained by way of introduction. "And you are the *bella Americana* who walks by my house each day with a knapsack and many friends, no?"

Suddenly shy, I blushed and looked away. "I'm Marcia," I mumbled. "I'm here with a group of law students for a summer program at the University of Siena."

His eyes widened, and he seemed to smile even more. "But I am a law student as well," he said. "My friends and I, we all study law or medicine. This is our house." He pointed to the yard behind us as if to satisfy any doubt I might have had about his veracity. "How long do you stay in Siena?"

I found his broken English and heavy accent exceedingly charming. "I'm here through August," I responded. "It will be hard to leave. I've already fallen in love with Italy."

"Ah, but you must let me show you Siena. There is much beauty here. Also, I have a *moto*, the best for—how you say—sightseeing?"

A vision of me perched precariously on the back of an Italian motorbike while Nico steered us through Siena's winding alleyways flashed suddenly and impertinently through my brain. I blushed. "I think . . . that would be . . . nice," I finally managed to stammer.

And that was how our whirlwind romance began, a satisfying blend of mutual attraction peppered with a willingness to expand our boundaries and break through cultural impediments. There were many occasions when my rudimentary grasp of the Italian language and his rough English could not adequately convey the thoughts we yearned to exchange and the stories we longed to tell. During those times, we laughed, gestured wildly, and in extreme cases, called on a mutual friend to translate.

To my surprise and delight, I soon learned that Nico expressed himself in the true Italian way—through food. His mama had raised a thoroughly modern man, as strong and macho as they come, but with the skills and desire to create potfuls of aromatic offerings for me and others in his ramshackle kitchen. I spent countless blissful hours seated at the long wooden table there, breathing in the delicious smells, warm air, and endless conversations with our friends in a multicultural feast for the senses. We would talk and sip *grappa* late into the night, reveling in the opportunity to expand our worlds.

One night, not long before I was scheduled to board a plane that would return me to my everyday U.S. existence, Nico surprised me with a special meal. We dined on wild boar with truffles, clinked broad-rimmed juice glasses filled with Chianti, and toasted our romance. Later, satisfied, I began to clear the plates from the table. Reaching for my hand, he said, "Wait. There is more."

Before I could register my protest, he dove, head-first, into the refrigerator and emerged triumphant with an enormous custard-filled bowl in his hands. *"Il dolce,"* he proclaimed proudly.

Today, as I clumsily attempt to replicate Nico's sweet cream trifle within the confines of my small American kitchen, I am reminded of everything that was good about him, about us. Ten years have chipped away at my optimism and willingness to take risks. I feel grounded, weighted down unnecessarily by bills, the mortgage, the predictability of this mundane life.

I sigh, hands trembling, and set down the whisk. Eyes closed, I breathe in softly and remember. And I vow, right there in between the berries and the egg yolks, to let magic enter my life again.

MARCIA ("MARCI") HANNEWALD is a gypsy soul based in Ann Arbor, Michigan, who believes in the transformative power of travel to open minds and unlock hearts. Through her writing, she seeks to foster cross-cultural curiosity and encourage others to step out of their comfort zones. Reach Marci at her website at www .writtenjourneys.com or by e-mail at marci@writtenjourneys.com.

 ## Nico's Sweet Cream Trifle

Adapted from a recipe from Marcia Hannewald

SERVES 8 TO 10

⅓ cup sugar

4 egg yolks

1½ to 2 teaspoons vanilla
  4 to 5 ounces Neufchâtel (low-fat) cream cheese
  1 cup whipping cream
  1 angel food cake
  1 cup very strong coffee (strong espresso is perfect), cooled
  1 to 2 pints fresh strawberries (sliced), blueberries,
      raspberries, and/or blackberries

Whisk the sugar and egg yolks together in a large bowl set over boiling water until the sugar is dissolved. (Make sure the internal temperature of the mixture reaches 160°F if you are worried about using raw eggs.) Add the vanilla and Neufchâtel, and blend (by hand or with a mixer) until creamy.

In a medium bowl, beat the whipping cream until stiff peaks form. Add to the cheese mixture, and chill.

Break or cut the cake into bite-sized chunks. Mix the cake pieces and coffee together in a large bowl until the cake pieces are coated but not soggy.

In a large, clear trifle bowl, alternate layers of cake, cheese mixture, and fresh berries. Chill until serving time.

....

Since angel food cake does not exist in Mexico, I made my own for the first time in my life. I used less sugar than the cake recipe called for. The wonderful thing about making trifle is that cake mistakes go unnoticed. I split the cake in half horizontally and heated it in a low oven for a few minutes. This way it absorbed all the coffee without getting soggy and had a nice espresso taste. A combination of blueberries and blackberries was my favorite. The trifle can also be arranged in individual, clear dessert dishes. An absolutely divine recipe—and I don't like desserts. —ma

Chapati Love Remembered

Jean Allen

Love may come but once; it may never come again. Yet if it does, it will never be the same.

Remembering chapati love has me caught up in the past—remembering who he was and how it was then.

I was living in Nassau at the time and had arranged to meet a friend for a glass of wine on the beach. We were deep in conversation when his friend arrived. I felt his presence before I ever saw him. As I turned, I watched him move across the sand like an evening shadow, lengthening and looming as he drew near. My friend offered introductions. We needed none.

I remember him as a six-foot-two-inch pillar of tightly woven innuendos. He radiated a disturbing calm and a tranquil potency. His hair was black as inky water, edged with moonlit silver; it cascaded past his ears, down his neck, pooling on his collar.

His eyes, luminous and velvet brown, beckoned me with waves of warmth, flashing with the phosphorescence of a storm-tossed blackened sea. His lashes were long and full, and his brows were knitted in the fashion of scholars.

His nose was aquiline, a proud member of the ruling caste; his mouth was disciplined and restrained except when disarmed with laughter. His voice was smoky honey, dark and liquid. It flowed into my mind with sticking sweetness. He spoke about microorganisms with incantations and Vedic songs.

His body was granite softness, a statue yearning to be carved. His back was straight, his waist small, his skin soft—glowing and touchable.

His touch was as gentle as a morning raga, as playful as an afternoon frolic—and hungry. Always hungry.

When he ran, as he did early in the morning, he was a mighty jaguar.

We sun-baked our naked bodies on deserted beaches. I gloried in the sun-sparked freedom. He watched me, lying on his stomach, pressing his obvious passion deep into warm sand. We tempted the Fates on visits to his office, daring someone to catch us. We wept for movie heroes felled by some villain in the middle of their colorful song. We sipped the vintage wine called "life."

Together we created curries, interrupted and spiced with frenetic lovemaking, causing hunger to become even more seductive. He taught me how to eat with my hand while sitting on the floor. He also taught me how to make chapati.

It was a stormy afternoon in Nassau, rain lashing the window. We were in the kitchen, and he was working on a curry. We still had electricity—great music was playing. He decided it was time I learned to make chapati. He opened a bottle of wine, poured us a glass, and went about gathering the ingredients: flour, salt, water. He put a large mixing bowl on the counter and into it, measured about 1½ cups whole wheat flour and ¾ cup white flour. He moved behind me and pressed extremely close, his arms around me, and told me to sprinkle some salt onto the flour. He gave me a sip of wine and took one himself.

He reached for a cup of water, pushed my hands into the flour-salt mixture, and slowly poured water over them, instructing me to mix. The flour flew, dusting us both. The dough became very sticky, and we were a mess. He had me put flour on the counter and turn the dough from the bowl onto the flour. At this point, he poured more wine and gave me another sip, spilling it down my front. He turned me around, unbuttoned my blouse and expertly removed it along with a couple other items that might interfere with the chapati-making process.

Aprons were certainly optional at this point.

It was time to knead.

Kneading together is an excellent way to tighten up the "chest" muscles and extremely sexy without blouse, shirt, and assorted other things, especially with a dusting of flour and sticky hands. It is also hysterically funny. It took about fifteen minutes for him to decide our kneading was finished along with the wine. We covered the dough with a damp towel and let it sit for about a half hour or so, long enough for him to put the finishing touch on the curry and me. We listened to the rain hitting the window and felt the force of the storm electrify the kitchen—and us. A new bottle of wine appeared. The lights went out. Candles were lit.

Curry aside and waiting, he began heating a griddle over a medium flame. He wanted it very hot. He then uncovered the dough, and I dusted the counter with more flying flour. We pulled the dough into twelve small balls, rolled them in the flour, and flattened them until they were about five inches across. Then we patted them between our hands to knock off some of the flour. He slapped a chapati onto the hot griddle for about one minute, turned it with tongs, and cooked it for about thirty seconds on the flip side. He handed it to me, and I put it onto a second flame, as instructed, and watched it swell. We continued this until all the chapati were cooked, sharing another glass of wine. We lightly buttered them and kept them warm on a plate covered with a towel.

The storm still raged, the candles flickered, the curry was finished, and the chapati were ready. We sat on the kitchen floor, curry and chapati between us, sharing the wine, feeding each other, dipping chapati into the curry, and kissing/licking away any that escaped—laughing as lovers often do at such silly things.

Outside the wind howled, lightning struck, thunder roared, and the rain continued to come in torrents.

Inside, with spilled flour and dribbled wine on the kitchen floor, the curry and chapati were forgotten. With wine bottle and glasses accidentally knocked over, lightning flashing, and thunder crashing, my chapati-making lesson was concluded.

We journeyed through more than a year of waking, sleeping—a time of dreams and nightmares.

Finally, a nightmare won. His wife, a stranger chosen by his family many years before, had quit her job in Delhi and decided to come to Nassau.

Now is nothing compared to *then*. Other loves have come and gone—and no, they weren't the same. I have already forgotten many of them. But I will always remember chapati love!

JEAN ALLEN, whose drawings enliven this book, has lived in forty-nine different cities and four foreign countries. Wherever she goes, she tries to study art. She is divorced and has two sons. DeWayne is living in London and has two children, Thomas and Neisha. Steve and his wife, Bichthi, are living in Florida with their three children, Nina, Cody, and Kacy. For now, Jean is living in Pátzcuaro, Mexico, something always subject to change.

Food

The Ho Mok Story

Rita Golden Gelman

Ho mok happened to me one day in 1999. It has bubbled in my head ever since. *Ho mok* is a coconut milk fish mousse that sits on a bed of basil leaves and steams in individual banana-leaf baskets. Just thinking about it makes me want to rush out and buy a ticket to Thailand.

I met *ho mok* when I was living in a bungalow in the village of Ban Krud, about four hours south of Bangkok. My friend Fon, the manager of the family resort, knocked on my door one day and said, pretty much exhausting her English, "Lita, come, eat."

I put on my flip-flops and followed her across the compound, but instead of taking me to a table, she sat me on the floor of the dining room among a group of women who were cutting saucer-size circles out of huge banana leaves. Fon was stapling the circles into little baskets. (In Bali I had often stapled leaves with toothpick-thin bamboo "needles"; Fon was stapling with metal staples!)

When I sat down, the chubby Thai woman next to me

smiled and pointed at me. "Same fat," she said, clearly pleased. Then she handed me some scissors and showed me how to cut out circles. Together we cut and stapled, smiling a lot, which is what you do when you can't talk.

When we had a few hundred baskets, we put them into a giant cloth rice-bag. Fon handed me the bag and motioned for me to get onto the back of her motorcycle. I had no idea where I was going. But my credo was and is, if someone says, "Come," I go.

After a couple of minutes we turned off the paved street onto a wooded dirt road, where we bounced and splashed through mud puddles until we finally stopped at a sunny, busy clearing where dozens of women, assembled on colorful mats, were cleaning, chopping, grinding, mashing, milling, mixing, stirring, spooning, and pouring. Grouped in orderly piles were meats, poultry, vegetables, shrimp, sea bass, squid, noodles, rice, lemongrass, cilantro, basil, palm sugar, and more. (I found out later that they were cooking for a community ceremony that would be attended by hundreds of locals. There wasn't anyone there who spoke English, so I just patiently waited for things to happen.)

The *ho mok* contingent was off in one corner, not too far from the cooking burners, which the men were assembling. We dropped our bag of two-inch baskets next to a woman in a lacy white blouse who was energetically stirring a huge pot of coconut milk, white ocean fish, and hot, red curry paste. The pot was sitting on a mat while she sat on a stool, mixing the white liquid with a three-foot-long firm spine of a palm leaf. She stirred for at least half an hour. Occasionally others would come by and relieve her. Some would add more coconut milk. Some added red paste. Others just took over the stirring.

Finally they added tiny strips of Kaffir-lime leaves to the pot and stirred some more. I never saw anyone add a thickener, but the liquid thickened until it was about the consistency of too-thin mashed potatoes.

When the cooks were satisfied, they spooned the mixture into our banana-leaf baskets on top of a handful of basil leaves that we'd stuffed into the bottom of each basket. Then they packed the baskets into steamers, set them on top of a pot of rapidly boiling water, and put on the cover.

Fon and I wandered and watched as dozens of cooked dishes were set up on rocks, tables, tree stumps, and mats, awaiting the eaters. I was the only Westerner there. I smiled a lot at the many welcoming locals. And I ate and smiled even more as they put a variety of foods in my hands and mouth. Thai cuisine is my favorite in the world. I was liking this a lot.

Meanwhile Fon kept looking over at the *ho mok* makers. Then suddenly she grabbed my arm and pulled. "*Ho mok. Ho mok,*" she said as we rushed toward the crowd gathered around the steaming green baskets.

The finished coconut-fish mousse was incredible. As I ate, I moaned in pleasure. Fon just stood there, smiling. I knew I would have to learn how to make it. And if I couldn't get it right, I would have to move to Thailand, forever eating *ho mok*.

Well, the rest of the story is that until I started this book, I had never even tried to make *ho mok*—it was just too intimidating. I knew that in the United States all the ingredients would be different. Coconut milk would come from a can instead of a coconut; the banana leaves, if I could find them, would be frozen; and the basil would probably be the Italian kind, not the purple-stemmed Thai kind. And I had no idea about the proportions of the ingredients. Nor could I figure out what thickened the mixture.

But I had to include *ho mok* in this book—readers of *Tales of a Female Nomad* constantly ask me about it. So Maria and I tried it several times in Mexico. I was never 100 percent happy. Then I settled into Seattle for a while and cooked it again and again. I've even cooked it in Lars's kitchen in Nantes, France (see page 6). The recipe below is not totally authentic (I added eggs as a thickener), but it's pretty wonderful. And I have to admit that I actually like the cabbage baskets better than the banana leaves; you can eat the cabbage. I made the switch because I couldn't assume that everyone cooking from this book would have a banana tree in her backyard.

In Thailand, food is regional; even well-known dishes differ dramatically from place to place. When I was in the country, I ate *ho mok* whenever I could, wherever I was. There is even a version in Laos that I found wonderful. Different, but delicious. But my favorite *ho mok* is still the custardy delicacy that they make at Fon's family resort, Rim Haad, in the village of Ban Krud. When they know I'm coming, they buy the fish! If you go there, and you should, you have to request it; it's not on the menu. You can buy *ho mok* in the night market in Rim Haad, but it's fully wrapped and grilled and the consistency is firmer.

I've only seen it once on the menu of a Thai restaurant in the United States. I ordered it, of course, but neither the taste nor the consistency was right. I didn't even recognize it. If you have a favorite Thai restaurant, you could try preordering it. Maybe if you smile, they'll make it a menu special some night. The recipe that follows is actually easy and fabulous. And I'm excited that so many of you out there will be introduced to this extraordinary taste. Feel free to moan with pleasure when you take that first spoonful.

 Ho Mok

Adapted from a traditional Thai recipe

SERVES 6 AS AN APPETIZER

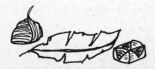

*T*his is one of my favorite foods in the world. Italian basil can be used, but the Thai basil with purple stems is milder and less dominant. You can find the basil, frozen banana leaves, kaffir lime leaves, curry paste, fish sauce, and coconut milk at an Asian market. www.amazon.com/grocery will have everything but the frozen leaves. Try your supermarket first. You never know. The cabbage baskets are my variation for people who don't have banana trees in their backyards. I like the flavor even more than the custards made in banana-leaf baskets, and I like being able to eat the basket!

  1 package of frozen banana leaves or 1 big fresh banana leaf, or a whole, medium green cabbage
  1 tablespoon fish sauce
  1 tablespoon sugar (or less)
  ½ pound white ocean fish, cut into ½-inch pieces
  1 to 2 tablespoons red curry paste
  1 cup thick coconut cream, the thicker the better (If you cannot find a can labeled "coconut cream," use the heavy cream from 2 cans of coconut milk. Don't shake the cans. Make sure the coconut milk is unsweetened. A Thai brand is usually a safe bet.)

  2 large eggs, beaten
  1 tablespoon needle-thin strips of Kaffir lime leaves, ½-inch
     long
 40 Thai basil leaves
  1 tablespoon needle-thin strips of red hot pepper, 1-inch long
 12 needle-thin strips of Kaffir lime leaves, 1-inch long

If you are using frozen banana leaves, thaw them for at least
two hours before handling. Flush them under warm water.
Lay them out on a flat surface and dry thoroughly, being
careful to rub only with the grain of the leaf to avoid tearing.

If you are using a fresh banana leaf, pass it over a flame, or dip
it very briefly in boiling water. This makes the leaf pliable
and easier to handle.

To make the baskets, cut six 5-inch circles out of the banana
leaf. (If you're using the fresh leaf, avoid the center vein.)
Form four ½-inch pleats around each circle to make a basket, securing each pleat with half a toothpick as you go.

If you are using cabbage leaves, first cut out the core.

Put the whole cabbage into a big pot of boiling water, and peel
off the leaves, one by one, as soon as they soften. The smaller
inner leaves almost form baskets naturally .

Do the best you can with toothpicks to make small baskets.
Use as little of the thick rib near the base as possible. (Shav-
ing the rib to make it thinner also works.)

Put the fish sauce and sugar in a big bowl with the fish.

Add the curry paste, the coconut cream or milk, and the beaten
eggs. Stir energetically by hand with a wooden spoon for
10 minutes or more.

Add the ½-inch strips of Kaffir lime leaves.

Place five or six basil leaves in the bottom of each banana leaf or cabbage basket.

Fill the baskets with the fish-coconut-milk mixture, trying to keep the amount of fish in each basket equal.

Arrange two tiny strips of red pepper on top of each custard, and add a few tiny slivers of 1-inch Kaffir lime leaves.

Cook the baskets in a covered steamer. Or use a colander or steam basket set inside a pot of boiling water. Make sure there is an inch between the water and the baskets. If your steamer setup isn't airtight, you might have to add more boiling water to the pot during the cooking process.

Steam, covered, for fifteen minutes, or until the custard is set.

Any Pan Is a No-stick Pan If You No-cook in It!

Bobbi Zehner

The comfort of washing dishes by hand in warm soapy water or sitting at the counter reminiscing with a friend makes my kitchen a special, almost sacred space. The appliances, however, hold no such allure. The refrigerator, of course, is the one exception without which I could not survive. But the stove and I barely manage to peacefully coexist. When and if I cook, it is because food is a vital necessity, and regular dining out is too costly. But I never entertain dinner guests in my home.

Have I reached a point in life for resting on my culinary laurels? Absolutely not. I have none! Do fewer and fewer dinner invitations come my way? Definitely! However, I do have one angelic chef friend with exquisite skills and more than a dollop of understanding. She continues to nourish me, body and soul, even though I do not reciprocate. Okay, I may spring for an occasional dinner at Lombardino's, but in no measure could it ever be deemed reciprocal. I remain positively phobic about cooking for others.

My sense of dread got its roots in the sixties with a

Thanksgiving Jell-O mold that kept me up half the night slicing bananas. No one told me specifically how many layers to make, so I kept resetting the alarm clock. When morning came, I fleetingly wondered why so much unused Jell-O still sat on the stove. When friends unmolded my masterpiece, it proved to be a mound of sliced bananas, merely grouted with red Jell-O, weighing close to seven pounds.

The following Thanksgiving I baked a turkey with the little bag of innards still inside the bird. Somewhat comforted to learn that this is a fairly common mistake for a novice, I further wondered how many beginners made turkey gravy my way.

I started off fine, even remembering to add the flour slowly to a separate bottle of water and mix well before adding it to the turkey renderings, just like Mom used to do. How then could I have forgotten the most important ingredient? Heat!

"Oh please, just tell me what that was supposed to be?" begged a former sweetheart when he caught me discarding the greasy, cold concoction.

Age never did bring a lick of wisdom to my kitchen. Larry's first visit to Chicago in 1977 found me trying to replicate Mom's poached eggs, a sure route to a man's heart. Larry slowly ate one and a half of the three eggs on toast before "feeling stuffed." He later bravely informed me that the egg whites were supposed to be just that: white. Mine were jiggly and transparent.

While visiting his family in Madison, early in our courtship, Larry bragged about my cold tuna casserole. I couldn't believe what I was hearing when his mom added, "I've got all the fixings. Why don't you whip some up for us?"

Flummoxed, but hoping to please the future in-laws, out to

their kitchen I went. In a huge kettle I began making enough Creamettes to feed eight people. Sharon, Larry's sister, came along to keep me company while I chopped and diced the standard onions, celery, and Velveeta cheese. When I moved to stir the macaroni atop the stove, I gasped. In front of me bubbled a kettle of pasta mush. Laughing, Sharon and I conspired to make another batch since there was plenty of macaroni for a second go-round without anyone's knowing about my blunder. Trying to ditch the evidence, I dumped the mushy Creamettes into the toilet, where they lodged like a bowling ball refusing to budge. Amid tears of laughter, I 'fessed up, and Larry plumbed the depths of my chagrin—with a Roto-rooter rotor.

It's been twenty-nine years, and his family still drags out this story, along with my cookie caper, as proof that I should be permanently banned from all kitchens.

See, Larry's mom used to make fabulous refrigerator cookies, and having copied her recipe, I decided to make them myself. Following the directions to a T, I rolled the ingredients into sliced logs wrapped in wax paper and put them in the refrigerator.

Periodically I would peek to see what was happening, and nothing was. Finally, I phoned Sharon, asking if she'd ever made her mother's cookies. "All the time," she replied.

"Well," I said, "what happens in the refrigerator to turn them into cookies?"

"What do you mean?" she said. "They have to go into the oven!"

"The oven? The recipe never mentioned an oven!" Puleeze, see why I hate stoves?

Sure enough, when Sharon checked her mother's recipe

card, there was no mention of ten minutes at 350 degrees in any oven. Everyone just knew to do it.

And so it has gone to date. Cooking seems to have a logic that eludes me. Sure, I need sustenance. Therefore I cook, minimally, in order to feed myself and Larry. But dinner parties, so to speak, "are not even on the table."

AS A SIGN LANGUAGE interpreter, Bobbi Zehner is thrilled to help Rita's kids in India. "This is right up there with my News-week essay about my mother receiving aid from a stranger." A writer of memoir and fiction, often with a humorous bent, Bobbi is working on her own anthology. She is collecting tales of coincidence or synchronicity, like the woman who drove to the top of Haleakala and found that the only other person on the volcano was a woman from her exercise club in Wisconsin. Got a story to share? Contact Bobbi at bobbiz@sbcglobal.net.

Paneer Sailor

Lily Morris

The first things I noticed about Ben when he arrived on board the *Pride of Baltimore II* were his funny little knit hat that didn't quite cover his ears, and the way he towered half a foot above me and the rest of the crew.

After a week or so of sailing alongside each other, we began running together. Every morning at six, from across the chilly cabin, we would roll out from under warm blankets into cold sweat suits. Half an hour later, sleepy, coffee-sipping fellow crew would find us stretching on deck, winding down from the run before racing below to change.

Our friendship grew and thrived as we discovered many common interests and new ideas. I taught Ben how to knit, and we spent many evenings cozied up in his bunk with needles clicking away. He taught me about the raw food diet he had recently discovered and inspired me to eat more fresh fruit and veggies. He was famous for eating as much salad as the rest of the crew put together. On our days off, we drove to the nearby reservoir to walk in the woods, and afterward we sniffed out new health food stores. But the romance I was hoping for wasn't happening.

I had come to believe that the way to a man's heart is through his stomach (yummy, homemade chow), his feet (warm, hand-knit socks), and his shoulders (a sensuous back massage).

So I went to work. The local yarn store had his favorite color in stock. I purchased a couple of skeins and cast on forty-eight stitches for a pair of dark purple socks. I offered up my services as ship's masseuse and let my fingers do the talking. Fellow crew members came to me when they were aching and broken. Ben soon realized that I had hands that could heal, and he too showed up for treatment.

The final key, the one I figured would go directly to his heart, started with the discovery of some unbleached cheesecloth at the local health food store. I was inspired to make *paneer*, a simple and delicious Indian cheese. I stopped at the Save-a-Lot that night and purchased milk and lemons. I was practically skipping with excitement through the rain on my way back to the dock. I put the milk to warm on our temperamental diesel stove, Chernobyl. After fielding questions from nearly every member of the crew about my curious concoction, I posted a note on the bulkhead behind the stove. It read: "This is paneer Indian cheese. It is to eat, but not for tonight."

Finally the milk came to a boil; I added lemon juice, stirring gently and watched with delight as the curds formed, leaving a pale yellow whey behind. I strained the mixture through my new cheesecloth and let it drain overnight.

The next evening the cook and I prepared an Indian feast: *muttar paneer* (peas and cheese) with fresh chapatis, basmati rice, banana raita, and mango chutney to accompany the colorful main dish. I was excited for everyone to try one of my favorite meals, but I cared most about Ben's reaction.

There was no need to worry. Not only did he polish off a large plate of my *muttar paneer,* he went back for more—before a piece of lettuce even touched his plate. In one meal I had captured his taste buds and more.

Muttar paneer is a magical food. Combined with a pair of hand-knit wool socks and a sensuous massage, it's a sure way to anyone's heart.

LILY MORRIS is a massage therapist, artist, sailor, writer, and lover of good food. A native of Martha's Vineyard, Massachusetts, she recently returned to the island after traveling extensively as a crew member and teacher on tall ships. Her sailing experiences have exposed her to many different cultures and their diverse cuisines. Lily's patchwork of interests converge in her quarterly knot-tying column for Edible Vineyard *magazine. She is currently at work on logo and literature, as well as course design, for Vineyard Voyagers Inc., a local nonprofit offering maritime adventures for island youth. Contact Lily at lilykmorris@gmail.com.*

 Paneer, an Indian Cheese
   Adapted from a traditional recipe
   SERVES 4

*T*his is a wonderful kitchen activity to do with children. It's kind of like a science experiment.

   ½ gallon whole milk
   2 lemons
   Cheesecloth

Line a colander or strainer with two layers of cheesecloth. Squeeze lemon juice into a cup. Strain out the pulp and seeds.

In a heavy-bottomed pot, boil the milk. Don't let it burn. As soon as it boils, turn off the heat and add the lemon juice, a tablespoon at a time. The milk will curdle, making curds and whey. This will probably happen with only 3 or 4 table-spoons of juice.

When the milk turns into curds floating in a pale yellow liquid (the whey), let it sit for around 10 minutes. The curds will clump.

Strain off the liquid by carefully pouring it through the cheese-cloth. Make a package of curds by tying the cheesecloth and hanging it for at least an hour to drain the liquid. When no more liquid drips out, give the cheesecloth a final twist.

Place the package of curds between two cutting boards, and put heavy books on top of the upper board. Press down on the top board to flatten the curds. Try to square off the edges to form a block.

Leave it in the press for a couple of hours. It will turn into a firm ½-pound block of cheese. That's the *paneer* used in *muttar paneer* (recipe follows). The cheese can be crum-bled onto Indian dishes and cut into ½-inch chunks or 2-inch slices. The slices can also be fried in a little oil until browned. Sprinkle a pinch of salt and ground cumin on the frying slices if they are not going into recipes, and eat them as a snack with a squeeze of lemon or lime.

✧ *Muttar Paneer*

Adapted from a traditional Indian recipe

SERVES 4 TO 6

---

2   medium onions, chopped

4   cloves garlic, peeled and crushed

1   tablespoon grated fresh ginger root

1   tablespoon vegetable oil

1   teaspoon ground coriander

1   teaspoon ground cumin

½   teaspoon turmeric

¼   teaspoon cayenne pepper, or more to taste

1   teaspoon sea salt, or to taste

3   to 4 medium tomatoes (½ pound), peeled and cut into chunks

1-pound bag frozen green peas, thawed

2   tablespoons vegetable oil or ghee (clarified butter)

½   pound *paneer*, cut in 1-inch cubes (in a pinch you can use Mexican *panela* or *queso para freir*)

1   cup plain, unflavored yogurt, stirred

1   teaspoon garam masala (you might have to order this: www.amazon.com/grocery)

2   tablespoons chopped fresh cilantro

Place the onions, garlic, and ginger in a food processor or blender, and process into a puree. If using a blender, add a little water. Set aside.

Heat 1 tablespoon of the oil in a heavy-bottomed saucepan over medium-high heat. Add the onion puree, and cook 3 minutes, stirring to prevent burning.

Add the dry spices, and sauté 2 minutes to release the aroma of the spices.

Add the tomatoes, and simmer on medium-low heat 5 minutes. Add the peas, and simmer an additional 5 minutes.

Meanwhile heat a sauté pan over high heat, and add 2 tablespoons oil. Sear the *paneer* to golden brown. Drain on paper towels.

Add the *paneer* to the pea mixture. Stir in the yogurt and garam masala, and heat through. Add water, depending on the consistency you prefer.

Sprinkle with the cilantro, and taste for seasoning. Serve over rice, or eat with chapati.

....

Two hot green chiles and a handful of fresh cilantro leaves can be added to the blender or food processor. One of our testers added ½ teaspoon ground cardamom, ¼ teaspoon cinnamon, a pinch of ground cloves, and 2 bay leaves. Clearly this is a recipe where you can fool around. —ma

....

Bonjour, Friendship!

Patricia Lundquist

A newcomer, all alone with nothing to do in this foreign city of Nantes, France, I decided to visit the local park. It was a beautiful, sunny September afternoon, and the pathways were filled with promenaders—mothers with babies in strollers, groups of schoolchildren, older folks, lovers arm in arm. Mostly people *with* other people. I thought about my husband whom I'd left at home while I ventured to France to teach English to high school students. As I looked around at the beautifully sculpted gardens and brilliant blooms, I felt a knot of homesickness starting in my stomach. Then I noticed someone looking at me.

I smiled impulsively. The young dark-haired girl smiled tentatively back at me.

"*Bonjour*," I said awkwardly, wondering if I would understand her response. I recognized the girl as Véronique, one of the students in my English class. Her companion turned out to be an older sister whose name is the same as mine: Patricia.

Véronique asked if I would like to join them. Although

today was only the first day of class, she later explained that I had seemed friendly, so when she saw me in the park, she and her sister decided to approach me. She was hoping I spoke French and was relieved I did.

I understood instinctively that approaching someone they really didn't know was almost unthinkable. But for me, the sun suddenly seemed brighter, the trees, flowers, and shrubs more lush, and the crowds of people smaller, as the three of us walked round and round the park chattering away in French. Finally Véronique and Patricia invited me to come home with them. I hesitated, wondering what their parents would say. Both girls assured me I would be welcome. That proved to be an understatement.

Madame Cantel was on her knees paste-waxing a beautiful hardwood floor, hair in a kerchief, face slightly flushed. The smell of the wax reminded me of my own home and floors that I cleaned in exactly the same way.

She immediately rose and greeted me warmly and suggested to the girls that we go to their room where she would bring us "tea." Soon Madame Cantel arrived with a floral china tray with matching cups, a pot of hot tea, and a lovely plate of homemade pastry. She lingered a few minutes asking me questions and then turned to Véronique and said—almost as if I weren't there—"she will come to dinner here, so please invite her." Then she turned again to me warmly, taking both my hands in hers, and assured me I was welcome in their home anytime. I believed her.

Véronique asked me if I liked seafood and shellfish. Since I'm a native of the Pacific Northwest, a love of seafood is almost a given. Although I didn't find out until later, the Cantel family operated a small *poissonnerie*, one of the finest in Nantes, specializing in the freshest oysters, shellfish, and all kinds of seafood. M. Cantel was just as charming as his wife.

When I arrived a month later for the promised dinner, I nearly gasped with surprise. The entire dining room had been transformed into a floral paradise. The linens were imprinted with flowers in pink, orange, and red. China, glassware, and silver sparkled in the candlelight. Fresh flowers in coordinating colors arched out of crystal vases.

They were having an American to dinner and obviously wanted me to experience the "pleasures of the French table." I was honored and filled with affection for these people who had taken a complete stranger into their lives and home. I wondered to myself about the whispered reputation of the French for being aloof and never inviting people into their homes.

Needless to say, the meal was splendid. Each course was served with a wine chosen carefully to complement the delicate flavors of the dish. I ate like a man going to the gallows. I ate for America. I ate and ate and ate. They were smallish portions, but the courses kept coming. I knew without anyone ever having to tell me that to push away from the table now would be bad form at the least, and probably insulting after all the work and preparation that had been done.

At last, a pause! Some coffee, cheese, and fruit. I sighed inwardly with relief and adjusted my posterior into the chair cushion. I answered more questions about where I was from, what my husband did, and how long I would be in France. Did I like the school and teachers, and most prominently, did I like *La Belle France*? Madame smiled mysteriously when I said that Americans always talk about how beautiful France is and how wonderful the food is. I assured Madame that she had admirably acquitted herself where culinary exploits were concerned.

Conversation was easy and comfortable. I thought I might still be able to walk back to my dormitory. Then Madame requested, "Véronique, would you serve the *charlotte aux myrtilles*?"

I wasn't sure what a *charlotte* was, but it sounded rich and desserty to me, and I wondered if I could squeeze down yet more food. While Veronique was serving the dessert, Madame reached for a gaily wrapped package next to her chair and handed it to me with a brilliant smile. Véronique entered the room with individually plated servings of *charlotte* and set the tray on the coffee table.

"Open the package," she urged.

I took off the wrapping and saw a gilded maroon book with a grosgrain ribbon bookmark. Inside the cover it was inscribed in French: "To Patricia with all our affection. These are all the recipes you were served this evening so that when you return home you can prepare them for your husband. We hope you will remember this 25th day of October 1977, and us, whenever you open this book." Signed "Famille Cantel: Luc, Henriette, Patricia, et Véronique."

The women in the family had all taken turns, carefully handwriting into this blank book each recipe that had been lovingly prepared for my first meal with them. It was divided into sections, with plenty of blank pages for me to fill in. And fill them in, I have! But my favorite recipes are those that were entered first in the book. Not only are they excellent, but the measure of love with which the dishes were served warms me to this day.

The rest of my teaching year was a delight because of the hospitality of this wonderful family. And their openness with me gave me the courage to be open and trusting of others I met, widening the circle of friendship in a city where I had come knowing no one.

And to think it all began with an impulsive smile in the city park.

A FASCINATION WITH other peoples and places inspired Patricia Lundquist to earn an undergraduate degree in French language and literature after which she was awarded a Fulbright-Hayes teaching assistantship in France. She continues to explore the complex art of communication as a writer and illustrator of horticultural essays, as a French language tutor, and by maintaining an extensive international correspondence. She lives in Bellingham, Washington, with her husband Robert, a gifted teacher, musician, poet, and composer. The beautiful, tranquil garden they are creating on a verdant acre surrounding their cottage is artistic inspiration for themselves and many others. E-mail Patricia at lundquiststudio@comcast.net.

✂ Salmon Tartare Aller Retour

Created by Lars Johannsen (Lars and Nirin, Rita's friends from Nantes, live a few blocks from where "Bonjour, Friendship!" took place.)

SERVES 6

S *erve this dish with a dry Loire Valley wine: Sancerre, Muscadet, or Quincy. —lj*

Tartare

   1 pound skinless, boneless salmon

  ⅓ pound cooked shrimp

2 tablespoons chopped dill

½ teaspoon sea salt

⅛ teaspoon freshly ground black pepper

Caramelized Shallots

15 medium shallots

2 tablespoons unsalted butter

Sauce

Pinch of saffron

¼ cup dry white wine

½ cup whipping cream

¼ teaspoon sea salt

⅛ teaspoon white pepper

For Frying

2 tablespoons unsalted butter

Mince the salmon and the shrimp.

Mix the salmon and shrimp with the dill in a medium bowl. Add the salt and pepper. Mix and taste.

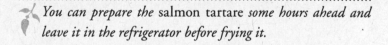

You can prepare the salmon tartare *some hours ahead and leave it in the refrigerator before frying it.*

Peel and cut the shallots into thin slices. Fry them slowly in butter in a heavy frying pan for 25 to 30 minutes, until they become translucent and lightly caramelized. If they start to stick to the pan, add a little water and reduce the heat.

Add the saffron and white wine to the whipping cream, and

reduce the mixture by heating it in a saucepan for 10 minutes. As you stir the sauce, it will become thicker and creamier. Add salt and pepper to taste.

Make 6 burgerlike *tartares,* and fry them in butter in a very hot pan for 2 to 3 minutes on each side. The center should still be raw and tender.

Put one *tartare* on each plate. Serve these with homemade mashed potatoes, one scoop on the side of the *tartare.* Pour the sauce around the *tartare* and the mashed potatoes, and top them both with the caramelized shallots.

The sauce also makes a dynamite coating for pasta served up with whole shrimp cooked in a little olive oil, crushed garlic, and white wine. A little goes a long way. Thin with a bit of the pasta water. —ma

Foreign Flavors

Karen van der Zee

Living in Ghana, West Africa, for a number of years, I'd enjoyed eating groundnut soup many times, but the most memorable occasion was at the house of friends who lived in a small village. Paul was a former Peace Corps Volunteer, and his wife, Patience, was a Ghanaian elementary school teacher. One day they invited GD, our little daughter, and me to spend the day and have a meal.

We arrived in the village about nine in the morning to find Patience chasing a squawking, wing-flapping chicken around the compound. The bird appeared to be in fear for its life, as I would be: it was meant for the soup pot.

Having caught the unfortunate fowl, Patience disappeared around the corner of the house, and I decided to keep the men company on the front porch rather than witness the next step in soup preparation, which involved, of course, the demise of the aforementioned chicken.

Sometime later I ventured a visit to the courtyard, where

Patience was busy chopping the plucked hen into pieces, the bird no longer recognizable as something alive, squawking, and loved by its mother. We chatted about babies—we both had one—and all the other things that women talk about all over the world, although I'm not sure we discussed sex.

The bird duly butchered, Patience set out to make the groundnut paste (peanut butter to us), an ingredient essential to the soup she was crafting for our dinner. After shelling the raw peanuts, she dry-roasted them on top of the stove, then took off the skins. This accomplished, she placed them in a small mortar and pounded them with a small stone, after which she rolled the smashed nuts into a fine paste with a beer bottle.

It took her the greater part of the day to prepare the soup and the *fufu* that was to be served with it. The latter involved the boiling and pounding of plantain and yam until it resembled a big white ball of raw bread dough. This is what you call cooking from scratch.

In the middle of the afternoon we sat down to the meal. We ate from rough black clay bowls and used our hands, pulling off chunks of the doughy *fufu* and scooping up some soup that had been ladled over it. It was very flavorful and peppery hot and not at all boring. We had a wonderful time, aided by a glass or two of fresh palm wine which the men had procured from a neighbor who had hacked down a palm tree. (The sap is the wine, which ferments quickly.)

To this day when I think of groundnut soup, I see in my mind Patience chasing a wing-flapping chicken around the compound.

Groundnut Soup

Adapted by Karen van der Zee

SERVES 6 TO 8

roundnut soup is found in many variations all over West Africa and is usually spicy hot. It is very popular made with chicken, but many kinds of protein foods can be used, such as beef, goat, smoked fish, snails (big fat ones are for sale by the road), and grasscutter, a tasty rodent often irreverently referred to as bush rat. "Bush meat" usually means grasscutter but may refer to meat from any kind of wild critter caught in the bush. Yes, that one too. If you're squeamish, don't ask. —kvdz

    2 onions, finely chopped
    2 tomatoes, peeled and cut in small pieces or 2 tablespoons
       tomato paste
    2 pounds stew beef
    ½ to 2 teaspoons cayenne pepper
    Salt to taste
    2 to 2½ cups boiling water
    ¾ cup natural, unsweetened peanut butter, or more to taste

Place the onions, tomatoes, and beef in a Dutch oven. Sprinkle with salt (if used) and cayenne pepper. Heat over high heat, and stir until the meat loses its color. (You are not browning the meat as you would for American beef stew.) Turn the heat to low, cover the pot, and allow the mixture to simmer in its own juices for 15 minutes.

Add boiling water, cover, and continue simmering for 1 hour 15 minutes, stirring occasionally.

Place the peanut butter in a small heatproof dish. Ladle ½ cup of the liquid out of the pot, and mix it into the peanut butter to soften. Add this mixture to the stew, and blend it well. Cover and simmer for an additional 30 minutes or until the meat is very tender.

Check the seasoning, adding more salt and cayenne pepper to taste. Serve over rice or instant *fufu* if available in your area.

Instead of beef, you can use one chicken, cut in fairly small pieces, including skin and bone, or use cubed chicken breast. Cooking time will be much less. —kvdz

It's not traditional, but one or two red peppers, chopped and sautéed, can be added during cooking to give a little extra punch. Even 1 tablespoon of curry powder can be used. —ma

Cajeta and the Spirits

Maria Altobelli

The focal point of the room on the top floor of the Radisson
Hotel in Minneapolis was a round, six-foot *Noche de Muertos*
altar, filled with photographs and memorabilia from the life
of Mercedes. Paul and I had driven down from our central
Minnesota home to be with Arturo, our longtime friend and
fellow Spanish teacher, for the traditional memorial service to
celebrate his mother's life and death. As we walked into the
room, we smelled the heady scent of marigolds and calendu-
las. Mixed among the traditional *cempasúchitl* flowers and
the chayote were plates of Mercedes's favorite foods, the sheet
music she loved to play on the piano, and her ancient and bat-
tered typewriter that had served her well. Her long and schol-
arly life had moved from Puerto Rico to Cuba to Florida and,
at the end, to Minnesota.

Guests sat in a circle around the table as musicians sang
and played on drums, flute, guitar, and panpipes. People interrupted the music to tell stories about the deceased.

Glenn, the first in the group to share a story, told how he

had gone to Florida to visit Arturo. The two friends took Mercedes to a restaurant. All three ordered coffee, and Glenn sat mesmerized as Mercedes opened packet after packet of sugar from a bowl on the table and stirred the contents of each packet into her cup.

He waited for the critical point to be reached where the liquid would overflow onto the saucer, but Mercedes continued to stir her coffee as the pile of sugar wrappers accumulated at the side of the plate. Finally, she lifted the cup to her lips, sipped delicately, gave a satisfied sigh, and smiled.

Years later Arturo brought Mercedes, now in her early nineties and still smiling, to a hospice, a facility designed for those in their final days. Mercedes lived at the hospice over four years. Her problem, as she stated to Arturo, was that she just couldn't make up her mind to "cross over." She traveled back and forth comfortably from the world of the living to the next without ever leaving her bed.

Though bedridden, Mercedes took an avid interest in the comings and goings of the visitors to the hospice. Friends and family members of other residents came to chat with her before leaving. Her winsome smile, quick wit, and engaging conversation never failed to lighten the hearts and the step of those who stopped by her room.

Two sisters in their twenties saw Mercedes often. Their mother, only in her midforties, was dying of cancer. The two could forget for a time their sad reality by visiting with the lighthearted woman over twice their mother's age.

At the service, one of the hospice staff told how she had come in one morning to find Mercedes already sitting up in bed, propped up against her pillows, smiling. "My goodness, Mercedes, you're certainly awake bright and early today. What's the occasion?"

"I've just had the most pleasant conversation with an extremely nice young woman, dressed in the most beautiful long white dress. She was wearing a large blue hat that was stunning with her blond hair. I always like to see young people wearing a hat. Don't you think it's rather a shame the custom has gone out of vogue? Such a pretty woman and so friendly . . ."

The aide told how she had tried not to look at her watch since she knew it was far too early for visitors. "Really? That's nice, Mercedes. Now why don't you get some rest, you hear, hon?"

She went on to say how later in the day, she had gone into the room of the mother of the two sisters and found an empty bed and the two daughters poking about in the closet. As they caught her puzzled gaze, they stopped and explained.

"Mom died last night. One of her last requests to us was to be buried in her wedding dress." They indicated the floor-length white dress draped over the armchair in the corner. "Now we're trying to find her favorite hat. Where could it have gone? The blue went so well with her blond hair."

As one story after another came to an end, people shifted in their chairs and vied to tell the next tale.

A niece recounted one escapade her aunt and she had traipsing around half the city looking for what a friend had said was *the* shop to buy *the* perfect earrings. "Mercedes was in her seventies at the time, but she still loved odd jewelry. She only had a vague idea where the store was located, but did she ever have stamina. She was forty years older than me, and I was exhausted by four in the afternoon. She was still raring to go.

"Finally, we found the shop, and Mercedes bought her perfect set of earrings. She turned to me and smiled. 'My dear, you must be starving. Shall we have lunch?' "

Arturo told the group how, after returning from one of her cross-over visits, his mom told him that the next world was quite pleasant, and sometimes it was rather hard to convince herself to return. But then, as she put it, "When I go, I want to walk in through the front door. I don't want to be climbing over any walls." Her eyes twinkled. "I'm way too old to be climbing over much of anything these days."

One day the director telephoned Arturo. "We think that your mom is nearing the end. Please come." He entered a room filled with teary employees. His mother was lying motionless on the bed with her eyes closed. She was barely breathing.

Arturo sat next to Mercedes for a bit and then opened a jar of *cajeta,* a creamy, sweet, caramel confection made from cooked goat milk. He scooped out a small spoonful and rested it just inside his mother's lips. The quiet breathing continued for a time, and then her body shifted. Her eyes blinked and opened. Then she reached for the spoon and smiled.

"Ay, Arturito," she said. "This time the door was finally beginning to open. But for a really good *cajeta,* I'm willing to come back for a bit."

I never met Mercedes except through the stories of Arturo and all those who knew and loved her. But she taught me that sometimes good earrings are just too hard to pass up and that life can never have enough sweetness.

⚘ Flan Natural de Cajeta

From Susi Santiago, Restaurante Mistongo, *Pátzcuaro*

SERVES 6 TO 8

8 tablespoons sugar

4 fat tablespoons *cajeta*, also called *dulce de leche* (available in many supermarkets, Latino markets, and at www.Amazon .com/grocery)

7 medium eggs

1 quart whole milk

Preheat oven to 300°F.

Put 4 tablespoons of the sugar in a nonstick frying pan. Set it over medium heat, and shake it until the sugar becomes liquid and caramelizes. Pour the liquid into a pudding pan or a mold for flan. Tilt the pan or mold back and forth so the liquid covers the entire bottom.

Put the *cajeta,* eggs, and 4 tablespoons sugar in a blender, and blend for 1 minute. Add the milk, and continue to blend 1 minute more. Pour the mixture into a pudding pan or flan mold, set the pan or mold in a pan of water, and cook in oven for 1 hour. If a toothpick comes out clean, the flan is done. At higher altitudes, baking time is greatly increased. Just keep checking the consistency of the flan after an hour.

Cool to room temperature, and then refrigerate, preferably overnight. Place a plate over the pan or mold, and carefully invert to unmold the flan. If the caramel on the bottom of the pan has hardened in the mold, place it very briefly in a pan of hot water to soften before inverting.

Serve with a thin layer of *cajeta* on top, whipped cream, and
   chopped nuts.

Cajeta *is made by boiling down either cow's milk or goat's
milk. There are recipes for doing this at home, but it's certainly not foolproof. Susi's grandmother could make any dessert
with success but had spotty luck with* cajeta. *Sometimes it worked,
but other times it separated and had to be thrown out, even though
she followed the same procedure each time.*

It can be used as well in crepas de cajeta, alfajores *(the Argentina cookie that was a great favorite of my Spanish classes in
Minnesota), as a topping for ice cream or fruit, or as a dessert in
its own right. You might even want to experiment making your
own caramel corn with* cajeta. *My neighbor Lusmila told me that
if no dessert is available and you are left with a taste for something
sweet after a meal, spread a little* cajeta *on a saltine cracker! I
think Mercedes would have approved. —ma*

Thanksgiving: A Different Perspective

Åsa Maria Bradley

I'm in the middle of a wonderful dream about being back home in my own country where people speak a language that I can understand without getting a headache from staring at mouths, concentrating on every shaped sound, every syllable of their words so that I can make sense of what they mean. In my dream I am back in the country where my family and friends live. The people who understand who I am. The people who don't need an explanation of my history or traditions to understand me. But why are they all eating turkey? In Sweden we eat chickens and geese but not turkey. Besides, I am a vegetarian, on principle, so I eat no birds at all. I start to ask my mom about this curious new culinary habit when a little voice intercepts my happy reunion.

"Åsa, Åsa, wake up, Åsa! It's the butt-crack of dawn, but Mama is already cooking. You have to come see!" Five-year-old Erin has launched herself onto my bed and is pulling on my arm to wake me up. "Butt-crack of dawn" is her new favorite expression. If her mom hears her using it, she'll be in serious trouble.

I don't want to leave my dream. If I wake up, I have to return to this strange country where nobody speaks anything close to the English I've been studying for the past seven years. In this odd place, they speak without consonants, but each vowel is drawn out to infinity.

What were my parents thinking, sending a seventeen-year-old Swede to Texas as an exchange student? I truly feel like an alien, and I am more homesick than I could ever imagine.

Erin's method of getting me to wake up has changed to lightly slapping my cheeks. Her seven-year-old sister, Rian, has joined her on the bed and takes over the arm-pulling duties. These two kids and their parents are the best thing about my stay. My host family has opened not only their home but also their hearts.

We are all drawn to the kitchen where Donna, the mom, has been cooking since the wee hours of the morning. We are expecting a full house. Erin and Rian are jumping up and down with anticipation because of the big turkey and because they can't wait to see all their aunts, uncles, cousins, and grandparents. Their joy is contagious.

Donna lets us peek at the turkey in the oven. It is the biggest fowl I have ever seen. Everything in Texas is much bigger than what I am used to.

The guests start to arrive early afternoon, bringing the side dishes and lots of desserts. The house fills with happy voices.

I lurk around on the fringes of the festive gathering, wondering if there will be vegetarian options, feeling a little overwhelmed by the exuberance of this large family. It doesn't take long for them to spot me, though. They pull me in to join their group whether I want to or not. The extended family members echo the generosity and hospitality of my host family.

I'm asked a thousand and one questions about me, my country, and my family. It's hard to keep up with them.

"How do you like it here then? Is everyone at school taking good care of you? You'd better tell me if they're not, and I'll come up there to that school of yours and tell them folks a thing or two about taking care of our Norwegian gal."

Dicki's dad is a little confused about the geography of Scandinavia, but he means well. I have a hard time deciphering his East Texas accent; his words are drawled even longer than they are in other parts of the state. Before I have a chance to say anything, his wife asks me a question.

"And how are your parents celebrating this Thanksgiving without you then? I bet they are missing you especially on this holiday that is all about family."

Before I can answer, she's moved on to talk to someone else. After a while I'm mentally exhausted by being the center of attention, but I also feel like a member of the family and not at all like an alien anymore. I notice that all the men are in the living room talking about hunting and fishing, and the women are in the kitchen. I join the women.

The kitchen counter sags under all the food. Most of the dishes I have never seen before. The only thing that looks vaguely familiar is the green bean casserole, but it has fried onions on top. The baked yams look delicious—golden brown and caramelized. The stuffing is flawlessly fluffed and contains bits of celery that break up the landscape of various browns with little areas of greenery.

A dish made especially for me by Dorina's mom has steaming vegetables under a gooey cheese, blistered to golden brown perfection. The cranberry sauce in a fancy glass bowl glistens with red wetness.

Next to it I see what must be a misplaced dish. Obviously, it should be on the side table with the rest of the desserts. The dish contains whipped cream with bits of marshmallows, Jell-O, and cranberries. By my standards it must be meant for consumption after the main course. I am a big connoisseur of sweets, so I should know. I'm already planning my main meal in accordance with leaving enough room for a taste of each and every one of the other desserts: pecan pie that looks so perfect I can taste its nuttiness on my tongue already, pumpkin pie with an impeccable crusted surface, and for the kids, ice cream in everyone's favorite flavor.

My contribution to the meal also resides at this table. I have made *kladdkaka,* a Swedish chocolate dessert whose name loosely translates into "gooey cake." It is a classic Swedish recipe, but I add my own twist to it—some orange zest in the batter, which gives it a more sophisticated flavor.

The women make the final preparations, but they are at the same time deep in conversation in that wonderful way of multitasking that only women seem to possess. They see to the food, mind the kids, and socialize with their peers all at the same time.

I am struck by how much this could be my mother's kitchen at one of our family gatherings. Swedish women gather in the kitchen the same way. Even the conversation topics sound familiar: sharing advice about a child having problems with math in school ("Åsa could probably tutor him, she's doing well in math."), whether heels go with shorts ("If you can wear short skirts with heels, why not shorts?"), giving sympathy over a husband forgetting an anniversary ("Honey, if you don't drop hints, they will never remember.").

Then there are the more emotional things to talk about, those that women share only with other women who are family or close friends. Subjects like hot flashes ("Dress in layers."), mother and wifehood exhaustion ("Red wine and chocolate are the remedy"), and the young, good-looking waiter at the local steak house flirting with you ("Tip him good, and he'll do it again next time—it works better than red wine and chocolate.").

I don't participate in the conversation much since I'm at that awkward stage where I'm not a kid anymore but not yet quite at home in the grown-up world. I'm content to just listen, to let the warm southern accents wash over me; I feel cocooned by their easy companionship. The smoothness of it, the light teasing, and the quick laughter are all part of the same atmosphere I experience in my mother's kitchen and in my friends' mothers' kitchens at any large gathering at home.

It lulls me; then suddenly, their words make perfect sense. I don't have to concentrate as hard to understand their meaning. Something has clicked in my brain, and the long vowels shape proper words, not just sounds.

The oven timer goes off, and like a school bell, the signal causes a stampede toward the kitchen. Donna carries the turkey to its place of honor in the middle of the table. It is magnificent. I have never seen anything like it, steaming hot with crisp golden skin. After saying grace, Dicki carves the big bird, and an amazing elaborate process of passing plates and scooping up food begins.

In seconds everyone has a heap of food on their plate and

digs in, talking and laughing through it all. It happens so quickly I don't have time to make special requests as to what should and should not go on my plate. My plate, like everyone else's, is heaped with turkey and a bit of every side dish, including the strange whipped cream concoction.

I learn that it is called Jell-O salad and is not considered a dessert. "Honey, how could it be a dessert? It has cranberries in it?!"

I feel so much a part of the group, a part of the family, that it would be rude not to eat the food in front of me. Besides, I have lived with the wonderful smell of this turkey cooking for close to eight hours now. It invaded my dreams. How could I not taste even just a small piece of it?

It is absolutely delicious, and the end of my vegetarianism. I feel a little guilty, but also relieved to not have to always make a fuss at each meal. Vegetarianism has not yet caught on in Texas.

That night I go to bed with a full belly and a full heart. My very first Thanksgiving, and I am thankful for these wonderful, warm people with their funny accents. I finally feel relaxed enough to open up to the possibilities of my year abroad. I fall asleep dreaming not of things left behind but of amazing adventures that lie ahead.

AFTER HER HIGH SCHOOL exchange year, Åsa Maria Bradley stayed in the United States to complete college and graduate school. She then spent eight years working as an engineer and technical writer for various software companies in Silicon Valley. She currently lives in eastern Washington where she teaches physics and writes. Her work has appeared in Wire Harp, eWag, Auntie's Notes, Inland NW Homes & Living, *and* Bylines Writers'

Calendar. *She travels often and still loves events involving lots of food, especially if chocolate cake is served. Find out more about Åsa Maria and read her blog at www.asamariabradley.com.*

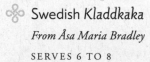 Swedish Kladdkaka
From Åsa Maria Bradley
SERVES 6 TO 8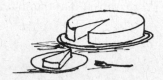

The two best chocolate desserts I have ever had in my life are this one from a former Swedish au pair, and the mousse from Lars, which appears on page 161. I don't know what other secrets those Swedes are hiding, but I'm thinking it might be time for me to head out to Sweden! —rgg

- 5 ounces salted butter, melted
- 2½ cups sugar
- 3 large eggs
- 1 teaspoon vanilla extract
- 6 tablespoons unsweetened cocoa powder
- 1 cup all-purpose flour
- Zest of ½ orange
- 1 teaspoon powdered sugar

Preheat oven to 350°F.

Grease a round springform cake pan and line the bottom with parchment paper.

Using an electric hand or stand mixer, mix the butter and sugar to a crumbly paste. Add the eggs and vanilla, and beat on the highest setting.

Add the cocoa powder, flour, and orange zest. Beat on medium setting. The batter will be very thick.

Pour into the springform pan and bake for 35 to 45 minutes. When done, the cake should have a crust on the outside and be very moist in the center . . . almost liquid. Insert a toothpick into the middle of the cake. It should come out gooey with chocolate.

Let the cake cool a bit, move it from pan to platter, and then sift a thin layer of powdered sugar over it.

Serve warm or at room temperature.

Riding Out the Storm

Victoria Allman

Yesterday was a day of tropical storms like none I had ever seen. Rain fell hard and from every direction, large heavy drops that bounced off a vengeful sea. The ominous gray and purple-rimmed clouds blanketed low in the ever-darkening sky, and the noise of the storm vibrated through the steel hull of the 185-foot yacht, the *Pangaea,* driving us inside. We pitched uncomfortably back and forth in the swells. Sleep was a challenge; the boat's continual motion, plus the clanging of the anchor, kept all of us awake.

We started this voyage in Australia and were now traveling through the Solomon Islands to Tahiti, where we were meeting our guests. A 3,500-mile run.

I am the chef onboard, and I'm responsible for breakfast, lunch, and dinner for my twelve crewmates. Since I usually do this, as well as cook for the yacht's guests, this light duty left a lot of down time that I had been looking forward to.

The Pacific Ocean can be beautiful and calm, like a glass mirror, or rough and agitated like margaritas in a blender. We had seen it all on this trip. The first few days were spent pleasantly reading and catching up on sleep. Then the storm happened.

The *Pangaea* has four levels of decks, six staterooms, a dining room, a gym, and two large living rooms, most of them off limits to the crew. We were confined to our cabins and the crew mess. The same twelve humans, in the same rooms, every hour of every day, every day for thirty-six days of storm. It was like a prison sentence.

Some days were too scary to go outside with a wind blowing so strongly that I feared being picked up like a newspaper and tossed into the water to drown. Some nights the wind increased to over forty knots and roared outside our porthole. Waves ranging from eight to ten feet crashed against the boat and sent us rocking. Those with a delicate constitution spent most of the night curled up beside the toilet.

We'd just about had enough when the captain decided to anchor in Marovo Lagoon. The next day looked only marginally better. The clouds were still threatening to explode on us, but there was at least a little light peaking through. It was just enough encouragement to give Patrick and me the confidence to take a Wave Runner and go for lunch at Uepi Lodge, seven miles and three islands away. I didn't care if we got rained on. I just wanted off that boat.

Patrick is a blond, blue-eyed surfer and one of the happiest men I have ever known, but even he was showing signs of weariness and feeling a little batty from the storm. We put on sunscreen, more from habit than from any chance that the sun would break through the clouds, placed our money and a change of clothes in a dry sack, and donned our life jackets.

The minute we left the *Pangaea*, we knew this was going to

be tough going. The usual translucent blue waters had turned ugly again. Menacing waves grew larger and threatened to upend us. I sat behind Patrick wrapping my arms around his waist and holding on for dear life. I had been tossed off once before, and I was trying to avoid a second swim. As the Wave Runner rode up the crest of the waves and fell, crashing down into the water with alarming speed, it sent spray up and over the front of the ski. As quickly as we dropped, another wave appeared in front of us. I barely had time to wipe the salt water from my glasses before we would drop again, sending another torrent of water up and over us.

After two hours of constant pounding, we arrived at Uepi Island. We had a map and a rough idea that the lodge was located on the eastern side of the island, but little else to go on. We circled the area twice before we saw the sign. *Uepi Lodge* was engraved on a piece of wood no larger than a paperback book. The lodge itself was obscured from view. Large coconut palm trees concealed the building, and a small dock amidst the tropical rain forest was all that signaled its existence to those passing. It is a small resort where guests go to relax and scuba dive.

Although we arrived unannounced and in an unconventional way, Jill and Grant, the lodge's owners, led us up a pebbled path, past green flowering bushes to the main house. Lunch was being served in the open-air restaurant. The timber veranda was shaded with a palm-frond roof and overlooked the white sandbars and turquoise shallows of the lagoon. The ominous day disappeared. Half a dozen tables and chairs were set up, and a hammock for reading in the afternoon. The place screamed of total escapism from the outside world. Jill was a petite Australian pixie of a woman with sharp features and the air of one in charge. "I fell in love with Uepi Lodge twenty years ago when we were here as guests. We bought the place and raised a family on this island," she told me. As Patrick and Grant discussed fishing and diving possibilities in the area, Jill and I talked about food.

Her size was misleading. She was a strong woman whose passion was on fierce display when she spoke of food and living on the island. After buying the lodge from the previous owners, she had commandeered the kitchen and started creating the fabulous dishes and fastidious reputation that Uepi Lodge is known for.

"Our guests are normally from Australia and are used to lots of fresh vegetables that are just not available in the Solomon Islands, so I planted a garden on the property. Today I grow my own herbs and lettuces for each meal," she said with a hint of pride.

Lunch arrived at the table as we spoke. A South Pacific yellowfin tuna pie, Jill's healthy version of an Australian meat pie, was placed before me. Enveloped in a flaky buttery crust were chunks of tender sweet yellowfin tuna coated with coconut milk, ginger, lime, and cilantro. This was topped with fluffy mashed potatoes and baked until golden. I had never had anything like it. The coconut milk reminded me of Thai food but without the heat. I could distinctly pick out the taste of ginger and lime in the velvety-smooth sauce. The yellowfin, a top-quality tuna that is plentiful in South Pacific waters, was just barely cooked, so it was moist and full of flavor. The pastry was still crisp instead of soggy or overloaded with sauce. I eagerly poured sweet chili sauce (an Asian staple used like ketchup) onto my plate to accompany the pie. It was delicious.

"There must be just a little of the sauce peeking through

the potato layer . . ." I could barely concentrate on what Jill was saying as I took another bite. All I could think about was how I could re-create this dish. It was that good. I had to replicate it.

Our harrowing journey to get to Uepi Lodge and the endless hours I had spent on the boat were now forgotten as I sat on the porch with Jill and her guests, absorbed in the quiet, laid-back atmosphere. There was no fuss or formality, just a feeling of comfort. This was Eden, our secret oasis, hidden not only from the *Pangaea* but also from the world. No telephones rang, no television blared. There was no movie theater on the island and no Starbucks. Patrick and I were on solid ground that didn't sway and tilt under us. We had succeeded in escaping our floating prison.

Unfortunately as the day progressed, I was forced out of my euphoric state by reality. No matter how good the tuna pie was, it could not stop time, and the daylight hours were dwindling fast. Patrick and I faced two more hours pounding through whitecaps on the Wave Runner to return to the boat.

Grant, who had been watching storms from this vantage point for twenty years, felt the weather was about to get rougher; the next storm was approaching. "You'd better get going, mate, or you'll be here for the night," he advised us.

The idea of being stranded on the island appealed to me as I imagined devouring more of Jill's culinary creations. But Patrick was a little more responsible and insisted that we go before it was too late.

With good-byes from everyone and a rough idea of how Jill had made such a fantastic lunch, we walked along the flower-laden path to the shallow, warm water of the dock. I climbed on board our Wave Runner, and Patrick started it up.

We had only gone a hundred feet when I turned to wave good-bye. But it was too late. Surrounded by the coconut palms, Uepi Lodge was lost from sight. Once again, hidden from the world.

VICTORIA ALLMAN has been following her stomach around the globe for ten years as a yacht chef. She writes about her float-ing culinary adventures through Europe, the Caribbean, Nepal, Vietnam, Africa, and the South Pacific in Sea Fare: A Culinary Odyssey: A Chef's Journey Across the Ocean, *available from NorLightsPress.com. Read more of Victoria's food-driven esca-pades by visiting her website, www.victoriaallman.com.*

 Mary, the woman who first tested this in Mexico, goes deep-sea fishing with her husband. She made it with home-canned tuna. The taste was outstanding. I've tried it several times since with one pound equivalent packets of dry-packed yellowfin tuna in water. It worked very well. Victoria tried canned yellowfin tuna and felt the canned was quite satisfactory. Rita winces at this; she made it with tuna from a fish store and loved it. —ma

✧ Jill's Tuna Pie

*Adapted by Victoria Allman from a dish
at Uepi Lodge, Solomon Islands*

SERVES 5 TO 6

1 9-inch pie crust (recipe follows)
2 tablespoons vegetable oil
3 cloves garlic, minced

2   leeks, white part only, sliced thin
1   tablespoon grated fresh ginger root
6   small or 3 large kaffir lime leaves, chopped fine (or zest
    of 2 limes) (If you can't find kaffir lime leaves, or the next
    ingredient, go to www.amazon.com/grocery.)
1   teaspoon sambal olek (hot Indonesian sauce in a jar—
    or substitute any hot sauce)
1   cup chicken stock or white wine
1   can of coconut milk
1   pound yellowfin tuna, diced into 1-inch cubes
1   teaspoon salt
½   cup chopped fresh cilantro
2½ cups mashed potatoes, however you make them
    (leftovers are perfect)

Preheat oven to 350°F.

Bake the pie crust (page 286) for 10 minutes until golden brown. Remove from the oven, and raise oven temperature to 375°F.

In a large heavy skillet, heat the vegetable oil, and sauté the garlic until golden. Add the leeks, and sauté an additional 5 minutes. Add the ginger, lime leaves, sambal olek, and chicken stock or wine. Simmer 5 minutes. Add the coconut milk, and simmer 5 minutes more.

Remove from heat, and add the tuna, salt, and cilantro. Place the tuna mixture in the baked crust, and top with mashed potatoes. Start the mashed potatoes on the outer edge of the circle and work them into the middle.

Bake for 20 minutes, until the coconut milk bubbles under the potatoes.

Serve with sweet chili sauce and a big green salad. Most su-permarkets carry my favorite brand of sweet chile sauce: Mae Ploy. —rgg

✤ Never-Fail Pie Crust

MAKES TWO SINGLE-SHELL, 8- OR 9-INCH PIE CRUSTS

- 2 cups all-purpose white flour
- Pinch of baking powder
- Pinch of salt
- 12 tablespoons hard vegetable shortening (chilled)
- 7 to 8 tablespoons ice water

Combine the flour, baking powder, and salt. Mix the short-ening into the flour mixture with your fingers. Work it in until it is the consistency of rough cornmeal.

Sprinkle with the ice water. *Do not* work the dough. Simply press it together into a ball with the least handling possible. Chilling it is fine but not necessary. Divide in two and roll out on a lightly floured surface. Freeze the extra dough.

Just Call Me Garlic

Carolyn McKibbin

It was my turn to contribute a dish to the communal meal. Every night of my two-week stay at Il Campeggio, a campground in a town called Agerola in the hills above Italy's Amalfi Coast, I had been treated to the best six-, seven-, and eight-course meals of my life. Grilled fish and crustaceans were transported directly from the Mediterranean below to the camp grill, my plate, and then my mouth, day in and day out. Fresh, soft, milky mozzarella from the *formaggeria* down the street complemented explosive tomatoes and pungent basil in my *caprese* salad. Gnocchi disintegrated on my tongue. At the finish, a dainty glass of *limoncello* washed it all down with lemony-sour, sugary-sweet pleasure.

For a foreigner (especially an American), making your first dish for a group of Italians is like performing your first brain surgery: it's no easy feat, and there are possible victims involved. The victim? She would be me. Impressing them with your food is all but impossible. Italians don't need advice on how to dress and certainly not on how to cook. And one more thing: my mom's tuna casserole wasn't going to cut it here. Italians like eating Italian food.

I was twenty, and this was the summer between my sophomore and junior years of college. I had been studying in Siena, in Tuscany, and living with my Italian grandmother, Franca, so that I could improve my language ability. Toward the end of the season my girlfriend Ali and I decided to travel. We ended up in Agerola on a whim. We wanted to go to the southern coast, but low on funds and therefore "auto stopping," as they call hitchhiking, we would go wherever anyone would take us for free.

As we loitered, confused, outside a small train station somewhere beyond Naples, two filthy, smiling men in their rickety Jeep-like vehicle came to our rescue. Our thirtyish male chauffeurs followed a curving, narrow road for a few hours, stopping twice so that they could toke joints in the woods and we could take photos of the shoreline below and Mount Vesuvius above. The ride stopped at Agerola, a tiny town with stray dogs dodging dodgy young men on Vespas, teenagers loitering on street corners, and locals leisurely drinking sparkling water and Campari at lazy outdoor cafés. We soon found one of the few places to stay and certainly the cheapest.

It was getting late in the evening, and the dormitory-style rooms sounded like a five-star hotel to us. The price was right, about eight dollars a night. After a shower and a change of clothes, Ali and I had barely put our sandal-clad feet out of the dorm door when two new men appeared: Giorgio and Davide.

"Ciao, belle. Di dove siete?" Hi, beautiful ladies (Italian men truly are romantic), where are you from? Giorgio, a rotund fiftyish man with shoulder-length black hair, asked. *"Dai, venite con noi!"* Come on, join us!

Quite the trusting travelers, we boarded their red Fiat and went on a drive down the steep, winding road into the towns of Amalfi and Positano below. The lights dotting the curved coast leading southward to Salerno resembled a distant string of glowing pearls. The sky was clear, the breeze warm, the stars bright. That night we ate, drank, danced, practiced our Italian, and met true friends—friends whom I would return to visit in Italy, friends who would come to visit me in Boston.

And so Ali and I stayed. What was to be a few days in Agerola turned into two weeks. Toward the end of our visit I decided I wanted to contribute to the nightly feast, to help the mothers, neighbors, and other campers cook. It looked like fun, and it would be a way to express my gratitude. But what could I make for these innately food-snobby people without making a complete fool of myself?

Franca, my Sienese grandmother, whom I couldn't understand because of her thick, raspy Tuscan accent (an accent tainted by H-sounds muffling the Cs), had introduced me to Italian cooking. She served me every luscious, fresh, tasteful supper out on her warm garden terrace. Olive-oily *bruschette* started every dinner, followed by homemade thin-crust pizzas with tangy *salsa di pomodoro* (tomato sauce), anchovies, and olives. The simplest ingredients, she told me, are what make Italian cooking the best in the world. The dear, muumuu-wearing woman served me as if I were royalty. Not once was I allowed to help make dinner, slice a tomato, boil a spaghetto (one piece of spaghetti), or wash a dish. And I tried—I'm not a heathen. It's just the nature of the Italian mamma to humbly serve her children and guests.

Franca knew I loved her *bruschette*. She explained, but evidently ingredient amounts were lost in translation, what it consisted of: fresh chopped tomatoes and basil from her garden, garlic, salt, and loads of extra-virgin olive oil, harvested locally, of course. All scooped lavishly onto a piece of saltless Tuscan bread. Easy enough, right?

So I thought. My day for cooking arrived, and those five ingredients, or just one of them in particular, were to be my downfall.

In the large bowl the women gave me, I chopped maybe ten or fifteen medium-sized tomatoes (we were usually a big crowd of at least a dozen) and a bouquet of basil. I tossed in a good palmful of salt and drizzled half a liter of olive oil. And because I tend to like garlic (my dad's motto is "Too much garlic is just enough"), I thought a whole head of Dracula's worst enemy would be my best friend. *Mamma mia,* was I wrong.

While all were delighted by my intention, only the little girls were nice enough to eat a whole piece of bread dipped into this garlic-toxic concoction made by the *americana*. The rest of the bunch took one bite and all but spit it out. Okay, so I added a lot of garlic, what was the big deal? *"Hai dovuto mettere uno o due pezzi, non tutto intero!"* Giorgio told me, laughing hysterically, making guttural Neapolitan noises and waving his hands in the air. "You should have added one or two cloves, *not the whole head*!" It was repulsive to them, not bad to me. But what did this hamburger-eating, fast-food-dining American know anyway? (As I'm sure they thought, although I indulge in neither.)

My eternal punishment: I have returned to Il Campeggio several times to visit friends, and because of the garlic incident I shall forever have the nickname "Aglio." I could have handled Bruschetta, but Aglio, the Italian word for garlic, just isn't appetizing.

DON'T LET ANYONE tell you studying a foreign language is a waste. Even though Carolyn McKibbin's degree in Italian studies did little to help her career in Web editing and search engine optimization, when she goes back to the bell paese, *where she studied abroad in college, she is treated like a* principessa. *Speak a foreign language, live in a foreign country, see life through an entirely different perspective. It's an investment in lifelong friendships and a certain enlightenment found only through cultural exchange. You won't regret it. Find Carolyn at www.ideaLaunch.com and contact her at CarolynHMcKibbin@gmail.com.*

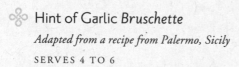

Hint of Garlic *Bruschette*

Adapted from a recipe from Palermo, Sicily

SERVES 4 TO 6

*E*ven a die-hard garlic fan like myself finds these bruschette perfect. —ma

- 12 slices crusty baguette, ½ to 1 inch thick
- 2 to 3 juicy tomatoes, halved
- 6 cloves garlic peeled and cut in half

Good-quality extra-virgin olive oil

- 1 cup of the best-tasting tomatoes you can find, peeled, seeded, and chopped

Coarse-ground sea salt and freshly ground black pepper

Basil leaves, at least 12 large ones

Preheat oven to 485°F.

Toast bread in oven until lightly golden (about 4 minutes).

Remove, and while still warm, rub each slice with a cut tomato half and then with a garlic half.

Pour a layer of olive oil in a saucer, and coat the side rubbed
with the tomato and garlic.

Moisten the chopped tomatoes with a little olive oil, and spoon
them on top of the bread slices.

Season with sea salt and freshly ground pepper.

Top with basil leaves, roughly torn with fingers.

The Café Chapín

Janna Rudler

The Café Chapín is something of a misnomer. *Chapín* is the slang term for Guatemalan people, but the cook is from El Salvador. She is the one who works tirelessly in the kitchen patting out *pupusas* (the national dish of her country), filling tamales, and creating those golden treasures that need no filling—*tamales de elote* (corn).

It doesn't matter, since the place is actually named for its clientele, humble, industrious *guatemaltecos* with ready smiles. They can never forget what they left behind in Guatemala: work-weary and aging parents, younger brothers trying to stay in school, desperate cousins stealing to live, lonely girlfriends trying not to cry on the phone, babies growing up without them. Celebrations come and go without their presence. The dead go to graves without a final goodbye.

The clientele of the Café Chapín can never forget the grinding poverty of their beautiful but violent, beloved but impoverished homeland. It is what sent them to the States looking for work so they can send money back to Guatemala to help sustain their families.

These *guatemaltecos* spend their few free hours in the Café Chapín satisfying their hunger for the familiar music and food that both sharpens the pang of their memories and brings unspoken comfort.

Walking into the café on a lazy Sunday afternoon, I was the cause of much curiosity and the object of hushed questions aimed at my boyfriend, Jaime. The teenage Guatemalan girl behind the counter surprised me by her first, and what I thought oddest, question. "Is she an *American*?" This is a question I have never heard directed at me in my home state of New York. The girl was polite and kind, but her eyes looked directly into mine with unabashed curiosity. Our Mexican companion, Victor, felt as foreign as I did in this little Guatemalan enclave; he stuck close to my side and let our *chapín* friend order for him. The girl was surprised to hear me speak Spanish and further mystified by my familiarity with and enthusiasm for *pupusas*.

Jaime tried to explain to me how exactly the waitress was related to him, but the convoluted lineage was lost on me. He finally summed up his explanation by describing her as a cousin. The two distant cousins exchanged the latest gossip about family both here and back in Guatemala and shared cell phone numbers of several mutual friends and relatives.

Jaime, Victor, and I finally wandered over to the corner jukebox. My homesick Jaime chose the sublime sweet sadness and longing in the deceptively cheerful-sounding strains of a *bachata* song, while Victor satisfied his craving for home with the more buoyant sounds that only *Los Tigres del Norte* can deliver. When our food arrived, we eagerly shared bites with each other, jealously eyeing one another's tamales. Tall glasses of *horchata* (a milky rice-based drink) provided the perfect chaser for each mouthful of our *maiz*-encased Latin American delicacies.

I have found shared meals to be a particularly binding way to promote understanding and camaraderie with my expatriate Latino friends. I basked in the glow of a belonging born of the mutual satisfaction of our different kinds of hunger. Victor iced the cake of togetherness with the type of good-natured jab that always makes me feel even more at home with these guys. He had noticed that I shunned the spicy condiments normally eaten with *pupusas*—a pickled cabbage salad called *curtido* and a pungent orange salsa—in favor of eating them plain.

After trying unsuccessfully to persuade me to eat the *pupusas* the way any self-respecting Latina would, he gave up with an exasperated "*¡Gabacha, aprenda a comer!*" Gringa, learn how to eat!

JANNA RUDLER is an archaeologist by trade and a migrant advocate by her heart's choosing. She writes about the lives of Latina immigrants at http://mariposaenlapared.blogspot.com and is a contributing blogger for http://www.citizenorange.com/orange/. Janna lives in upstate New York.

 Pupusas

Adapted from a traditional recipe

MAKES ABOUT 8 *PUPUSAS*

*S*alvadoreños *are justifiably proud of these masa-based morsels. There's even a National Pupusa Day the second Sunday in November. The cheese-filled ones are the easiest to make* *and very tasty. See the recipe note for other filling ideas. This is a recipe that would be fun to do with kids, and they're bound to enjoy the results. If some of the cheese leaks out, don't worry. It becomes crispy with the cooking and tastes delicious. —ma*

1 cup masa harina, sometimes called corn flour, not corn meal (Masa harina can be found in Latino markets and many supermarkets.)

½ teaspoon salt

Pinch of baking powder

¾ cup warm water (possibly more, to get the right consistency)

1 cup shredded melting cheese, like manchego, mozzarella, farmer's cheese, or queso blanco

¼ to ½ cup minced jalapeños, seeds and veins removed (optional)

Mix together the dry ingredients, and add the water in ¼-cup increments. Stir with a spoon, or mush the dough between your fingers. As you work the dough, it becomes drier. If it cracks when patted out, it is too dry. Sprinkle a bit more water on the dough, and work it in. It should be soft but not too sticky. Let it sit for 5 to 10 minutes.

Combine the cheese and jalapeños to make the filling.

Divide the dough into eight equal balls. Flatten each ball in the palm of your hands. (If the dough sticks, lightly coat your palms with oil.) Using your thumb, gently press down on the center of the dough, working your way outward. The flattened dough will be about the size of your palm. Leave a raised rim ¼-inch all around.

Fill the indentation with 2 tablespoons filling, pushing the filling slightly into the dough.

Press the raised rim together around the filled center, and form
a ball. Roll it in your palms to even out the dough around
the filling. (You might need to rub a bit more water over the
ball to seal the edges.)

Pat the ball lightly between your palms to flatten.

Cut open two sides of a freezer bag. Set the *pupusa* on one side
of the bag, and cover with the other side. In order to flatten the *pupusa*, you will need two cutting boards. Put the
pupusa, covered with the bag, on one board, and press down
lightly with the other. Flatten to a circle ½-inch thick.

Heat a cast-iron griddle, heavy frying pan, or *comal* over
medium-high heat, and rub the surface with a paper towel
dipped in olive oil. Carefully peel back the plastic bag, and
gently set the *pupusa* on the griddle. Cook for 3 to 4 minutes and flip over. Cook for another 3 to 4 minutes. *Pupusas*
should be browned on the outside and slightly moist in the
middle. Serve warm.

....

Pupusas *lend themselves to numerous fillings. Seasoned cooked
pork, cheese, and beans (or combinations) are the traditional
fillings. The meat and beans are usually pureed before using. Be
adventurous. —ma*

....

A Desert Mirage

Maria Altobelli

Paul stomped hard on the brakes, jammed the gearshift into reverse, and pushed the gas pedal to the floor. The car jerked backward, accelerating north in the southbound lane of Mexico's Highway 57.

"What the hell are you doing?" I yelled at my husband. "You'll get us killed!" I swung around to look out the back window, mesmerized by the shape of an eighteen-wheeler barreling toward us.

Paul swung off the highway. "Hey, I saw a sign. If they're advertising Fanta, they gotta have beer."

I sat immobile, staring straight ahead, waiting for the semi to whoosh by. Paul draped his arm over the seat back, giving my shoulder a squeeze. "See? No big deal, Ducky. We had plenty of time."

Taros, our German shepherd cross, panted in the backseat, oblivious, squeezed in between our camping gear and bags of dog food.

It was June 1972.

Paul shut off the ignition. I turned my head and saw a thatched roof supported by skinny wooden poles covering a hard-packed dirt floor. Metal card tables with the semivisible words *Cerveza Corona* painted on the corners and an assortment of folding chairs (some with the red and white Coca-Cola logo peeking through the rust) littered the compound. I thought the place abandoned. Off to the side, a primitive shack made from wood slabs, tarpaper, and corrugated metal looked as if it had been blown together by the dry desert wind.

A couple emerged from the shack.

Both had the lean, leathery look of people exposed to years of hard work in the desert sun and wind. He wore a faded shirt, dusty jeans, and scuffed cowboy boots and squinted at us from under the brim of a sweat-stained sombrero. The woman wore a simple red, short-sleeved blouse that hung outside her conservative dark blue skirt.

"We're going to look like freaks," I muttered as we got out of the car. After all, we could have been the poster couple for Haight-Ashbury hippiedom. The couple's eyes went from Paul's long hair, bushy beard, and scruffy clothes down to his leather sandals, and over to my sandals. They winced at the ridiculous long skirt I had purchased after reading a guidebook's advice. Their gaze skimmed over my bralessness and settled on Taros.

The dog had the highest approval rating.

"Buenas tardes. ¿Ustedes están abiertos los domingos?" Three years in Bolivia in the Peace Corps gave Paul's polite greeting and the question about being open Sundays a nice zing. Three years at the University of Minnesota gave me a knowledge of the Golden Century of Spanish Literature and nothing whatsoever in the way of conversational skills.

Yes, they were open. Yes, Paul could get his beer. They

looked at me and waited. *I'll have a beer as well,* almost slipped out before I figured I'd better follow the 1970 guidebook's advice about women drinking in public. "I'll have a Fanta, I guess." No way could Mexico's version of orange soda pop compare to a frosty beer, but I figured I'd try to play by the rules our first time in the country.

The beer came out of an ice-filled chest; the beads of condensation on the bottle attested to its coldness. I watched Paul lift the bottle to his lips and could almost taste the cool bubbly liquid sliding down his throat. My Fanta came out of a plastic container only partially shaded by a shrub. The warm, orange syrup stuck to the roof of my mouth, and I swallowed over and over to get rid of the sweet taste.

Introductions took place with multiple handshakes. With my limited Spanish, I could understand the guy's name was Fulgencio and his wife's, Esperanza. Paul always welcomed the opportunity for a conversation, so he motioned to Fulgencio to sit down at the table with us. Esperanza hovered off to the side until her husband signaled for her to sit down with us as well.

An expert at luring country people into conversation after his stint in Bolivia, it didn't take Paul long to get an animated conversation going. I sat and listened, trying to focus on any words sounding a bit like English. I heard "Costa Rica" and figured Paul was relaying the final destination for our summer-long camping trip. Here and there I extracted an actual word or a phrase and felt a fleeting smugness before my attention wandered again. In one of these attention gaps I noticed a couple of pickups off in the distance.

My interest perked as they slowed and turned into the compound, wheels spitting gravel. A boisterous group of men climbed out.

I eyed the expensive belt buckles, the new sombreros, and the quantity of grilled chicken they brought and raised my eyebrows at Paul.

"Local ranch owners," he muttered while Fulgencio and Esperanza excused themselves and bustled about supplying piles of fresh-made tortillas, bowls of roasted chiles, and unlimited beer. The men ate, drank, and laughed. Every so often they cast curious glances at the two of us.

In between beers and tortillas, Fulgencio and Esperanza returned to our table and continued their conversation with Paul while keeping a watchful eye on the men. Fulgencio jumped up often and ran to replenish the beers, and Esperanza disappeared from time to time into the shack to make more tortillas.

Bottles of Victoria continued to appear long after the chicken and tortillas were gone, and the men soon entered the gregarious stage of drunk.

One in the group stumbled over to our table, lager in hand, and sat down. He ignored the couple and talked to Paul. Fulgencio and Esperanza sat immobile, lips set in a rigid line and hands clasped together, knuckles almost white. In piecemeal fashion I caught the Spanish words for *pigs, animals,* and *dead.* At one point he looked at the couple, turned, and spat on the ground.

Paul's rapid-fire Spanish comment prevented me from even a glimmer of understanding. Fulgencio and Esperanza relaxed their clenched hands, and the slightest of smiles broke the tight line of their mouths. The rancher paused and tilted his head. I thought he was deciding if he had been insulted or not and if a fight needed to be fought. Paul made another comment, and the man laughed and pounded Paul on the back before weaving back to his cronies.

"Whatcha say? Come on! Whatcha say?" I whispered to Paul.

"Shhh!" he hissed.

Damn! I gotta learn Spanish.

Whatever Paul had said made Fulgencio very happy. He asked us something, and Paul smiled and nodded.

"What'd he say?"

"Nothing. Just wants to know if we're hungry."

I knew Paul's answer—this was a man who was always hungry. But for me, the question presented what I thought to be a life-and-death decision. The same guidebooks that advised wearing long skirts and drinking warm soda pop, also warned about the possible hazards of all food except soup. Like the naïve tourist I was, I resorted to a set guidebook phrase: "*¿Hay sopa?*"

Fulgencio smiled even broader. He and his wife disappeared into the shack.

"What is going on?" I asked Paul. "Are they bringing us food? Is it soup? What should we do? Can we eat here? Are we going to get sick?"

Paul acquired the beatific expression of a man about to be fed and said nothing. I paled as Fulgencio and Experanza set down a plate of meat, a pile of hot tortillas wrapped in an embroidered cloth, a bowl of salt, and a larger bowl of roasted chiles on the table. The couple stood by waiting for us to eat. A clear choice—refuse to eat and insult our hosts or eat this dubious concoction and promptly die. Or at least invite a horde of intestinal villains into my system.

Seeing Paul reach for the food, I tentatively followed suit. The meat was tasty and succulent.

Fulgencio nodded at the table. "*Cabrito. Muy bueno, ¿no?*"

Paul muttered to me around a mouthful of food. "Goat."

The tortillas had the toasted, substantial taste of corn

roasted over a fire. I closed my eyes and savored those tortillas, the salty, grilled flavor of the crispy goat meat, and the burning heat of the chiles.

After eating, we took Taros for a walk down the dusty dirt road.

"C'mon. Tell me what you said back there to the rancher."

"It was no big deal. There are tons of double entendres in Spanish. Fulgencio took the words to be a dig against the rancher, as I intended. It could have gotten nasty, but I lucked out. The rancher took it as a joke. That's it. The words just slipped out."

Paul grinned and poked me with his elbow. "Besides, it doesn't translate. You'll just have to learn Spanish. I am surprised, though."

"What? That the guy didn't start a fight?"

"No. The meal. I figured Esperanza might offer tortillas and beans. But goat? How often do you think those two eat goat? I bet they gave us their Sunday afternoon *comida*. And it's probably the only time during the week they eat meat."

I kept quiet and thought how close I had come to letting my fear make me refuse the food.

 ### Crema Poblano Mistongo

From Susi Santiago

SERVES 4

No wonder guidebooks teach the phrase ¿Hay sopa? *Soups in Mexico are universally wonderful.* Sopa de tortilla, caldo Tlalpeño, *and Michoacán's* sopa Tarasca *are just a few of the great mixtures. Here's another from Restaurante Mistongo, Pátzcuaro.*
—*ma*

2   poblano chiles, chopped

1   Roma or other small tomato, chopped

¼   onion, chopped

1   tablespoon salted butter

1   small can of corn, drained (just under ⅔ cup)

½   quart chicken stock

½   quart whole milk

Salt and freshly ground black pepper to taste

Toasted bread rounds or croutons

Sauté 1 chile, the tomato, and the onion in the butter.

Put the corn and the remaining chile in a blender with the chicken stock, and blend. Add the mixture to the sautéed ingredients. Simmer for 10 to 15 minutes. Add the milk, and simmer gently to thicken.

Add salt and pepper. (Make sure to taste before adding salt. If the chicken stock is made from dry bouillon cubes or powder, it might be salty enough.)

Serve with toasted bread rounds or croutons.

I've blended a whole can of corn, drained (a little more than one cup), with the chicken stock for a heartier soup. I've also used extra poblano chiles. But then I love poblanos. —ma

Cow Feet Soup for Breakfast

Karen van der Zee

The most interesting items for sale in an Armenian food market are cow hooves. To me, they appear to be a rather inedible substance, but I am wrong. I learn they're the essential ingredient for making *khash:* cow feet soup.

Khash is not just any soup. It's Armenian soul food. An ancient traditional dish, originally poor-people food, cow feet soup has now been elevated to gourmet status, and the Armenians go into raptures over it. Eating *khash* is an event, a party, an experience. It's eaten early in the morning in the winter months, consumed with copious amounts of vodka. Foreigners will say this is the only way to get it down and keep it down.

The stories I've heard about *khash* have been interesting. The Armenians revere and adore it and the foreigners revile and abhor it. But there are exceptions. My friend Yulia, a true Armenian, detests the stuff.

"Karen-jahn, it's disgusting," she tells me succinctly.

Khash is prepared from what was left over from the cow after the good stuff had been used by the monied folks. What goes into the *khash* then are the hooves and the stomach. These take days of soaking in water and scraping with knives to clean properly, and many hours of cooking.

One cold February day I too must experience this winter ritual of eating cow feet soup. My husband and I have been invited to a *khash* party to celebrate a friend's birthday. For more than two years now a *khash* invitation has eluded me. Most expats will find this a lucky circumstance. But since there are those who believe you are not allowed out of the country without having attended, at least once, a *khash* party, I might as well approach the inevitable invitation with a sense of adventure.

We meet several of the partygoers at a convenient location in town, and together we set off on foot toward the *khash* venue. We turn down an arched alley, slosh through the slushy snow, and make a few turns behind and around dilapidated buildings, past overflowing garbage containers being raided by skinny cats, and end up in front of a big gray gloomy Soviet block of flats. Inside we find a private apartment that has been set up as a commercial eating place by a venturesome woman. Her food is very good, it is said, but she only feeds people by prior arrangement.

It looks like a roomy place from what I know Soviet-style apartments to be and might actually be two apartments that have been combined. In the living room a long table is set and ready with plates of pickles, fresh herbs, sliced large radishes, bread, dishes of salt, and chopped garlic. And of course the usual forest of soft drinks, wine, brandy, and vodka bottles.

As soon as we sit down, somebody reaches for the vodka and pours all around. It's just after ten in the morning. I'm sitting next to Arson who helps me to some water as well.

Toasting begins immediately, a *bari luis* (good light) to all, and down goes the vodka. I sip a careful drop, realizing that this is a new experience for me; I've never had strong alcohol so early in the day.

I take in my surroundings while munching on radish slices. The windows are decorated with elaborately draped forest-green curtains festooned with a fringe of gold tassels. The tablecloth is green too. Paintings decorate the walls, from brownish bucolic scenes in ornate frames to a bare-breasted maiden with happy nipples. A piano stands quietly in a corner. In another corner a seating arrangement with heavy sofas and chairs invites lingering. It all looks rather cozy in a very old-fashioned way, sort of what your great-grandparents might have had in the early part of the last century—minus the naked nymph perhaps. However, this is the new millennium, and to prove it there's a state-of-the-art silver CD player looking anachronistic in the old-world room. Next to it, a stack of CDs that someone has brought is ready and waiting. There must be music, of course. And dancing, naturally. This is an Armenian party.

Khash arrives, in bowls the size of the Caspian Sea. I study the soup in front of me with trepidation. It's colorless and greasy and has a white, flabby piece of gelatinous cow foot in it. I take a spoonful of the broth and taste it. Nothing. No flavor worth mentioning. I'm not sure if I'm disappointed or relieved.

"You've never had *khash* yet?" Arson asks, surprised, and I tell him no.

He hands me a dish of salt and a spoon. "You must put salt in it," he says.

No kidding. I put in a couple of heaping spoonfuls.

"And garlic." A dish with smashed garlic appears in front of my nose. I avail myself of a generous amount. Maybe there is hope yet.

"Now you take the meat out and put it on your plate and cover it up with *lavash* to keep it warm."

I'm all for liberating my sea of soup from that white flabby stuff—if that is what is called meat. I don't see meat, but they've got to call it something. I do as instructed and take a fresh sheet of *lavash,* a very thin wrap-bread, and cover the glob up real good.

"Why do we do that?" I ask.

"Because it's the best part, and we save it for last."

I smile politely. "Okay."

"Now you take the dry pieces of *lavash* and put as much as you can get into the soup."

A bowl on the table holds a pile of dry *lavash,* broken into small pieces. People are grabbing them by the handful and dropping them in their soup, the way Americans use oyster crackers. So I follow suit.

There is another toast, but I miss what this one is about as I am watching, transfixed, as the bread sops up the soup, turning it into a gloppy, greasy, gray mess. I raise my glass, clink it all around, and take a fortifying gulp of vodka.

So here I am, spooning in the bread soaked with grease and broth and garlic, practically feeling my arteries clogging up. It tastes fine—salty, garlicky, bready—and greasy.

Everybody eats with gusto, some of the men emptying the enormous bowls as if they were starved desert nomads. Several of them get seconds. And all the while there's the toasting and the downing of vodka. At ten and eleven in the morning.

"Don't worry," says Arson next to me. "The hoof fat in the soup coats the stomach and makes it possible to drink a lot of vodka."

Is this good news? I'm not sure. But people are certainly enjoying themselves.

"You need to try some of the meat," Arson tells me several toasts later.

Lifting a corner of the sheet of *lavash,* I cut off a piece of the quivering white jelly stuff pretending to be meat. I put it in my mouth. It tastes like soft quivering jelly stuff. I spoon in some more garlicky bread soup. I have another sip of vodka, stomach weighted down with *khash.* But dancing is what you do, always, no matter how full your stomach or how little the floor space.

"Why is *khash* always eaten in the morning?" I ask Sona, who sits across from me.

"Because it takes all day to digest," she says promptly. *Well, there's that.*

But it isn't only the *khash* that needs digesting. When finally people have eaten to their soul's content, the bowls are taken away, and it is announced that we should go entertain ourselves until the *khorovats* is ready.

My husband and I look at each other, horror stricken. *Khorovats?* After this, these *khash*-gorgers have room for barbecued meat?

Yes. But not right away, because they haven't even started the fire yet outside in the barbecue. Someone is playing the piano, and people huddle close and sing sad, melancholy songs about the beauty of Armenia and the soldiers who have died and the loss of Mount Ararat. Then another CD is put on, and some people start to dance. Others play cards, or backgammon, all the while drinking to keep their spirits up until the next sad song. Apparently, people are settling in to feast away the whole day. Along with the cigarette smoke, conviviality fills the air.

And we thought we were having breakfast.

Soul Food

Melanie Ehler

When I was a child, my nana would take me along to the Old Reg'lar Baptist meetings at her church. Full of good-hearted people, we had a much higher preacher-to-sinner ratio than your average church. The Old Reg'lar Baptist meetings generally went through three or four different preachers during the same service, and the sermons often lasted several hours.

To a kid, they seemed interminable, as infinite as salvation itself, though not nearly so sweet. Most Sunday mornings I would busy myself in ways other than spiritual. First I would rearrange the contents of my nana's patent-leather purse, eating all the interred peppermints and circus peanuts. Then I'd lean back in exaggerated repose and vigorously wave one of the church's paper fans, overly enthusiastic in my attempt to be mistaken for a Southern belle. The fans were the old-fashioned paddle-type that had a vibrant biblical scene on one side with the name of a funeral home underneath it. The message seemed to be *Just because Lazarus was revived after four days, it doesn't mean you'll be. Buy your coffin early.*

I would interrupt my fanning five or six times to make trips to the drinking fountain. All these activities never took up more than fifteen minutes. Once I'd gone through my routine, I'd stretch out on one of the wooden pews for a nice long nap. My casual attitude provoked a story that still circulates in my family. Upon being asked how I liked church, I purportedly answered in a peevish tone of voice, "It's fine for the most part, but the preachers keep waking me up when they holler 'Amen!' "

At any rate, for somnolent sinners and for attentive saints, a certain earthly reward was attached to the church meetings, and that was the church supper. All the good ladies of that church knew how to cook, and they did not waste their talents doling out dainty portions of haute cuisine. No, these soft-bellied, gentle souls served up homey foods, comfort foods, soul food, every Sunday creating a sumptuous spread that covered three fold-out tables. Immediately following the service, a line of people gathered in front of those tables. The prayer that was given before supper was always the shortest one.

Not even the everlastingest preacher could ignore the tables laden with home-cooked food. There were mashed potatoes piled in high, snowy peaks, sitting side by side with thick pools of gravy; there were mounds of dandelion and turnip greens picked fresh from the nearby woods and gardens. There were tureens of red beans in savory sauce; there were round cakes of golden-grained cornbread and white cornpone. On occasion, there was turkey with stuffing or dumplings bobbing in gravy. And there was fried chicken. Always and forever, there was fried chicken, a crowd pleaser that just about everybody piled on their plates.

And so it was, many years later as a graduate student, living far from the comforts of home, alone and hungry and perhaps a bit homesick, that I got a hankering for fried chicken. Now, in those lean years, meat of any sort was not a regular part of my diet. I was supported solely by the money garnered from my assistantship. As per the usual assistantship tradeoff, in return for teaching freshman classes, the university paid my full tuition, along with a bit extra to cover living expenses—so long as said living expenses didn't include luxury items such as heat in my room or more than one meal a day.

I lived on the thin of things, always on the fringe of hunger. I existed on a diet that consisted chiefly of bananas and cereal moistened by water.

Upon occasion, I would see fit to reallocate my meager food budget. That is to say, I would sometimes spend my grocery money on admission to a local swing dance. After such occasions I would, from necessity, scavenge samples at the local grocer's for my next meal. Whatever food samples were being offered, I would take two, sly vulture that I was, and after circulating the store twice, my stomach would be full, or at least it would stop growling for a few hours. I certainly had nothing in my budget that would allow for eating out, not even at the most humble establishment.

Yet there I was, this one particular day, hungry as could be; and nothing could divert my mind from fried chicken. I could not make fried chicken—my cuisine art was limited to microwave food and toast—and so, with little-exercised extravagance, I went into a local diner.

"How many pieces are in the adult portion of chicken?" I asked the waitress. "Five pieces," she answered. "And in the small?" I asked. "Three," she responded.

I did not need to finger the money in my pocket to know

how much I had. The thing with being poor was that I always knew, down to the last cent, how much money I owned. I had enough for the large portion, unless they charged tax. I could never remember if restaurants charged tax, and then there was also the embarrassment of leaving a cheap, nearly nonexistent tip.

"I'll have the small portion," I said in a tiny voice. Perhaps my eyes looked hungry. I might have also sighed.

When the waitress brought me the plate, it was heaped with fried chicken. It did not contain three pieces, or even five pieces—it brimmed with ten pieces of chicken, all coated in a crisp, peppered golden skin and, as I found out by sampling, with tender white meat inside. Thin curls of steam rose from the chicken. I ate and ate and ate. I ate that hot, delicious chicken until I was full, and then—oh, unheard-of luxury—I kept going and ate past being full. Even so, I couldn't manage to eat all the chicken. I carefully wrapped the remaining pieces in paper napkins and discreetly deposited them in my purse. They would be for tomorrow. When I got the bill, the total cost was listed as $3.99, the price for a child-size portion.

I was too embarrassed to thank my waitress properly. I just smiled shyly when paying, hoping she'd understand. Some hunger can be satisfied with food, but there is also another, more intimate type of hunger that can only be appeased by kindness. I was filled that day with both food and compassion. I've never felt more full. And I've never been richer.

MELANIE EHLER has paddled a gondola down Venice's Grand Canal, fallen asleep during a root canal, and eaten at Burger King when they ran out of burgers. She has danced the tango in Prague, the blues in St. Louis, and the lindy hop everywhere from grocery aisles in Ohio to cocktail clubs in Oahu. Several years after obtaining her master's degree in English, she decided to spend a year living in Seoul, South Korea, and from there she will circumnavigate the globe. Follow Melanie's most recent adventures at http://odysseusdrifts.blogspot.com.

✂ Grandma's Fried Chicken
(What else, after a story like this?)

From Jean Allen

SERVES 4 TO 6

---

1 frying chicken, cut up (or pieces of breast, thighs, and legs)

1 cup milk or buttermilk

1 to 2 large eggs

1½ cups all-purpose flour (more if needed)

Pinch of cayenne pepper, to taste

Onion powder, to taste

Garlic powder, to taste

Salt and freshly ground pepper, to taste

Vegetable oil or shortening

Cover the chicken pieces with the milk or buttermilk, and put them in the refrigerator for a couple hours.

Combine the dry ingredients.

In a shallow bowl, whisk an egg with a bit of water. Depending on how many pieces of chicken you are using, you may need another egg.

Place 2 or 3 chicken pieces into a paper or plastic bag with the flour mixture, shake and remove. Dip the chicken pieces into the egg mixture, then put them back into the flour and shake gently. Place the chicken on a rack and let it sit for at least ½ hour to let the coating adhere. If you are not cooking the coated chicken pieces within 30 minutes, put them into the refrigerator.

Preheat oven to 250°F.

In a heavy cast-iron skillet or other heavy-bottomed pan, heat 1 to 2 inches vegetable oil or shortening to 350°F. If you prefer, use a deep-fat fryer and follow fryer directions.

Using tongs, lower the chicken pieces into the hot fat, being careful of spatters. Do not crowd them. Cook until one side is done, then carefully turn using tongs. Cook the chicken pieces until they are golden brown and have reached an internal temperature of 165°F, or when pierced with a fork, the juices run clear. Carefully remove the chicken from the skillet and drain it on brown paper or paper towels.

Keep warm in the oven until ready to serve.

If you prefer, brine the chicken pieces. Make a brine by dissolving 2 tablespoons salt in 2 quarts water with 1 teaspoon sugar (optional). Leave the chicken in brine in the refrigerator for 2 hours. Rinse pieces and pat dry with paper towels. The brining will make the chicken breast much more moist. —ja

✤ Baked Beans

Adapted from a traditional recipe

SERVES 8 TO 10

---

2 cups dry white medium-size beans (will yield 5 to 6 cups cooked beans)

1 teaspoon salt

½ pound thick, very lean bacon, cut in 1-inch pieces

1 onion, finely diced

2 to 3 cloves garlic, minced

½ cup ketchup or barbecue sauce (add a little hot sauce if desired)

¼ cup (packed) dark brown sugar

2 tablespoons maple syrup

1 tablespoon Worcestershire sauce

1 teaspoon dry mustard

Freshly ground black pepper, to taste

Cover the beans with hot water and soak them for 1 to 2 hours. Drain, and cover the beans with several inches of fresh water. Simmer the beans 1 to 2 hours or until quite soft but still holding their shape. Add 1 teaspoon of salt after 1 hour of simmering. Drain the beans, and reserve the liquid.

Preheat oven to 350°F.

Layer the beans in a casserole with the bacon, onion, and garlic. If the bacon is fatty, cook it briefly to render off some of the fat.

Mix together the ketchup or barbecue sauce, sugar, syrup, Worcestershire, and mustard. Pour it over the beans, adding enough bean liquid to cover. Make sure the beans do not come to the top of the casserole or the sauce will bubble over.

Cover the casserole, and bake it for 3 to 4 hours. Stir every 30 minutes or so, adding more bean liquid when needed.

Taste after 2 hours. If you want to spike up the flavor, add more ketchup, mixed with the other five ingredients (about half the amounts listed).

The beans will absorb much of the liquid during cooking. Make sure to add more of the bean-cooking liquid to ensure they do not dry out.

I like to cook the dry beans with quartered onions, peeled garlic cloves, peppercorns, and fresh sage leaves. Make sure to add salt only after the beans are soft and then simmer ½ hour more. Adding salt at the beginning of the cooking time makes for tough beans. —ma

Maasai Moments

Rita Golden Gelman

We see six giraffes, four ostriches, and three leaping dik-dik antelope that are only fourteen inches high during the three-hour ride to the *boma*. The lions and elephants disappeared years ago from this part of Tanzania, but hundreds of weaver birds and their basket nests, dozens of termite hills (some taller than the car), and thousands of white, yellow, and blue butterflies are still very much there. And so are the "splendid starlings," birds whose coloring can match the peacock in a contest for shimmering, iridescent beauty. The landscape has a spectral magnificence, dry and brown and seemingly endless.

I had been invited to spend two days in a traditional Maasai homestead called a *boma*. My friend Alais, whose family I have been living with for several months, keeps his cows and goats at the *boma*. He is driving our borrowed car over bumpy dirt roads, and I share the excitement he feels as we go deeper and deeper into the bush.

But before we get too deep, let me tell you how we met.

One of the questions I'm most often asked is *How do you find the families you stay with?*

My moving into Alais's home came about in a wonderfully serendipitous way. I was in Seattle, Washington, visiting my daughter, just before I left for a working visit to the international school in Arusha, Tanzania. A week before my flight, I gave a talk at Plymouth Church in downtown Seattle and mentioned my upcoming adventure.

The day after my talk I got an e-mail from a woman who had been in the audience. She wrote that she was active in an organization called EarthCorps, which works on environmental projects in the area. Young people come to Seattle from all over the world to learn about protecting the environment and to develop leadership skills that they can take home and share. One of the foreign visitors last year, she wrote, was Alan, a young man from Tanzania. "He was here for a year and a half, and we all loved him. He's back in Tanzania now. You might like to get in touch with him." She gave me his e-mail, and I wrote immediately asking him if perhaps we could have dinner when I arrived.

He wrote back to say he would be happy to have dinner and talk to me about his country. Then he asked, "What are your intentions while you are here?" I replied that after my two weeks at the school, I wanted to move to a village, live with a family, and learn some Swahili.

He answered immediately. "My parents can't wait for you to arrive." And that was how I met Alais and Judith, and Alan's two brothers and two sisters. They are Maasai.

Alais grew up in a *boma*. These days he lives in a house in a transitional Maasai village in the northeastern part of Tanzania. There is no electricity in his village, but Alais is an optimist; when he built his house, he had it fully wired. Every room has a light switch—ready and waiting for the day when electricity arrives!

The *boma* we are about to visit is the home of three adults, three young men under twenty-five, and an assortment of children. One of the adults is Mama Nanyori, the sixth wife of Alais's deceased father. The other two are a couple, friends of Alais. The three youths are *morani* (warriors), who are certain to be wrapped in their red (with black or blue) plaid blankets called *shukas*. Alais tells me that the *morani* take the goats and cattle out to graze early every morning and bring them home at the end of the day.

A traditional *boma* is a multihousehold compound that is circled by a three- or four-foot-deep fence of acacia branches, pressed tightly together. It's virtually impenetrable by human or animal. Every branch, and there are thousands, is covered with thorns that resemble rose thorns—and spines that look and feel like porcupine quills.

Most *bomas* have a separate entrance through the fence for each family that lives inside, and a traditional order to the living arrangements. In this polygamous culture, wife number one lives with her children on the right of the entrance, wife number two on the left, and then right and left again, until there are no more wives.

Alais's father had eight wives and forty-eight children. But today Alais lives with his only wife, Judith, in a house, in the predominantly Maasai town of Longido, in the northeastern part of Tanzania. Two of his five children are in high school; the other two have graduated and gone on to study further. With parental encouragement, they have all learned to speak English.

Alais's roots are deep in the Maasai culture, but he dresses in modern clothes, speaks English well, and is a community leader. His main concern is figuring out how to preserve the Maasai culture while bringing his people into the twenty-first century. He knows that the traditions and vitality of the Maasai culture are in danger of disappearing.

I spend the hours in our borrowed car asking questions and trying to take notes while bouncing over the bumps and the holes in the dirt roads. I ask about wives and cows, and rites and responsibilities. Alais seems pleased to be teaching me about his people, and I am thrilled to have this time alone with him.

"There it is," says Alais after we have been driving for several hours. And rising out of the dry, brown landscape is the *boma*. We park under a tree and go through the acacia-wall entrance. None of the adults is home, just a couple of children.

Mama Nanyori lives here. She is the mother of Nanyori, a fourteen-year-old who lives with Alais when she is not away at a Lutheran boarding school. Nanyori is beautiful, smart, and funny. I've grown to love her. This will be the first time I've met her mother who has gone off this morning to the mountains with a donkey to get water, a job that will take her many hours. There was no way to let her know we were coming with water.

We walk into the empty acacia-fence enclosure that later will be filled with goats and cattle. The people in a *boma* live side by side with the animals. During the day the animals graze far from home; only the cattle and goat dung and thousands of flies and fleas remain.

Dozens of flies cluster on the oiled skin of the kids, on their mouths, on their eyelids, on their bodies. The flies are more than an annoyance; they cause eye infections and diarrhea.

What seem like hundreds are circling and settling on me. Unlike the kids who appear not to notice them, I swish them away, but they come right back.

As Alais shows me the huts and explains who lives where, I look at his face. He appears peaceful here. His life has taken him far from his roots, but a part of him is obviously still comfortable with the *boma* part of himself.

At the end of the afternoon, Mama Nanyori arrives with the water—and the cows and goats arrive shortly after her.

Alais decides that we will eat one of his goats for dinner. We are standing surrounded by the animals in the enclosure in the middle of the *boma* when Alais turns to me. "Choose one," he says. I laugh. No way am I going to play God and decide who shall live and who shall die. Alais chooses.

The *morani* are in charge of killing the goat. They do it by suffocating him. Two *morani* hold the legs and the third holds the nose. There are a few minutes of twitching, and then the animal is still.

The skinning and butchering are bloody. More than once blood accumulates in the carcass and one of the *morani* leans over and drinks it. When the heart is taken out, one of the young warriors squeezes the blood into a glass and drinks. One of my rules of the road is to eat or drink everything I'm offered; I am thankful I'm not offered a sip.

Dinner is goat meat, cooked over a fire. The men sit in one hut and get the choicest pieces. Women and children eat in a separate hut and chew diligently on the fringe cuts. If there were old people, I'm told, they would get the liver because they might not have teeth. Because of my status as a visitor and guest of Alais, I sit with the men.

The meat is delicious, moist and chewy. It is a treat for all.

Livestock is rarely eaten. Milked, yes, but killed for food—only on special occasions. A Maasai man's wealth is determined by his cattle and his goats.

On the way over I had asked Alais how he happened to leave the traditional life. He explained that Julius Nyerere, the first president of Tanzania who had been a teacher, asked every Maasai family to send one boy to school. Alais was the one chosen in his family. He was a star pupil and ended up a trained veterinarian, a concerned and aware young man, and a devout Christian. Until he went off to a missionary-founded school, he did not even know what Christianity was. Today at his home in Longido, there are prayers before every meal and four-part-harmony hymns before bed. I love the resonance of the harmonizing voices and join in enthusiastically, reading the Swahili words by lantern light.

Religion is a living, active element in Alais's home. But when we are in the *boma,* it is clear that Alais, standing among his sixty goats and twenty cows, sitting on a low stool talking with his friend, or eating roasted goat meat with his fingers, is very much "at home" in the *boma.*

I sleep that night in Mama Nanyori's hut, on a hard goatskin-over-board bed. (I wake up with hundreds of flea bites that plague me for the next week.) I have displaced the three *morani* who usually sleep there. Mama, a beautiful woman still in her thirties, is up before dawn, milking the goats and cows before they go off for the day; cooking *uji,* a porridge of cornmeal, goat milk, and sugar; and getting ready for the day's tasks. Maasai women build the houses, make the fences, patch the problems, care for the children, fetch the water, chop the firewood, and cook.

In many *bomas,* kids between five and ten take the animals

out for the day. Here, in the absence of young boys in that age group, the *morani* tend to the animals. Traditionally it is the job of *morani* warriors to protect the *boma* from lions and marauding groups of cattle stealers. But there are rarely lions around anymore; and cattle stealing, at least in Tanzania, is rare. Kenya to the north still has problems.

Wherever you go in Tanzania, the *morani,* all young men between fifteen and twenty-five, spend a lot of time primping and parading and flirting and sleeping with young uncircumcised girls. They are proud and handsome, and they know it.

Mostly what the elder men do is talk, make family decisions while swishing the flies away with fly-swishers (the long-hair tails of cows attached to sticks), and discuss and solve tribal problems.

The traditional Maasai culture does not much respect the value of schooled education. The Maasai believe that skills learned at school have little to do with the life skills needed by the young men and women. Some of the boys attend school, but rarely the girls.

The three *morani* in our *boma* have been brought in by Alais and his friend to take care of the animals. They are young, lean, and very good-looking. We joke a little in mime, and I debate whether to break the tranquil scene by introducing the bubbles and balloons I have brought with me. There are a bunch of pretty serious kids running around, covered but unbothered by hundreds of flies, kids who would have fun chasing bubbles and taking balloon animals to their hut. Yeah, why not?

I show the kids how to blow bubbles, and they learn quickly and laugh while they blow and chase the bubbles. I teach the *morani* how to make balloon animals and let them present their creations to the kids. The flies have not gone away, but now there is laughter.

As we are blowing bubbles, an elder from another *boma* stops to watch. He observes for a while, standing straight and tall and dignified in his red and black *shuka*. After a while I hand him the wand and the bottle of soapy liquid. Never once losing his dignity, he slowly blows one masterpiece after another while the kids run about shrieking with glee and chasing his ephemeral creations.

We are there for two nights. I would like to stay longer, but Alais has a meeting in his village of Longido, a meeting that will discuss how to preserve the Maasai culture. Over the years, grazing lands have been diminishing as national parks serving safari tourists have taken them over. Once the Maasai were exclusively pastoralists; now they have to learn to plant corn and other crops. The Maasai have been pushed and squeezed into smaller and smaller areas, much like indigenous people all over the world. There are Maasai customs such as female circumcision and polygamy that are not a very good fit with growing Christianity. School education, long considered a dangerous and worthless endeavor for Maasai kids, is being reassessed. Educated Maasai like Alais and Judith are thinking about how lessons learned in school can be tailored to the customs of the tribe.

Alais leaves the *boma* with thoughts of his upcoming meeting racing about in his head. Which customs must be kept in order to preserve the culture? Which must be eliminated so that the tribe will survive in the twenty-first century? What new skills must the Maasai learn to protect themselves and their tribe, not from lions, but from modernization?

I applaud Alais and men like him whose bodies and souls

have moved to another place but whose roots and sensitivities are still very much with their brothers and sisters in the *boma*. I am thankful to Alais for having brought me into the heart of his people, and I feel honored to have shared a small piece of the beautiful and threatened world of the Maasai people.

Afterword

I hope you enjoyed your varied journeys with our authors. Many thanks for buying *Female Nomad and Friends*. Thanks in advance from Lal Singh, Gulshan, Roshan, Mukesh, Paramlal, Haridas, Pramod, Bablu, Sukhpal, Sunil, Ram Devi, Pushpa, and Shoba, and from the hundreds, maybe even thousands, of young men and women and their families whose lives your book purchases will profoundly enrich.

I wish you and your families numerous opportunities to connect and learn around the world as the authors here have done. Your life will be richer, your perspective broader, and you will feel a new sense of yourself and your place in the world.

Interacting across cultures creates a unique kind of joy that can come only when borders are crossed, meals are shared, smiles are exchanged—and hearts connect.

Before you go, I'd like to share with you my current passion. I'm deeply involved in a national movement called LET'S GET GLOBAL (www.letsgetglobal.org). Its mission is to dramatically increase the number of U.S. youth who spend time living in other cultures. Spending a year in a village somewhere changes lives forever—even a few weeks can make a dramatic difference. Young people who are fortunate enough to experience other cultures return with a new way of seeing the world and themselves. If we encourage and assist our youth to go abroad, we will soon have a population that has shared games and laughter and songs across cultures, and we will have made a major move toward peace and understanding in the world.

If you would like to join the LET'S GET GLOBAL movement to make the "international experience" a popular practice among the youth in our country, contact us at info@letsgetglobal.org.

Much love and best wishes for wonderful journeys,

Rita Golden Gelman

Acknowledgments

Female Nomad and Friends is the culmination of the work and effort of many people. We would especially like to thank Victor Velazquez at VIX Solutions in Pátzcuaro, Mexico (www.vix.com.mx) for being the computer guru for the manuscript and especially for formatting the illustrations done by Jean Allen. Without both Victor's and Jean's help and support throughout the project, the book would look nothing like it does.

And without the devoted cooks and tasters in Mexico, the United States, and Australia, and especially Victoria Allman on the yacht *Cocoa Bean,* the recipes wouldn't be as delicious as they are. It was great to have a professional chef test all the recipes with her crew and her guests as they moved around the Mediterranean. Check out Victoria's book *Sea Fare: A Culinary Odyssey: A Chef's Journey Across the Ocean.*

Thanks to Lars Johanssen in Nantes, France, for his initial book idea and for the recipes he shared.

Bonnie Betts provided indispensible help by organizing names and stories and permissions and setting up a system so that no one got lost. She also contacted all the authors, for various reasons, many, many times. Thanks.

Special thanks go out to our editor Heather Lazare at Three Rivers Press who enthusiastically championed this book and thoughtfully edited the text.

Thanks to Rita's agent Elaine Markson and her assistant Gary Johnson. And warm regards to all the people in Rotary International who continue to work between Maryland and New Delhi to administer the monies and vet the students, especially Chris Perlick and Manjit Sawhney. Our work in New Delhi is just beginning. Hopefully it will go on for many years.

Rita sends a big thank-you to Jan, Bill, Mitch, and Melissa, "who continue to put up with and support me in my nomadic life." And to Cris, "who makes me laugh."

Maria wants to thank her husband Paul Kundzins, who delayed his trip to Latvia to help her see this project through. "He witnessed my rants, ignored my screams, and helped with all the dirty dishes from the recipe testing. And he still wants me along in Latvia."

And from both of us, to the many authors who submitted their wonderful stories, even the ones that didn't make the cut, thank you for connecting around the world through smiles, food, and love. We all hope the stories here will inspire readers to jump on a plane, bus, boat, or car, cross borders, and experience the joy of their own adventures.

Happy traveling and happy eating.

Rita Golden Gelman and
Maria Altobelli

Reading Group Guide

Hey, Readers and Book Clubs,

There are a lot of interesting themes that run through these stories, and they make for pretty lively and challenging discussions. We thought we'd throw out some ideas for you to think about or discuss at your meeting—after you have eaten a meal made from some of the recipes in the book. Or, you don't have to wait until after—we give you permission to talk and eat at the same time!

1. Probably the most common theme in the book is the concept of trust. Most of these "connecting" stories involve trusting strangers. For many of the authors, extraordinary experiences resulted from saying yes to invitations, asking for help, accepting a hand, or offering theirs—when they had no idea of the outcome. Trust can be difficult if you don't know the people, the culture, the circumstances. Yet, without

trust, fear prevents you from opening up and enriching your life. For most people, safe, comfortable, and predictable are far better places to be than walking into the unknown. Do you agree? What is your comfort zone? We've all learned from childhood that we're not supposed to talk to strangers. Is it a valid concept in adulthood? Sometimes trusting too much can be dangerous. How does one balance caution with adventure?

2. Another characteristic that many of the authors share is the willingness to take risks. Think about the risks you've taken in your life, risks that took you away from the norm and allowed you to break free of what you were expected to do. Did you find out some interesting things about yourself—and about the positive side of taking risks? What did you learn?

3. How about risks in the kitchen? Food is often a common theme around which connections are made. Sometimes the best quality time spent with others is the time spent preparing the meal together. Has the book motivated you to try new foods, play with recipes, invent your own? Would you feel comfortable having a dinner party in which everyone participated in the creation of the meal? Why or why not?

4. Some of the stories take the reader through some pretty dramatic moments. Though all of the authors of the stories have taken risks and made connections, each situation is unique. Which ones made you laugh

or cry or want to shout, "Hooray!"? Which authors do you identify with the most? The least? Why do you think you feel that way?

5. Have a look at the many different kinds of connections in these stories. Think about the role of connecting in your own life. Do you think the ability to connect is something that can be developed or is it wired into people's personality-genome?

6. Did the stories inspire you to think about breaking free and taking off? To revisit your dreams? If you were given ten thousand dollars to travel for three months, where would you go, what would you do?

If you'd like to share your thoughts or report on your club's discussion, we'd love to hear from you. Thanks for choosing *Female Nomad & Friends*. If you enjoyed the book, please tell your friends. Don't forget that all the royalties are going to The Golden Fund which has been set up to send poor kids in India to vocational schools.

Thanks.

Best,

Rita and Maria, editors
Bonnie Betts, author representative

Send your comments to:
femalenomadandfriends@gmail.com

Also by Rita Golden Gelman

*"I move throughout the world without a plan, guided by
instinct, connecting through trust, and constantly watching for
serendipitous opportunities."* —From the Preface

At the age of forty-eight, on the
verge of a divorce, Rita Golden
Gelman left an elegant life in L.A.
to follow her dream of connecting
with people in cultures all over
the world. In 1986 she sold
her possessions and became a
nomad, living in a Zapotec village
in Mexico, sleeping with sea
lions on the Galápagos Islands,
and residing everywhere from
thatched huts to regal palaces.
Rita's example encourages us all to
dust off our dreams and rediscover
the joy, the exuberance, and the
hidden spirit that so many of us
bury when we become adults.

Tales of a Female Nomad:
Living at Large in the World
$14.95 paper ($19.95 Canada)
978-0-609-80954-9